MIDWEST MADE

BIG, BOLD BAKING
from the HEARTLAND

SHAUNA SEVER

Photographs by Paul Strabbing

RUNNING PRESS

PHILADELPHIA

Running Press
Hachette Book Group
1290 Avenue of the Americas, New York, NY 10104
www.runningpress.com
@Running_Press

Printed in China

First Edition: October 2019

Published by Running Press, an imprint of Perseus Books, LLC, a subsidiary of Hachette Book
Group, Inc. The Running Press name and logo is a trademark of the Hachette Book Group.

The Hachette Speakers Bureau provides a wide range of authors for speaking events.
To find out more, go to www.hachettespeakersbureau.com or call (866) 376-6591.

The publisher is not responsible for websites (or their content)
that are not owned by the publisher.

Print book cover and interior design by Susan Van Horn

Library of Congress Control Number: 2018964555

ISBNs: 978-0-7624-6450-0 (hardcover), 978-0-7624-6451-7 (ebook)

1010

10 9 8 7 6 5 4 3 2 1

TO SCOTT, CAROLINE, AND ANDREW:
HOME IS WHEREVER I'M WITH YOU.

CONTENTS

INTRODUCTION

*Because it is the Midwest, no one
really glitters because no one has to,
it's more of a dull shine, like frequently
used silverware.*

— Charles Baxter, *A Feast of Love*

I N THE MIDWEST, OUR LOVE OF BAKING IS REAL AND IT'S DEEP. As "America's Bread Basket," we believe in No Carb Left Behind. We love our local bakeries where we're treated like family as much as we love to bake at home. Firing up our ovens gets us through long, cold winters, while our kitschy-but-irresistible icebox desserts delight at every summer picnic and potluck.

Midwestern recipes tend to be handed down through generations, most with dynamic immigrant influences. While the big cities of the Midwest have become culinary hotspots, in many of the rural communities, your neighbors are far more likely to be farmers. The bounty of native grains, top-quality dairy, and vibrant seasonal fruits here are legendary. From the Dakotas to Ohio, from Minnesota to Missouri, the Midwest is a veritable quilt of twelve states full of history, values, recipes, people, and places that make up the baking culture of the Heartland.

But up until a few years ago, I thought about all this as much as I wondered about the differences between *kolacky* and *kolaches*. I was thousands of miles away from my own culinary history, and I felt great about the whole thing. When I'd left the Midwest for California at the age of twenty-five, a newly minted bride with my Ohio-born husband, I had no curiosity about the place where we grew up, especially not the food. I was all about heading west and discovering a life that was, to me, "actually interesting." I was all about the glitter.

1

With my journalism degree in hand, I managed to work fairly often as a "generalist" television host and reporter, talking about everything from pop culture and red carpets to sports, cars, or technology. After several years, even with some of the world's most gorgeous movie stars inches from my face and all that glittering, it started to feel stale. Glittering is exhausting.

As a counterpoint, to keep a record of my baking hobby and exercise my atrophying writing muscles, I set up a blog. During a textbook quarter-life crisis, it allowed me to consider what I actually loved doing. Landing a part-time job as a recipe writer for a Michelin-starred chef taught me volumes about great food and pastry, and the craft of writing recipes.

In late 2007, we left Los Angeles for San Francisco. Moving to one of the world's great food cities accelerated all the second thoughts I was having about my already-shaky career path. And as a capper to all of that, within weeks of moving to the Bay Area, I was expecting our first baby. Sometimes the universe whispers to you to get your attention, and sometimes it lobs a few grenades at your head.

Once our daughter, Caroline, was born in August 2008, the blog became a place for me to not lose my mind as a new mother, and help overcome my postpartum depression. (I would throw myself back into work much sooner after our son, Andrew, was born in 2013 to avoid slipping back into the depths, which was exhausting, but relatively effective.) As the blog grew with intention, it was inspired by what was happening in California's vibrant food scene and trend-focused bakeries. Through a series of fortuitous events, I was introduced to a marvelous editor who would open the door for me to write my first cookbook in 2012. I wrote two more cookbooks after that, and got back to doing television, but this time the food-focused kind, loving the work and feeling that any glittering that was required by the job was an honest, low-key sort that I could get behind.

In California, I never really thought much about the food from the Midwest, and especially not the baking. Why would I? Other parts of the country have much more definitive food personalities—we all know what to expect from sweets in the South, the edgy bakeries of Brooklyn, or even dessert in California (and yes, they do occasionally eat dessert out there). And I wasn't alone in this thinking; not much light has been shone on the baking culture of the enormous swath of land in between those hotspots.

But with all the inventiveness encouraged in California, I still always craved tradition. I'd revisit it time and again, through family recipes, feeling almost rebellious for making my mom's cherry shortcake squares with their lollipop red canned pie filling in my San Francisco kitchen, when loads of fresh cherries awaited at my neighborhood farmers' market.

Over our five years in LA, and eight more in San Francisco, Scott and I started to wonder whether we were really meant to raise California kids. We'd talk about all the what-ifs, here and there, as most big transitions tend to begin. There weren't really any serious plans in place to leave. But you know what happens when you start to put ideas out into the universe like that. Just as a tube pan of benign batter emerges from the oven as an airy, showstopping angel food cake, things were rising.

In October 2015, after thirteen years of California living, Scott got a job offer that would really change up his commute. With just a couple days' consideration, we headed back to Chicago to be close to family and friends, increase our hot dog intake, and give our two young kids more seasons and less exposure to kale.

With a one-way flight, I left my flip-flops-in-January days behind, and moved back to my home state of Illinois. I didn't know what I'd do next personally or professionally, or what motherhood would look like in the suburbs of Chicago, a place I had only known as a child-free person. But halfway through the flight, I had my answer. Barely off the tarmac, I planned to reexamine my midwestern roots and show them to my kids the best way I knew how—by firing up my oven. Even before my baking pans were unpacked, I was digging for recipes, newspaper clippings, and old community cookbooks. People I barely knew lent me their favorite church recipe collections, tabbed with Post-its to indicate their favorites. Exchanging recipes with a midwesterner is a bit like playing therapist—deeply buried memories are revealed, and everyone takes home extra reading material.

Taking a closer look at recipes I'd always considered pedestrian, I started connecting the dots. Visiting local bakeries and asking questions about things I'd eaten since childhood without a second thought was like peeling a big, juicy September apple. I began to see that within the simplest or most kitschy recipes lay a whole lot of intention and character. Here are my Five Baking Tenets of the Great Midwest.

BAKE BIG. Every cozy, big-batch recipe is a chance to slow down, gather, share, and connect. The 9 x 13 and the Bundt reign supreme.

BAKE EASY. Whether the recipe is old school or new, simple is beautiful. Be practical and resourceful with your time, effort, and ingredients. No fuss or fancy pants, please. And if there's an extra push required, the results need to be worth it.

BAKE WITH PURPOSE. The through line of midwestern baking is context. Be it a birthday or a Wednesday, let the distinct seasons, local traditions, seasonal produce, stellar grains and dairy, or just the fickle weather outside your kitchen window inspire you to bake with intention. Working with local and seasonal ingredients might be buzzwords to some, but it's a way of life in the Midwest. When Janice from up the block drops 11 pounds of backyard rhubarb on your front porch, you'll find purpose real quick.

BAKE IN THE PRESENT. The midwestern recipe box tends to sit happily at the intersection of tradition and modernity. You might find just as many handwritten, 1960s-motif notecards and recipe labels torn off bags and boxes as you do printouts from Epicurious. In this book, I've opted to tent-pole the recipe list with the beloved midwestern pillars of Pie, Bars, and casual Counter Cakes, and fill out the story with recipes inspired by seasons and occasions, sprinkling them with techniques and tricks I've discovered from years of developing fresher, smarter recipes that are low on prepackaged and processed ingredients.

BAKE FROM THE PAST. Perhaps the most important tenet of all. Bake what your mama (and grandmama, and her mama) gave you. Heirloom recipes and family traditions are the backbone of midwestern baking.

But if there can be only one, all-encompassing way to explain what makes the baking story of the Midwest so captivating, it's this: **Without immigrants, this book you're holding, its author, and the region's unique culinary landscape at large, simply wouldn't exist.**

As it happens, I'm an optimal cross-section of the various cultures that make up this region. From German to Swedish, Irish to Greek and Italian, I'm a true Midwestern Mutt, with a sweet tooth that was raised on everything from Sicilian butter cookies to baklava. One glance at a midwesterner's holiday cookie tin tells all you need to know about the impressive range of international influences in our baking traditions.

The second I defined these tenets of midwestern baking, I was all in. The fancy food world of the West Coast had nothing on this rediscovery. I had no problem telling whoever would listen that at Christmastime, I'd much rather pop open one of my family's old Hostess fruitcake tins with the certainty of finding Gramma's completely perfect sugar cookies, decorated only with a smattering of coarse rainbow sugar, than see the latest Pinterest hero on the dessert buffet. I was over the glittering. Give me that dull shine any day. It feels so good.

When I turned out the first batch of Gramma's sugar cookies in our new house and brought them along to Christmas dinner at my auntie Amy's, I became so much more emotional than any sane person should be over a cookie. When my kids grabbed two at a time from the tin, thinking no one saw them, just as I had at their ages, it sent me straight to the Kleenex zone. I was home, with my people, our food, our traditions, and so much more to learn with new eyes as a baker, writer, mother, and human.

As I unpacked the last of our boxes that December, leaving the sandals and skirts in storage, and clipping tags off my kids' first-ever pairs of snow pants, I thought about how much our lives would change beyond the weather. I thought about what I want my kids' midwestern upbringing to become, as they will now experience their childhood here, just as I did. I want my children to have detailed, active food memories tied to this place, to treasure the dull shine, and not have to run away from it to appreciate it, as I did.

I first wanted to create this book for them, a snapshot of the comfort baking from home—a new heirloom cookbook. But it's for you, too—I'm hoping that everyone can find a little bit of themselves in these pages. If you are indeed from the Midwest, I'm betting you'll find some things that are sweetly familiar. I'm so glad you're here.

There's a shocking amount of ground, heritage, and recipes to cover in a place so many people consider "fly-over country." But that's part of the beauty of the great Midwest. We like to lie low, and then out of nowhere, blow minds and take names with our hidden stories and talents. And then sort of play off the compliments. Dull shine at its very best.

With all the cultural input that coexists here from centuries of immigrant history, I hesitate to call the Midwest a "melting pot" as so many others do. As you cross state lines—and even just county lines—you begin to notice that communities hang onto their ancestral roots, and play them up. Recipes that show up in one place won't necessarily be found all over the region. The hometown of a person will greatly affect their perspective on the Midwest's culinary landscape.

My experience as a Chicago-born, Great Lakes–focused midwesterner is one thing; what my Bold North friends bake and eat in areas so far up in Minnesota that they're practically in Canada—is very different. As is the take of people who grew up farming in the Plains, or those in Ohio that can practically reach out their windows and touch Kentucky or Pennsylvania, or the palpable difference when crossing from northern to southern Illinois, Indiana, or Missouri.

That said, there's still just enough crossover from state to state that it's not really practical to categorize a Midwest cookbook by state. As you make your way through this book, you'll find some specialties unique to specific places and clear lines to their sources, alongside recipes with that broader, quintessential midwestern essence that's better tasted than told.

And with that, I hope to showcase the character of this great region, where the values of heritage and kindness are shown through the service and exchange of the homemade. Not for kudos, not for the purposes of "glittering," but to add to the patina of a place that calls you back home, no matter how long you've been away.

In My Pantry

A fully stocked baker's pantry is a thing of unparalleled joy and makes me feel that I have great control over my life. Here are my staples.

STARCHY

UNBLEACHED ALL-PURPOSE FLOUR. Nothing will influence the outcome of a baked good like the type of flour and how it's measured. I like working with unbleached all-purpose flour for most baked goods. My brands of choice in the North (where the wheat is hard winter wheat, and higher in protein than the soft wheat of the South) are Ceresota and King Arthur, with protein contents hovering around 11.5 percent that are great for doughs. I'm also happy to use Gold Medal unbleached, which is slightly lower in protein, consistent across state lines, and easy to find in American stores. Even if I use cups and spoons for the rest of the recipe, I'll always weigh my flour for ease and accuracy. In this book, **1 cup of unbleached all-purpose flour weighs 128 grams**. If you opt to measure by volume, whisk the container or flour first to aerate it, then spoon it into the cup, then level it off lightly with the back of a knife. If you use bleached flour, it won't throw off the entire recipe, but it will have a lower protein content and you can expect a slightly different result.

BREAD FLOUR. Even higher in protein than all-purpose, this is ideal for when you want a nice sturdy or chewy bread product, such as pizza crusts, pretzels, or sturdy sandwich loaves. I like King Arthur or Gold Medal unbleached bread flours. Because I use less bread flour than all-purpose, I often keep it sealed in the freezer for longer storage.

CAKE FLOUR. Bleached, and low-protein (about 7 percent), and more finely textured than all-purpose. Best for special occasion cakes needing a light, airy crumb. I don't often use cake flour, but when I do, I use Swans Down.

CORNSTARCH. The MVP. I know there are a million ways to thicken a pie filling or a custard, but I don't want all of them cluttering up my already chaotic cabinets. I just buy cornstarch. Cheap, easy, and versatile.

YEAST. Yeast is a thesis-level topic and it can be crazy-making trying to convert from one form or another. To keep it easy, I only use dry instant yeast, not active dry or cakes. I buy SAF brand in bulk or Fleischmann's in glass jars. If you buy packets, each envelope should contain 2¼ teaspoons/7 grams per envelope, but even with packets, I measure to be sure (I do this with unflavored gelatin packets, too, by the way, which should be 2½ teaspoons/5.8 grams each).

In theory, one should be able to just add instant yeast to a dough without first proofing it in a warm liquid. However, I find this to be iffy on its success rate, and after too many situations where I've been driven to the brink by a dough with visible yeast granules in it even after a long rise, I pretty much always give instant yeast a quick warm bath in a small amount of the liquid from a recipe while I pull the rest of my ingredients together. Also, I bake with yeast often enough that I buy it in larger quantities and keep it in the fridge, so this warm soak helps to "wake it up" a bit. So, in nearly every recipe involving yeast in this book, you'll see I have you dissolve instant yeast in a little liquid first, just to make everything a bit more foolproof.

CREAMY

BUTTER. I use salted butter on my bread like it's going out of style, but for baking, it's exclusively unsalted. In the centuries of baking, it's a relatively new school way of doing things, as most midwestern bakers tend to reach for salted butter, even now. Salted butter means well-preserved butter, and it lasts longer both in storage and on grocery store shelves. To that end, unsalted butter will be a fresher product. Additionally, the balance of salty and sweet is very important in great baked goods, and if you use salted butter and don't adjust the salt in these recipes, you'll end up with an oversalted product. Best just to use unsalted and avoid the guesswork.

You'll also notice several recipes calling for European-style butter, which has a slightly higher butterfat content than American butters, and can make a big difference in recipes deserving a bold, buttery flavor. When I need the extra richness from a European-style butter, I most often use Kerrygold, Plugra, or look for small-batch butters from local farms with a butterfat percentage of at least 82 percent. It's a little more spendy, but the flavor and texture payoff is worth it when it's called for. Cultured butter is also a fun thing to try for butter-forward baked goods to give a little edge. Regular unsalted butter can be substituted in the same amounts without the recipe failing, it just may not sing in exactly the same way.

HEAVY WHIPPING CREAM. There's plenty in these pages, in both whipped and liquid form. Make sure you are getting "heavy whipping cream" and not plain "whipping cream" or "light cream," which are lower in milkfat and don't behave the same way in recipes.

MILK. Again, with the full-fat! I always use whole for baking, low-fat for drinking. If a recipe just needs a little moisture and the amount is in tablespoons, such as to thin a mixture slightly or make an egg wash, low-fat is fine. But you will taste and see the difference when you use larger amounts in batters and doughs.

BUTTERMILK. This one can be low-fat. (Somewhere a nutritionist is exhaling.) Just make sure you shake it well every time you use it and don't heat it on its own or it will separate.

EGGS. Large eggs only, in the neighborhood of 50 grams per whole egg. If you need only the whites or the yolks for a recipe, store the remainder in the fridge for two or three days, tops. (Egg whites can be frozen individually in ice cubes trays, popped out, and stored in freezer bags for up to a year. I'm not a fan of freezing yolks, as they become oddly gelatinous unless you add sugar or salt, and even that isn't foolproof.) Save frustration and trying to remember how many whites or yolks you've stored by weighing out what you need for your next recipe. Whites weigh approximately 30 grams each; the yolks, 20 grams.

SWEET

WHITE GRANULATED SUGAR. The controversial queen of the larder. I like pure cane like Domino or C&H and usually weigh it—200 grams per cup.

LIGHT AND DARK BROWN SUGARS. Light brown sugar is a key ingredient in midwestern baking. Forever it seemed, I was a dark brown sugar devotee for flavor and color. And I still love it. But what I've learned is if the Midwest had a flavor, it would likely be the combination of butter and light brown sugar. Light brown sugar whispers instead of shouting, and still lends moisture and chew. Dark brown is great when you really need to punch up depth in some way. In extreme cases, such as for gingerbread-y things, I sometimes go even further and look for dark muscovado sugar. Measure these moist sugars by packing them firmly into your measuring cup, or even better, weigh them, too—225 grams per cup.

CONFECTIONERS' SUGAR. Nothing adds the pretty or conceals flaws like a dusting of this stuff. Sometimes you need it for frostings, sometimes for making doughs meltingly tender. Either way, its super annoying to be out of it, so I make it a staple. Spoon it into your measuring cup and level it off like flour, or weigh it at 120 grams per cup.

CORN SYRUP. Not many appearances in this book and not in great volume, but where it shows up, it's essential for texture, even if you just need a spoonful. Light is more versatile, and it keeps forever.

SALTY

FINE SEA SALT. My salt preference for baking. It dissolves easily and has a clean flavor, especially great for recipes where you really want that crave-worthy sweet-salty thing happening and the salt really needs to sing. It tends to come in boxes or in taller, narrower canisters than iodized. I even find it at the dollar store sometimes. Fine sea salt has a level of saltiness somewhere between regular iodized table salt and Diamond Crystal brand kosher salt (Morton brand kosher salt is coarser, denser, and the saltiest of them all, so I avoid it). So if you only have table salt, use scant measurements of what's called for. For Diamond Crystal, use a slightly rounded measurement.

FLAKY SEA SALT. The crown jewel of salts. I typically reach for Maldon brand, which is readily available. Can be used as a finishing salt sprinkled over the tops of cookies, bars, savory baked goods, and more. Flaky sea salt mixed into a cookie dough adds marvelous little surprise sparks of salt throughout, often combined with a light backdrop of fine sea salt (as in the Caramel Canvas Blondies on page 178). It's an easy way to bring a simple, old-school recipe up to modern tastes.

HARMONIZERS

VANILLA. I reach for pure vanilla extract for almost every recipe, and keep a jar of pure vanilla bean paste for when I want both vanilla flavor and the aesthetic of vanilla bean flecks in a light-colored frosting, filling, or ice cream without having to scrape beans.

SPICES. I have a fairly standard spice selection, but there are a few I upgrade for a little extra ka-pow in my baking. First is **Vietnamese cinnamon**, also labeled Saigon cinnamon. It tastes like Red Hots cinnamon candy and is a world away from the dusty stuff we grew up with. Same goes for using **whole nutmeg, freshly grated** with a Microplane, over preground. **Chinese five-spice powder** makes a few appearances, and its zippy character helps to elevate things that might only use, say, cinnamon, and is revelatory in fruit desserts, especially apples, pears, cherries, and other stone fruits, making people ask, "What's in this?!" (in a good way).

CITRUS ZEST. Finely grated with a Microplane. I'm happiest when I can get organic, unwaxed citrus fruits so I don't have to worry about scrubbing like crazy to avoid sprinkling pesticides into my efforts.

CHOCOLATE. I most often reach for 60% bittersweet chocolate, either in bar form or chips. I also have a bar or two of extra bittersweet chocolate, something in the neighborhood of 75%, when a really sweet base needs bitter contrast. Changing up the chocolate in a recipe, both in quality and cacao percentage, is the easiest way to modernize the flavor of a recipe and give it a little edge. High-quality semisweet is used here and there in this book, and even some milk chocolate, too, which, if we're being honest and not food snobs, is basically life-giving when it comes to eating straight up.

BLACK COCOA POWDER. This ultradark, insanely intense cocoa is the key player when I want to take a recipe running on cocoa powder to the next level (such as the Wednesday Night Brownies on page 163). I consider this cocoa to be "Oreo" flavored. I rarely swap out all the cocoa in a recipe for black cocoa, as a little of this—like just a couple tablespoons exchanged—goes a long way. Black cocoa is Dutch-processed, so keep that in mind when using it in a recipe.

NUTS. Other than sliced and slivered blanched almonds, I almost always buy nuts whole and raw. That way, I can transform them into whatever I need for a recipe—toasted or not, chopped or ground. Much more versatile and cost-effective.

My Top 10 Tools

OVEN THERMOMETER. The most basic way to avoid the vast majority of baking problems. It sounds so obvious, but then, most solutions in life are.

ELECTRIC STAND MIXER. Many things in this book can be made with an electric hand mixer, which is what I grew up with. But baking becomes extra fun if you can make the investment in one of these machines. I am also a big fan of paddle attachments with a squeegee-like edge on them to save bowl scraping time during mixing.

SMALL OFFSET SPATULAS. I cannot do without a couple of offsets in my drawer. Great for frosting cakes, smoothing batters into pans, and the ideal thin blade for loosening and lifting items from pans.

BENCH OR PASTRY SCRAPER. It goes by both names, but the general idea is a stainless-steel rectangle with a straight edge and a solid handle across the top. It's ideal for lifting and moving pastry while rolling, folding soft doughs, cutting doughs into neat portions, cleaning off a work surface, and more.

DIGITAL SCALE. For years I exclusively used cups and spoons. It's how our grandmothers and mothers baked. It's the American way. I totally get it. But when I got the hang of weighing ingredients, my baking life got even happier—better results, more efficient, and cleaner with fewer dirty dishes.

FLEXIBLE PLASTIC BOWL SCRAPER. The plastic card type. It's like an extension of your hand, so much better than a spatula. Get every last bit of dough or batter out of a bowl. Waste not, want not, and all of that.

SIEVES IN A COUPLE DIFFERENT SIZES. Next to peeling garlic and melting chocolate, sieving things is my most-hated kitchen task. But when it comes to remedying clumpy dry ingredients, removing errant lumps from custards, and making ice creams silky smooth, you've gotta get with the sieve.

FISH SPATULA. Of all the handled things rattling in my kitchen drawers, this is what I reach for the most, for both baking and cooking. Its thin, flexible, vented blade allows for lifting even the most delicate baked good from a pan or baking sheet. Try making pancakes with a fish spatula, and you'll never use anything else.

NONSTICK COOKING SPRAY. I don't use it much it for cooking, but for baking I do. For me, it's the most convenient, foolproof way to grease. I also like that it doesn't cause overbrowning or creating a thicker or firmer crust when I don't want it. So, you'll notice I prep almost every pan with it in these recipes, but use the method you prefer (butter, shortening, homemade concoctions, etc.), knowing the results may vary.

A HEAVY ROLLING DOWEL. It's my rolling pin of choice (see page 81 about choosing your forever pin). Mine is maple, about 19 inches/48 cm long, and I love it.

CHAPTER 1
SWEET DOUGHS

FOR THE LONGEST TIME, I HAD AN IRRATIONAL FEAR OF BAKING with yeast (*you're telling me I have to feed it, and it's ALIVE?*). In talking with other bakers, I've learned I wasn't alone. But now that I've broken free of that fear, I can say that learning to love the process of baking with yeast turns a person into the kind of intuitive baker that everyone deserves to become. Long-game baking like this is a craft, but a rewarding one to practice. It might require a little more attention than other types of baking, but there's a payoff—it earns you the ability to really feel the dough you're working on and determine what it needs, and frees you from always feeling chained to a written recipe. And that's a skill that will translate to all manner of baking recipes, yeasted or not.

Practical skills aside, there's nothing quite like a yeast-risen baked good to warm the house, the belly, and the heart. Of all the golden, pillowy baked goods appearing in midwestern bakeries and on breakfast tables, it's the sweet, enriched doughs I find most compelling. As yeast predates other leaveners by thousands of years, if you've got a yeast-risen cake or morning treat on your hands, chances are you've got something with an interesting history baked into it, too.

Kneading your way through this section is a terrific way to get to know some of the more prominent immigrant influences of the region and indulge in some old-world baking traditions. And given that most of these recipes are best eaten soon after baking (which in turn will fill your house with a delicious fragrance), they also offer a great excuse to invite some neighbors over for coffee.

POTICA

Serves 8 to 10

MIDWESTERNERS WITH SLOVENIAN BLOOD MIGHT CALL IT POTICA, CROATIANS know it as *povitica*, and some folks simply call it nut roll. But what's important to know is the building blocks here are a sweet, yeasted dough and a rich, sugary, spiced nut filling, rolled together. Some look more like a long, uncut log of cinnamon roll, with chunky, distinct layers of dough and filling, while others reveal a cross-section of impossibly thin layers. Considering Eastern Europe tends to crank out supermodels at a staggering rate, I thought I'd give my potica the beauty treatment of the latter, with fine layers creating smokelike swirls inside.

Now, I'm not going to gloss over it—the process of shaping potica is absolutely a case of practice making perfect. But I promise you, the first time you nail the shaping and cut into a loaf to find a dizzying interior of swirls, you will experience a sense of self-satisfaction very few things can match.

DOUGH:

3 tablespoons warm water
(110° to 115°F/43° to 46°C)

2¼ teaspoons instant yeast

4 tablespoons/57 g unsalted butter, melted

⅓ cup/75 g warm whole milk
(110° to 115°F/43° to 46°C)

2 tablespoons granulated sugar

1 large egg

2 cups/256 g unbleached all-purpose flour, spooned and leveled, plus more for dusting

½ teaspoon fine sea salt

Nonstick cooking spray or oil for bowl and loaf pan

FILLING:

2 cups/225 g raw walnut halves, finely ground*

½ teaspoon fine sea salt, plus a pinch

1 teaspoon ground cinnamon

¼ cup/84 g honey

¼ cup/57 g light brown sugar

1 large egg, separated

2 tablespoons unsalted butter, melted

2 teaspoons unsweetened natural or Dutch-processed cocoa powder

1 teaspoon pure vanilla extract

1 to 2 tablespoons whole milk, as needed

FINISHING:

1 large egg

1 tablespoon water

Pinch of fine sea salt

3 tablespoons/38 g granulated sugar for sprinkling

*You want the nuts very finely ground in a food processor or blender, nearly to a flour. It will keep the delicate dough from tearing when the filling is spread out. If you happen to find yourself with some wild black walnuts, native to the Midwest and particularly the Missouri Ozarks, this is a stellar place to use them. Just do a half-and-half mix of black walnuts and the lighter English walnuts typically found in grocery stores—a little of the bold, musky depth of black walnuts goes a long way.

Prepare the dough: In the bowl of an electric mixer, whisk together the warm water and yeast. Set aside for a couple minutes. Add the melted butter, milk, granulated sugar, and egg. Add the flour and salt to the bowl. Mix with a wooden spoon until a shaggy dough forms. Fit the bowl onto the mixer along with the dough hook. Knead the dough on medium speed until smooth and elastic, 6 to 7 minutes.

Lightly flour a work surface and turn out the dough onto it. Knead the dough by hand several times. Spray the mixer bowl with nonstick cooking spray or oil it lightly. Place the dough in the bowl and cover tightly with plastic wrap. Let rise in a warm place until doubled in bulk, about 1 hour.

Prepare the filling: In a large skillet over medium heat, toast the ground walnuts with ½ teaspoon of salt, stirring often, about 5 minutes. Remove the pan from the heat and stir in the cinnamon. Let cool completely.

In a medium bowl, whisk together the honey, brown sugar, egg yolk, melted butter, cocoa powder, and vanilla. Stir in the cooled walnuts.

Beat the egg white by hand with a pinch of salt until thickened and foamy. Fold the egg white into the walnut mixture, to loosen it slightly.

When the dough has finished its first rise, lightly flour a large work surface, at least 3 feet/92 cm square. Turn out the dough and press into a rough rectangle, with the longer side closest to you. Roll out the dough, keeping it in a rough rectangle shape, until you create a very thin sheet, 18 x 24 inches/46 x 61 cm. As you roll, stop every few strokes and stretch the dough with your hands from underneath, from the center gently outward, and then smooth it back onto the work surface with a quick flick, like a small bedsheet (if it's getting tacky at any point, scatter a little more flour under the dough).

Once you've reached the proper dimensions, use a small offset spatula to spread a little bit of the filling onto a small area of the dough to test it—does it spread easily into a thin layer without pulling the dough or causing it to tear (a little stretching is okay)? If not, add a bit of milk in 1-tablespoon increments until the filling is thick but spreadable. Dollop the filling in tablespoons all over the dough, then spread the filling thinly, leaving a ½-inch/1.25 cm bare border on all sides.

Roll the dough into a tight log, starting with the long side closest to you: Begin with a ½-inch/1.25 cm fold along the length of the dough, starting on the far right and moving left. Now go back toward the right, tightly rolling up the dough with typewriter fingertips as you go.

To finish the loaf: In a small cup, beat together the egg, water, and salt.

Moisten the exposed edge of the dough with egg wash and finish the roll, pinching the dough to create a tight seam. Trim the 2 ends of the log neatly and pinch them tightly to seal. Turn the log seam-side down. Spray a 9 x 5-inch/23 x 12.7 cm metal loaf pan with nonstick cooking spray.

Gently roll the log back and forth under your palms until the length is 3 times that of your loaf pan. Fold the log into thirds in a tight Z shape and tuck the ends under to form a neat loaf. Transfer the loaf to the pan. Cover with plastic wrap and allow to rise 1 hour.

Meanwhile, position a rack to the lower third of the oven and preheat it to 350°F/180°C. Brush the loaf with the egg wash and sprinkle with the granulated sugar.

Bake for 15 minutes at 350°F/180°C, then lower the oven temperature to 300°F/150°C. Continue to bake for 45 minutes more, or until deeply golden and hollow-sounding all over when tapped (the internal temperature should register at least 190°F/88°C on an instant-read thermometer). Allow the bread to cool in the pan on a wire rack for 20 minutes before unmolding. Let cool completely before slicing.

SWEDISH FLOP

Serves 12 to 15

I'LL JUST TELL YOU RIGHT NOW YOU'LL BE HEARING ABOUT MY GRANDMOTHER, the grand dame Esther Foropoulos, from time to time in these pages. Gramma passed a year before I began working on this book, but I still wear her influence buttoned up all around me, in so many ways that I'm probably not even aware of most of them.

But what I do know is that Gram was a wonderful example of a midwestern lady, lived her entire life in and around Chicago, and was a bona fide baked goods enthusiast. A faithful user of the midwesternism "Jeet?" (a loose contraction of "did you eat?" to be delivered only as a question), she was nearly always in possession of a good coffeecake and ready to share it. She had a great sense of humor that made her eyes sparkle, and was polite but not immune to sharing a bit gossip over coffee and kuchen. She also had a way of always picking the very best thing from a bakery case, and her opinions on the matter were strong.

Swedish Flop was one of her favorites, and it wasn't until I began writing this book that I realized just how obscure it is. Found mainly in the Chicago area, this combination of fluffy, yeasted cake and buttercream is, like Esther herself, a showstopper.

DOUGH:

Nonstick cooking spray for pan

1 recipe Buttery, Yeast-Raised Coffeecake Dough (page 23)

STREUSEL:

3/4 cup/96 g unbleached all-purpose flour, spooned and leveled

1/3 cup/75 g firmly packed light brown sugar

5 tablespoons/70 g unsalted butter, at cool room temperature

1/8 teaspoon fine sea salt

ASSEMBLY:

1 recipe Ermine Frosting (page 305)

1/2 cup/162 g Rhubarb and Raspberry Jam (page 300), or any good quality, sweet-tart jam

1/4 cup/30 g confectioners' sugar

Prepare the dough: Spray a 9 x 13-inch/23 x 33 cm light-colored metal baking pan with nonstick cooking spray and line it with a parchment paper, leaving a few inches of overhang on the 2 longer sides of the pan.

When the dough has completed its first rise, press it evenly into the prepared pan. Cover with plastic wrap and allow to rise again until doubled, about 45 minutes.

Meanwhile, position an oven rack in the center of the oven and preheat it to 350°F/180°C.

Prepare the streusel: In a medium bowl, combine the flour, brown sugar, butter, and salt. Use your fingertips to work the mixture together into a fine rubble, a combination of coarse crumbs and larger pea-size pieces. Set in the refrigerator to chill.

When the dough has risen, scatter the streusel evenly over the top. Bake until puffed, fragrant, and golden at the edges, about 30 minutes. Let cool completely in the pan on a wire rack.

Assemble the flop: Lift the cake from the pan, using the parchment "handles," and set on a cutting board or serving platter. Using a long, sharp serrated knife, shave off the outside browned edges of the cake, just about 1/4 inch/6 mm of the perimeter, so the yellow interior is exposed. Slice the cake horizontally into 2 even layers. Remove the streuseled lid. Smooth the frosting evenly over the bottom layer, then the spread with the jam. Replace the top. Dust the entire flop generously with confectioners' sugar before serving. Store any leftovers tightly wrapped for up to 2 days at room temperature, but this cake is best served the same day it's made.

VARIATION:
STREUSELKUCHEN

If your love for coffeecake is more about the streusel than the actual cake part, first, I feel you, and second, this is the recipe for you. Prepare 1 batch of Buttery, Yeast-Raised Coffeecake Dough (page 23), and let rise until doubled. Pat it into an oiled 13 x 9-inch/33 x 23 cm baking pan, cover with plastic wrap, and let rise again for 30 to 45 minutes. Meanwhile, double the streusel ingredients and mix as directed, adding 1/2 teaspoon of freshly grated nutmeg, ground cinnamon, or both. Sprinkle over dough. Bake at 350°F/180°C for 30 minutes. Cool for at least 30 minutes before dusting generously with confectioners' sugar.

BUTTERY, YEAST-RAISED COFFEECAKE DOUGH

Makes enough for one 9 x 13-inch/23 x 33 cm cake, or two 8-inch/20 cm rounds

THIS DOUGH IS AN AWESOME BUILDING BLOCK RECIPE FOR SO MANY BAKERY classics. Although many yeast doughs can be made unplugged, with just a wooden spoon and your hands, this recipe calls specifically for an electric stand mixer and a paddle attachment. The reason is that the precise amount of flour in this recipe is the key to its light, cakelike texture, and the dough itself is meant to be very loose. To knead it by hand, you'd need to way too much flour on your work surface to make it workable, making for a dry finished product. Using a mixer ensures a soft, pillowy, buttery dough.

2¼ teaspoons instant yeast

⅔ cup/148 g warm whole milk (110° to 115°F/43° to 46°C)

4 tablespoons/57 g unsalted butter, melted

¼ cup/50 g granulated sugar

2 large eggs, at room temperature

1 teaspoon pure vanilla extract

2 teaspoons finely grated lemon zest

2 cups/256 g unbleached all-purpose flour, spooned and leveled, plus more for dusting

½ teaspoon fine sea salt

Nonstick cooking spray for pan

In the bowl of an electric mixer, whisk together the yeast and milk. Set aside for a couple of minutes. Whisk in the melted butter, sugar, eggs, vanilla, and lemon zest. Add the flour and salt. Fit the bowl onto the mixer along with the paddle attachment. Mix on medium speed for 3 to 4 minutes, or until shiny. It will be a very loose dough-batter hybrid. Stop the mixer and scrape down the bowl well about halfway through the mixing time.

Spray a medium bowl with non-stick cooking spray or oil it lightly. Scrape the dough into the bowl and dust the surface of the dough with a couple of teaspoons of flour. Cover the bowl tightly with plastic wrap. Let rise in a warm place until doubled in bulk, 45 minutes to 1 hour.

Use as directed in the recipes that call for this dough.

COFFEE CARAMEL MONKEY BREAD

Serves 10 to 12

EVEN THOUGH MOST RESEARCH LEADS TO THIS HOMEY, PULL-APART BREAD coming from Southern California in the 1940s, to me monkey bread is pure Midwest. It's comfort food of the highest order, shareable by design, meant to be placed in the center of the table and immediately devoured. I plucked countless sweet, sticky nuggets from batches served at girlhood slumber parties, between Hello Kitty sticker swaps and spritzes of Electric Youth perfume. When we first moved back to Illinois and experienced our first real block party mere weeks after, a friendly neighbor busted out with a fresh, hot monkey bread within the first 30 minutes of the street barricades going up, and my heart nearly cracked out of my chest.

This is an unabashed celebration of butter and sugar, and when warm and fragrant straight from the oven, even the most refined lady will dive in and get her fingers sticky to score a coveted, caramelized outer piece. This recipe is a twist on the classic, with a scratch-made dough and a hit of coffee added to the dousing of buttery, salted caramel.

DOUGH*:

2¼ teaspoons instant yeast

¼ cup/57 g warm water (110° to 115°F/43° to 46°C)

3 tablespoons/38 g granulated sugar, divided

1 cup/225 g well-shaken buttermilk, at room temperature

3 large egg yolks, at room temperature

4 tablespoons/57 g unsalted butter, melted and cooled

4 cups/512 g unbleached all-purpose flour, spooned and leveled, plus more for dusting

¾ teaspoon fine sea salt

Nonstick cooking spray or oil for bowl and pan

COATINGS:

5 tablespoons/70 g unsalted butter, melted

¾ cup/150 g granulated sugar

2 teaspoons ground cinnamon

¼ teaspoon fine sea salt

COFFEE CARAMEL:

⅓ cup/75 g strong brewed coffee, hot or cooled

7 tablespoons/98 g unsalted butter, cut into ½-inch/1.25 cm pieces

1 cup/225 g firmly packed light brown sugar

½ teaspoon fine sea salt

1 teaspoon pure vanilla extract

*If you're feeling like a shortcut, use 2 pounds/905 g of high-quality frozen, store-bought white bread dough or dinner rolls from the freezer section of the grocery store. Let it come to room temperature and rise until doubled in bulk, then proceed with snipping the dough into small pieces.

Prepare the dough: In the bowl of an electric mixer, whisk together the yeast, warm water, and a couple of pinches of the granulated sugar. Let sit until the mixture is foamy, about 5 minutes. Whisk in the remaining sugar, buttermilk, egg yolks, and melted butter. Add the flour and salt. Mix with a wooden spoon to form a shaggy dough. Fit the bowl onto the mixer along with the dough hook. Knead the dough on medium speed until smooth and elastic, 6 to 7 minutes.

Lightly flour a work surface and turn out the dough onto it. Knead the dough by hand several times. Spray the mixer bowl with nonstick cooking spray or oil it lightly. Place the dough in the bowl and cover tightly with plastic wrap. Let rise in a warm place until doubled in bulk, 1 to 1½ hours.

Spray a 10-inch/25 cm Bundt or tube pan generously with nonstick cooking spray (don't forget the core of the pan!). Using kitchen scissors, snip the dough into small chunks and roll into 1-inch/2.5 cm balls.

Prepare the coatings: Pour the melted butter into a pie plate. In a medium bowl, whisk together the granulated sugar, cinnamon, and salt.

Working in small batches, coat the dough balls with the melted butter, then toss them in the cinnamon sugar to coat. Fit the balls snugly into the prepared pan. (The bottom of the pan will end up as the top when the bread is inverted, so arrange the first layer neatly.) Cover with plastic wrap and set on a baking sheet. Let rise in a warm place until doubled, about 1 hour (or in the refrigerator overnight, 8 to 12 hours).

Position a rack to the center of the oven and preheat the oven to 350°F/180°C.

During the last half of the rising time, prepare the caramel: In a 2- to 2½-quart/1.9 to 2.4 L saucepan over high heat, combine the coffee, butter, brown sugar, and salt. Bring the mixture to a full rolling boil, stirring often until the sugar is dissolved. Boil hard just until slightly thickened, about 2 minutes, depending on the size and depth of your pan. Stir in the vanilla. Let cool for about 10 minutes. Pour over the risen dough—it may not all sink down into the pan.

Bake until puffed and golden, 35 to 40 minutes (the internal temperature should register at least 190°F/88°C on an instant-read thermometer). Tent with foil during the last third of the baking time. Let the bread cool in the pan on a wire rack for 10 minutes (no longer, to avoid sticking) before inverting onto a platter and serving warm.

HOUSKA

Serves 8 to 10

NOT FAR FROM MY HOUSE IS THE QUINTESSENTIAL MIDWESTERN BAKERY—
Vesecky's in Berwyn, Illinois. It's on a stretch of Cermak Road that decades ago was a wonderland
of Czech-Bohemian bakeries, but only Vesecky's remains, nearly 100 years after it first opened. If
you get there early enough to see the spread as it first tumbles out, you'll never forget the sights
and smells. Vesecky's *houska*, a rich, eggy, challah-esque braid, has a feather-light, cottony interior studded with golden raisins, and it's the closest thing to heaven when toasted and buttered. In
fact, when you buy Vesecky's houska, you'll be asked whether you're planning to toast it, and offered
loaves with or without a topping of flaked almonds, which will burn in a toaster.

While collecting recipes from my own family for this book, a recipe for houska was one of the first
brought to my attention. Soon after, I was given a recipe from another relative for "Great Grandma
Enzenbacher's Norwegian Christmas Bread" and I realized the two recipes are nearly identical—the
only difference being that the Norwegian Christmas Bread has candied cherries in place of half of
the raisins, the addition of cinnamon, and is baked in loaf pans without braiding. So, I'm sharing
with you the houska version of my family's recipe, which is a bit more evergreen, and you can change
it up as you wish when red candied cherries make their way into supermarkets during the holidays.

DOUGH:

1 tablespoon instant yeast

1/4 cup/57 g warm water (110°
to 115°F/43° to 46°C)

1/2 cup/60 g golden raisins

1/3 cup/75 g boiling water

6 tablespoons/85 g unsalted
butter, at room temperature

1/4 cup/50 g granulated sugar

1 large egg

1 large egg yolk

1 teaspoon finely grated
lemon zest

2 1/2 cups/320 g unbleached
all-purpose flour, spooned
and leveled, divided, plus more
for dusting

1/2 cup/113 g warm whole milk
(110° to 115°F/43° to 46°C)

1/2 teaspoon fine sea salt

1/4 teaspoon freshly grated
nutmeg

Nonstick cooking spray or oil
for bowl

FINISHING:

1 large egg

1 tablespoon water

Pinch of fine sea salt

Prepare the dough: In a small
bowl, whisk together the yeast
and warm water. Set aside to
allow the yeast to dissolve,
about 5 minutes.

In a separate small heatproof bowl, combine the raisins and boiling water. Cover tightly with plastic wrap and set aside to soften for 5 minutes.

In the bowl of an electric mixer fitted with the paddle attachment, combine the butter and sugar. Beat on medium-high speed until light and fluffy, about 3 minutes. Beat in the egg, egg yolk, and lemon zest. Reduce the mixer speed to low and stir in about 1/2 cup/64 g of the flour until smooth. Slowly pour in the yeast mixture and the milk and mix until well blended.

Drain the raisins and pat them dry with a paper towel. If they're still hot, allow to cool slightly.

To the mixer bowl, add the remaining 2 cups/256 g of flour, raisins, salt, and nutmeg and mix until a shaggy dough forms. Stop the mixer and switch to the dough hook attachment. Knead the dough on medium speed until smooth and shiny, 6 to 7 minutes. Lightly flour a work surface and turn out the dough onto it. Knead the dough by hand several times, making sure the raisins are evenly distributed throughout. Spray the mixer bowl with nonstick cooking spray or oil it lightly, and place the dough back in the bowl. Cover tightly with plastic wrap and allow to rise in a warm place until doubled, about 1 hour.

Have ready a 9 x 5-inch/23 x 12.7 cm loaf pan. Lightly flour a work surface once again. Turn out the dough onto the work surface and divide into 3 equal pieces (weighing the ball of dough and dividing by 3 is the best way to ensure an even finished loaf). Shape each piece of dough into a thick rope about 10 inches/25 cm long. Lay the ropes parallel to one another. Beginning at the end farthest from you, pinch all 3 ropes together. Starting with the rope on the left, braid the 3 ropes together with a medium amount of tension—you want to have enough plaits to create an attractive loaf, but not so many that the braid is overly tight—too much tension will cause splitting down the center of the loaf. Pinch both ends of the braid together once more, then tuck the ends under neatly to form a loaf about 9 inches/23 cm long. Carefully transfer the dough to the loaf pan. Cover with plastic wrap and let rise until doubled, about 1 hour more.

Position a rack to the lower third of the oven and preheat the oven to 350°F/180°C.

In a small cup, whisk together the egg, water, and salt until liquefied. Brush the egg wash all over the top with a pastry brush, being sure to brush over the deep creases within the braid.

Bake until deeply golden and the bread sounds hollow when tapped, 35 to 40 minutes (the internal temperature should register between 190° and 200°F/88° and 93°C on an instant-read thermometer). Let cool in the pan for 10 minutes. Remove the bread from the pan and allow to cool completely on a wire rack before slicing.

FIVE-SPICE SWEET ROLLS

Makes 12 rolls

WITH THEIR SWEDISH ROOTS, A GOOD PAN OF CINNAMON ROLLS HAS JUST about everything a midwesterner could want in a cold-weather morning treat—abundance, warmth, goo, chew, and an intoxicating fragrance that warms up the inside of a frozen nose. It's the scent of home, wherever you are. I find a good hit of Chinese five-spice powder adds a little jazz to tradition, and gives the rolls just enough heat to balance out a healthy amount of butter and sugar. When you're shopping for Chinese five-spice powder, know the combinations can vary. Look for a mixture bending toward the sweeter side, with such spices as star anise, fennel, cloves, cinnamon, ginger, or nutmeg.

In regard to the frosting on these heavenly spiced swirls, there's plenty to be had here, which is the way a good sweet roll should be. I slather the warm rolls with about half of the frosting, and serve the rest alongside for those who require an extra schmear.

DOUGH:

1/2 cup/113 g unsalted butter, cut into tablespoons

3/4 cup/170 g well-shaken buttermilk, at room temperature

1/4 cup/113 g warm water (110° to 115°F/43° to 46°C)

2 1/4 teaspoons instant yeast

1/4 cup/50 g granulated sugar

2 large eggs

4 1/2 cups/576 g unbleached all-purpose flour, spooned and leveled, plus more as needed and for dusting

1 1/2 teaspoons fine sea salt

Nonstick cooking spray for pan

4 tablespoons/57 g unsalted butter, melted and cooled

FILLING:

3/4 cup/170 g dark brown sugar

1 tablespoon ground cinnamon

2 teaspoons Chinese five-spice powder

1/8 teaspoon fine sea salt

ICING:

4 ounces/113 g full-fat cream cheese, at room temperature

4 tablespoons/57 g unsalted butter, at room temperature

2 cups/240 g confectioners' sugar

1 teaspoon pure vanilla extract

1/8 teaspoon fine sea salt

Prepare the dough: In a large, microwave-safe measuring cup, melt the butter in a microwave on **HIGH**, about 1 minute—it should be hot, but not bubbling. Whisk in the buttermilk. You should now have a liquid just warm to the touch. Set it aside.

In the bowl of an electric mixer, whisk together the warm water and yeast. Allow the yeast to dissolve for a few minutes. Whisk in the buttermilk mixture, granulated sugar, and eggs. Add the flour and salt and mix with a wooden spoon until a shaggy dough forms. Attach the bowl to the mixer along with the dough hook. Knead on medium speed until the dough is smooth and freely clears the sides of the bowl, 6 to 7 minutes. If the dough is still clinging to the sides of the bowl after the first 2 minutes of kneading, add a bit of additional flour, 2 tablespoons at a time, until the dough clings just to the center 2 inches/5 cm of the bottom of the bowl while kneading.

Turn out the dough onto a lightly floured work surface and knead a few times by hand until smooth and springy. Shape the dough into a ball. Spray the mixer bowl with nonstick cooking spray and place the dough back in it. Cover the bowl with plastic wrap. Let the dough rise in a warm place until it has doubled in bulk, about 1½ hours.

When the dough has completed its first rise, lightly flour a work surface and turn out the dough onto it. Roll the dough into a rough 12 x 16-inch/30 x 40 cm rectangle, with a long side closest to you. Spray a 9 x 13-inch/23 x 33 cm baking pan with nonstick cooking spray.

Using a pastry brush or your hands, coat the dough with a thin layer of the melted butter.

Prepare the filling: In a small bowl, combine the brown sugar, cinnamon, Chinese five-spice powder, and salt. Sprinkle the spiced sugar evenly over the dough, leaving a ½-inch/1.25 cm bare border along the long end farthest from you. Roll up the dough into a tight log. Moisten the filling-free edge of the dough with wet fingertips and finish the roll, pinching to seal. Turn the roll seam-side down. Using a large sharp knife or bench scraper, cut the log into 12 equal pieces and place them in the prepared pan. Turn the rolls so the seams will face each other, so they will be less likely to unfurl. Cover with plastic wrap and let the rolls rise until doubled in bulk once again, about 1 hour, or refrigerate the shaped rolls overnight, up to 12 hours.

Position a rack to the center of the oven and preheat the oven to 350°F/180°C. If refrigerating the rolls overnight, remove from the refrigerator and allow to sit at room temperature for about 1 hour.

Bake the rolls for 25 to 30 minutes, or until they are golden brown (the internal temperature should register at least 190°F/88°C on an instant-read thermometer). Let the rolls cool in the pan set on a wire rack for 20 minutes.

While the rolls are cooling, prepare the icing: In the bowl of an electric mixer fitted with the paddle attachment, combine the cream cheese and butter. Beat on medium speed just until smooth. Add the confectioners' sugar, vanilla, and salt. Beat briefly until well blended. Slather the rolls with about half of the frosting and serve warm. Serve the remaining frosting on the side.

CLASSIC CIDER DONUTS

Makes about 16 donuts, plus donut holes

OF ALL THE DONUTS IN THE WORLD, THE CLASSIC CIDER DONUT TRULY SPEAKS to me. Of course, to speak loud enough to be heard over the heavenly call of a French cruller or Boston cream, a cider donut must be completely on point. That means fresh from the fryer, piping hot with a sparkling, crunchy coat of cinnamon sugar that's sexier than any mink, with a good grating of fresh nutmeg in the batter to suggest everything seductive about the early weeks of autumn.

Although some recipes for cider donuts actually contain cider, in my mind, the only "cider" necessary with a cider donut is on the side—ice-cold, unfiltered, and preferably sipped at the U-pick apple farm where it was pressed, while on a break from picking said apples. I've found buttermilk does a fine job of adding the tang and acidity needed to create a flavorful, tender donut, without the fuss of boiling down cider to add to the batter.

DOUGH:

3½ cups/450 g unbleached all-purpose flour, spooned and leveled, plus more for dusting

1 tablespoon plus 1 teaspoon baking powder

1¼ teaspoons fine sea salt

2 teaspoons freshly grated nutmeg

½ cup/113 g unsalted butter, at room temperature

⅔ cup/132 g granulated sugar

1 teaspoon pure vanilla extract

2 large eggs

1 cup/225 g well-shaken buttermilk, at room temperature

FRYING AND FINISHING:

2 quarts/1.6 kg vegetable or canola oil

1½ cups/300 g granulated sugar

2 tablespoons ground cinnamon

⅛ teaspoon fine sea salt

Prepare the dough: In a medium bowl, whisk together the flour, baking powder, salt, and nutmeg.

In the bowl of an electric mixer fitted with the paddle attachment, beat the butter on medium speed until creamy. Add the sugar and vanilla and beat until very light and fluffy, about 3 minutes. Beat in the eggs, 1 at a time—the mixture will look curdled. Reduce the mixer speed to low and mix in the dry ingredients and buttermilk in 5 alternating additions. Finish mixing the dough by hand with a spatula—it will be soft and sticky and somewhat loose, but will hold a shape.

To shape the donuts, dust a work surface with flour. Line a 12 x 17-inch/30 x 43 cm baking sheet with parchment paper. Turn out the dough onto the work surface and dust the top with flour. Pat the dough gently into a disk, and with a floured rolling pin, roll out the dough to just shy of ½-inch/1.25 cm thick. (Using a bench scraper to move the dough around the floured surface a bit from time to time at this stage will help with sticking.) Using a floured 3-inch/7.6 cm donut cutter, cut out the donuts, transferring each to the prepared baking sheet, along with the donut holes. You can gather the scraps, reroll them, and cut once more.

Place the baking sheet in the refrigerator to let the donuts firm up a bit while you heat the oil. In a deep 5-quart/4.75 L pot, such as a Dutch oven, over medium-high heat, heat 2 inches/5 cm of oil to 365°F/185°C.

Set up your frying station: Line a baking sheet with paper towels. Have ready a slotted spoon and/or a slotted spatula—a fish spatula works well. In a large bowl, whisk together the sugar, cinnamon, and salt for finishing the donuts.

Fry the donuts in small batches of 2 or 3 at a time, 3 minutes per batch, flipping the donuts halfway through cooking. Transfer the donuts to paper towels to drain briefly. While still hot, toss the donuts in the cinnamon sugar. Allow the oil to come back to 365°F/185°C before frying the next batch. These are best served on the day they're made, with any leftovers being stored in an airtight container and briefly warmed before serving the following day.

PĄCZKI

Makes about 12 pączki

NEARLY EVERY CULTURE HAS A NAME FOR THEIR VERSION OF A ROUND, YEAST-raised, filled donut, with names ranging from *sufganiyot* to *bombolone*, Berliners to *krapfen*. In the Midwest, they're most frequently found as Polish *pączki* (pronounced POONCH-key) and they create near-hysteria on Fat Tuesday—the day before the beginning of Lent—at bakeries making the best ones.

In my neighborhood, Oak Park Bakery goes positively insane leading up to Pączki Day, as Fat Tuesday is called in the Chicago area. Lines run out the door and down the block, and that's just the pickup queue for people who thought to call weeks ahead to secure their orders for their favorite flavors. Hell hath no fury like pączki-craving Chicagoans who can't get their fix from their favorite bakery. Man, I love this town.

But if you're going to go to the trouble of making pączki at home, and I urge you to try, go all in. Go big and poufy and fill them to bursting, and don't forget the powdery blanket of confectioners' sugar. The secret here is resting the dough overnight, and the addition of double-acting baking powder to give an extra fluff factor. It's a kitchen project well worth the effort.

DOUGH:

¼ cup/57 g warm water (110° to 115°F/43° to 46°C)

2¼ teaspoons instant yeast

¾ cup/168 g whole milk, at room temperature

¼ cup/50 g granulated sugar

2 large eggs

2 large egg yolks

4 tablespoons/57 g unsalted butter, melted and cooled slightly

1 teaspoon pure vanilla extract

3¾ cups/480 g unbleached all-purpose flour, spooned and leveled, plus more for dusting

1¼ teaspoons fine sea salt

1 teaspoon double-acting baking powder*

Nonstick cooking spray or oil for bowl

FRYING AND ASSEMBLY:

2 quarts/1.6 kg vegetable or canola oil

1½ cups/480 g filling of your choosing (see "Filling your pączki," next page)

Confectioners' or granulated sugar for coating

*Nearly all baking powder these days is double-acting, but check to make sure yours is. It's the key to making sure the dough gets the full effect of the baking powder given the overnight rest.

Prepare the dough: In the bowl of an electric mixer, whisk together the water and yeast. Set aside for a couple of minutes. Whisk in the milk, granulated sugar, eggs, egg yolks, melted butter, and vanilla. Add the flour, salt, and baking powder. Fit the mixer with the paddle attachment and begin mixing on low speed. Gradually increase the mixer speed to medium and mix for 5 minutes, stopping to scrape the bowl down occasionally. When the dough begins to pull away from the sides of the bowl, stop the mixer. The dough will still be quite sticky and have a glossy sheen. Spray a large bowl with nonstick cooking spray or oil it lightly. Place the dough in the bowl and cover tightly with plastic wrap. Refrigerate overnight (at least 8 hours).

The next day, lightly flour a work surface. Turn out the dough onto the surface and cut into 12 equal portions. Roll each piece into a smooth, taut ball. Working with 1 piece of dough at a time, use your fingertips to pull and fold the perimeter of the dough toward the center. Pinch the center together tightly, so it resembles a tiny drawstring purse. Flip the ball over onto the work surface and cup your hand over the ball. Roll the ball clockwise underneath your cupped hand to create a smooth orb. Place the donuts on a parchment-lined baking sheet and cover with a clean kitchen towel. Let rise until doubled in size, 3 to 4 hours (cold dough takes much longer to rise).

Set up your frying station: Line a baking sheet with paper towels. Have ready a slotted spoon and/or a slotted spatula—a fish spatula works well. To fry the pączki, pour 2½ inches/6.3 cm of vegetable oil into a 4- to 5-quart/3.75 to 4.75 L pot. Clip a deep-fry thermometer to the side of the pot. Over medium-high heat, heat the oil to 360°F/182°C. Fry the doughnuts in batches of no more than 4 at a time. Keep the donuts waiting to be fried covered loosely with plastic wrap to prevent them from drying out. Fry until deep golden brown all over, 1½ to 2 minutes per side, turning only once. The oil may not sizzle very much while frying. Transfer the pączki to paper towels to drain briefly. While hot, dust them generously with confectioners' sugar or toss in granulated sugar. Let cool completely before filling.

When cool, fill the donuts with the filling of your choosing (see below). Best served the same day. Store leftovers an airtight container (refrigerate for dairy-based fillings).

TIP › FILLING YOUR PĄCZKI. *So many options! A good-quality prepared jam is the simplest—raspberry, cherry, apricot, or even a jarred lemon curd are great. I love a vanilla custard filling (see Spoonable Vanilla Custard, page 309). With these fillings, use a skewer to drill a "pilot hole" in one side of the donut, then use a pastry bag fitted with a ¼- to ½-inch/6 mm to 1.25 cm tip to slowly fill them until they feel plump.*

You can also split and fill larger pączki like a donut sandwich, with whipped cream (see the Make-Ahead Whipped Cream, page 308) and sliced fresh strawberries for a classic, over-the-top Pączki Day presentation.

DAKOTA FRUIT KUCHEN

Serves 12 to 15

WHILE TRYING TO DECIDE WHICH STATES TO INCLUDE IN THIS BOOK, IT BECAME clear there are two camps: those who believe North and South Dakota belong in the category of "Midwest," and those who don't. I found most people who don't think these states count as the Midwest are Great Lakes–centric snobs like me, and I vowed to change my ways. When I widened the net to include these states, a jumble of irresistible stories, recipes, and immigrant influences came forth, namely the Dakotas' celebration of both German kuchen (South Dakota's state dessert) and Czech *kolaches*. It was official: the Dakotas were in.

As it happens, both kuchen and kolaches can be made from the same dough; it's just a matter of how you shape and fill them. In my travels, I've found that both *kuchen* and *kolache* can mean many things to different people—it seems there are as many versions of kuchen out there as there are families and bakeries. Generally speaking, kuchen is a coffeecake meant to be cut and shared and usually features seasonal fruit, whereas kolaches are smaller, handheld "pastries" with fillings cooked and prepared ahead of time. Whatever shape they take, they're all good with me.

DOUGH:

1 batch Buttery, Yeast-Raised Coffeecake Dough (page 23), unrisen

1/3 cup/43 g unbleached all-purpose flour, spooned and leveled, plus more for dusting

Nonstick cooking spray for pan

TOPPING:

1 cup/240 g full-fat sour cream

1/4 cup/50 g granulated sugar

1 large egg

1 tablespoon unbleached all-purpose flour

1/2 teaspoon ground cinnamon, finely grated lemon zest, or both

1/2 teaspoon pure vanilla extract

2 cups/340 g fresh blueberries, raspberries, or blackberries, or sliced firm-ripe stone fruits, such as peaches, Italian plums, or nectarines

Prepare the dough: Mix up a batch of Buttery, Yeast-Raised Coffeecake Dough, adding the extra 1/3 cup/43 g of flour to the dough. Allow to rise once, according to the directions on page 23. After the first rise, spray a 10 x 14-inch/25 x 38 cm light-colored metal baking pan or jelly-roll pan with nonstick cooking spray. Pat the dough evenly into the pan, creating a 1/2-inch/1.25 cm ridge up all 4 sides of the pan. Cover loosely with plastic wrap and allow to rise a second time until puffy, about 45 minutes.

Position a rack to the center of the oven and preheat the oven to 350°F/180°C.

Prepare the topping: In a medium bowl, whisk together the sour cream, sugar, egg, flour, cinnamon or lemon zest, and vanilla until smooth. Sprinkle the blueberries over the risen dough. Pour the sour cream mixture over the top.

Bake until puffed, fragrant, and golden at the edges, 35 to 40 minutes. The center will still appear very loose, but will set upon cooling. Let cool completely in the pan set on a wire rack.

VARIATION:

KOLACHES

Using the same dough as the kuchen, you can create another of the Dakotas' finest Czech imports, kolaches. After the dough completes its first rise, turn it out onto a floured surface. Line a 12 x 17-inch/30 x 43 cm baking sheet with parchment paper. Divide the dough into 12 to 15 equal pieces. Shape each piece into a taut ball. Place the dough balls on the prepared baking sheet, evenly spaced. Using your palm, flatten each ball into a disk about 1/2 inch/1.25 cm thick. Cover the sheet pan with plastic wrap and allow to rise for 20 minutes.

Position a rack to the center of the oven and preheat it to 350°F/180°C.

Using your thumbs, make an indentation in the center of each pastry, and add a spoonful of the fruit filling of your choice: a small dollop of jam, store-bought fruit filling, or prepared pie filling all work well. In a small cup, beat together 1 large egg, 1 tablespoon of water, and a pinch of fine sea salt until liquefied. Use a pastry brush to lightly brush the exposed edges of each pastry with egg wash. (For extra points, mix up a batch of the streusel from the Swedish Flop, page 21, and sprinkle over the tops.)

Bake until risen and golden brown, 20 to 25 minutes. Let cool slightly before serving.

REAL DEAL ST. LOUIS GOOEY BUTTER CAKE

Serves 12 to 15

THESE DAYS, WHEN PEOPLE HEAR ABOUT THIS CAKE, THEY'RE FAMILIAR WITH THE cake mix version involving all manner of instant puddings and what not, found on so many websites. I've always found that version cloying and more gloppy than gooey, and not really my style. Turns out, this popular version of "gooey butter cake" is just a shadow of what this midwestern classic was truly meant to be.

Then again, Gooey Butter Cake was never really meant to be at all. It was a happy accident when a baker in St. Louis, intending to make one of his bakery's traditional German yeasted coffeecakes, made a ratio-swapping mistake and way too much butter was added to the coffeecake topping. That mistake proved profitable, and people in St. Louis and beyond have loved the concept ever since. When you make it from scratch, it becomes more balanced in flavor and texture, and even more lovable. Some folks serve it as a coffeecake, some as a special occasion cake. I'll eat it whenever, especially with a few modern ingredient tweaks to improve levels of sweetness, richness, and crave-worthy chew.

DOUGH:

Nonstick cooking spray for pan

1 batch Buttery, Yeast-Raised Coffeecake Dough (page 23), first rise complete

All-purpose flour for dusting

TOPPING:

1/2 cup/113 g unsalted butter, at room temperature

4 ounces/113 g full-fat cream cheese, at room temperature

1 cup/200 g granulated sugar

1/3 cup/75 g firmly packed light brown sugar

1 tablespoon pure vanilla extract

1/2 teaspoon fine sea salt

1/4 cup/84 g light corn syrup

1 large egg, at room temperature

1 cup/128 g unbleached all-purpose flour, spooned and leveled

Confectioners' sugar for dusting

Prepare the dough: Position a rack to the center of the oven and preheat it to 325°F/170°C. Spray a 9 x 13-inch/23 x 33 cm glass baking dish with nonstick cooking spray.

After the dough has finished its first rise, flour your hands and pat the dough into an even layer into the prepared pan. Cover with plastic wrap and let rise a second time for 20 minutes.

Meanwhile, prepare the topping: In the bowl of an electric mixer fitted with the paddle attachment, beat together the butter and cream cheese on medium-high speed until smooth and creamy. Add the granulated and brown sugars, vanilla, and salt, and beat until light and fluffy, about 3 minutes. Add the corn syrup and egg and beat until

smooth. Reduce the mixer speed to low and gradually stir in the flour. Fold the batter by hand a few times with a large flexible spatula until well blended.

When the dough has finished its second rise, dollop the topping over the dough. Use a small offset spatula to spread it evenly.

Bake until puffed and golden, but still quite loose in the center, about 40 minutes (it will appear almost liquid under the surface in spots, but will quickly set upon cooling. Have a peek at the bottom of the cake through the glass dish; if it's deeply golden, you're in good shape). Let cool completely in the pan set on a wire rack. Dust with confectioners' sugar before slicing and serving.

BELGIAN PIE

Makes 4 Belgian pies

IN THE SPIRIT OF CREATING NEW MIDWESTERN TRADITIONS, WE'VE ESTABLISHED a summertime vacation taking place the week right before school starts up again, a last hurrah giving us all something to look forward to in the dog days. Door County, Wisconsin, has been our destination, a quirky part of the state offering rich maritime history, old-school supper clubs, and gorgeous scenery.

Tucked in the southern portion of Door County is a sprawling rural area established during the Belgian settlement, which began with just four families founding Brussels, Wisconsin, in 1853. Southern Door County is still home to the nation's largest Belgian American population, and the traditions continue, nearly 170 years later. During one trip, I happened to meet a woman named Gina Guth, well known in the area for making and teaching classes on Belgian pie, inspired by her generations-old family recipe, which she was very generous to share with me.

Belgian pie isn't really a "pie" at all, it's more like a shared pastry, with a yeasted dough as its base. The pies can have a number of different fillings (cherry, apple, prune, and a rice pudding–like cream are typical), with a sweet cheese topping made with a combination of regular and dry-curd cottage cheese (also known as farmer cheese). The spirit of the pies is one of celebration and abundance (and always made and served during the early-fall Belgian celebration of Kermiss), so many old recipes make at least a dozen pies or more. I riffed upon Gina's recipe and scaled it down to make just four, which is enough for sharing with a few neighbors, instead of distributing to an entire village.

DOUGH:

⅓ cup/75 g warm water (110° to 115°F/43° to 46°C)

1 tablespoon instant yeast

2 tablespoons granulated sugar, divided

⅓ cup/80 g warm heavy whipping cream (110° to 115°F/43° to 46°C)

2 large eggs, at room temperature

5 tablespoons/70 g unsalted butter, melted and slightly warm

3 cups/384 g unbleached all-purpose flour, spooned and leveled, plus more for dusting

½ teaspoon fine sea salt

Nonstick cooking spray or oil for bowl and pans

CHEESE TOPPING:

6 ounces/170 g dry-curd cottage cheese or farmer cheese

6 ounces/170 g small-curd cottage cheese

6 tablespoons/75 g granulated sugar

2 large egg yolks, beaten (reserve 1 white for egg wash)

½ teaspoon finely grated lemon zest

FILLING:

4 cups Homemade Cherry Pie Filling (page 301) or 2 (21-ounce/595 g) cans high-quality cherry pie filling

FINISHING:

1 large egg white

2 teaspoons water

Pinch of fine sea salt

Prepare the dough: In the bowl of an electric mixer, whisk together the water, yeast, and a pinch of sugar. Allow the yeast to dissolve for a few minutes. Whisk in the remaining sugar, cream, eggs, and melted butter. Add the flour and salt. Use a wooden spoon to stir until a shaggy dough forms. Fit the bowl onto the mixer along with the dough hook. Knead on medium speed for 6 to 7 minutes, until the dough is soft and shiny.

Spray a medium bowl with nonstick cooking spray or oil it lightly. Scrape the dough into the bowl and dust the surface of the dough with a couple of teaspoons of flour. Cover the bowl tightly with plastic wrap. Let rise in a warm place until doubled in bulk, 45 minutes to 1 hour.

To make the cheese topping, in the bowl of a food processor, blend together all the topping ingredients until smooth and creamy. Refrigerate until ready to use.

Spray four 9-inch/23 cm thin metal pie tins with nonstick cooking spray. Turn out the dough onto a lightly floured work surface. Divide the dough into 4 equal pieces. Press each portion of dough into a pan in an even layer. Cover each pan with plastic wrap and let rise a second time until slightly puffy, about 20 minutes.

Position racks to the upper and lower thirds of the oven and preheat it to 350°F/180°C.

Top each crust with one quarter of the fruit filling and cheese topping. In a small cup, beat together the egg white, water, and salt. Brush the exposed edges of the crusts with egg wash. Bake the pies, 2 per rack, until the crust is golden and the filling bubbling slightly, about 15 minutes, rotating the pies from top to bottom halfway through the baking time.

Allow the pies to cool slightly in the pans before transferring them to a wire rack to cool completely.

TIP › *Old-fashioned, thin metal pie plates are the way to go for this recipe. I have a small stack of tins I've thrifted with Belgian pie-making as my excuse, but you can also use those disposable foil pie plates from the supermarket— all the better to gift them with.*

CHAPTER 2
PASTRIES

DRESSIER THAN A QUICK BREAD, MORE DAZZLING THAN A DONUT,
nothing says "fancy coffee break" quite like a flaky, filled pastry. Some of that magic comes from the unique qualities a good pastry offers—it's at once airy and rich, firm and tender. It's strong enough to support fillings or add-ins, but melts in the mouth. It can be the building block of a recipe, or when made well, the star.

Generally speaking, it's interesting to note that many beloved pastries in the Midwest have Scandinavian and Western European roots, while most favorites made with yeasted, enriched doughs, like those in the previous chapter, tend to come from Eastern European settlers.

By definition, pastry differs from the sweet enriched doughs in the previous chapter because of the percentage of fat in the recipes (read: a whole lot more), and the ways in which that fat in a recipe is married with the starch (such as cold butter worked into flour) to create either many whisper-thin layers or a nubbly-yet-airy patchwork in the final product.

Some recipes here use yeast for lifting that network of fat and starch, whereas others use baking powder, or simply the power of eggs. In all cases, the alchemy of pastry making is pretty fascinating, and it doesn't have to be complicated. If you want to experience the sorcery of combining butter and flour, and impressing yourself along the way, this chapter is for you.

DANISH KRINGLE

Makes 2 kringle

MY HUSBAND IS AN EXCEPTIONAL PARENT. I OFTEN FEEL LIKE I SHOULD STEP IT up and mother a bit harder—more kitchen table crafts, more Lego construction sessions on the carpet, exciting field trips to all the spectacular museums in the city—because he is always doing these things with the kids every chance he gets. He revels in it. It makes me look bad.

But at some point, I realized there are things I do with the kids that are extremely important to their personal development that he would never think to do. For instance, who was the parent who drove the older child all the way to Racine, Wisconsin, for a day trip we called the Kringle Krawl? And brought said child to four different bakeries in the city, all known for their kringle, to sample them all, grill the bakers at each place about their methods, and determine once and for all who makes the best dang kringle in all of Racine? It was not her father, I will tell you that right now. It was all me, exposing my child to the greatness of Wisconsin's state pastry in a very scientific manner. Science, I tell you! Education! Artistry, history, and interpersonal skills! All wrapped into many, many layers of buttery pastry.

FILLING*:

6 ounces/170 g almond paste

4 tablespoons/57 g unsalted butter, at room temperature

1/4 cup/30 g confectioners' sugar

2 tablespoons well-beaten egg white

1/4 teaspoon freshly squeezed lemon juice

Pinch of fine sea salt

DOUGH:

All-purpose flour for dusting

1 batch Shortcut Danish Pastry (page 48)

ICING:

1 batch Five-Finger Icing (page 303)

*My favorite kringle has an almond filling as seen here, but mix it up by using any store-bought jam, lemon curd, or prepared fruit filling you like—you'll need 1 cup of filling to make 2 pastries.

Position racks to the upper and lower thirds of the oven, and preheat it to 375°F/190°C. Line two 12 x 17-inch/30 x 43 cm baking sheets with parchment paper.

Prepare the almond filling: Combine all the filling ingredients, reserving a little of the beaten egg white for brushing the dough, in a medium bowl. Use a handheld mixer to beat everything together until smooth.

Prepare the dough: Lightly flour a work surface. Divide the dough in half. Roll out each half to a long, narrow rectangle of dough, 6 x 24 inches/15.25 x 61 cm. Spread 1/2 cup/170 g of the filling in an even strip down the center. Fold in 1 side lengthwise, over the filling.

Using a pastry brush, slick the entire open border of dough with the reserved beaten egg white, on both the long end and the 2 short ends. Fold the second long side over the first toward the center. Pinch and press the seam tightly, sinking your fingertips into the pastry, all along the seam to create a tight seal. Remeasure the length of dough—if it's shrunken a bit, gently press and stretch it back out to at least 24 inches/61 cm. Form the strip of dough into an oval.

Insert 1 end of the pastry into the other by at least 1½ inches/3.8 cm, then tightly pinch and press the seam together. Flip the oval over, seam-side down, onto the prepared baking sheet. Cover loosely with plastic wrap. Repeat the filling and shaping with the second portion of dough. Allow the pastries to rise for 30 minutes, until slightly puffy.

Brush all over with beaten egg white.

Bake until golden, about 25 minutes, rotating the baking sheets from front to back and top to bottom halfway through the baking time. As soon as the pans come out of the oven and the pastries are piping hot, do something that seems a little crazy: Compress each pastry slightly by using the baking pan with the other pastry on it—just set the pan on top of the pastry and press gently to eliminate the air pocket between the pastry and filling. Allow the pastries to cool completely on the pans set over wire racks before icing.

Ice the kringles with Five-Finger Icing. Let the icing dry before slicing and serving.

SHORTCUT DANISH PASTRY

Makes 1 large braid, 2 kringles, or nine 5-inch/12.7 cm Danish pastries

THE LONG-GAME VERSION OF DANISH PASTRY INVOLVES MAKING A YEAST DOUGH and a "butter block"—a plank created from mashed-together sticks, and then wrapping the butter in dough before a rolling and folding process creates loads of whisper-thin layers of butter and dough. It's time-consuming, not foolproof, and honestly, I don't find this traditional version any more satisfying than a shortcut version once everything is shaped, baked, and filled. When I learned Scandinavian baking goddess and Minnesotan Beatrice Ojakangas swears by a shortcut recipe and claims no home baker in Denmark does it any other way, I was sold.

Making laminated dough—shortcut or not—might seem a bit intimidating at first. But look at it this way: with this method, it's not all that different from making a pie crust. You'll just be rolling the dough out a few more times, and folding it between rollings. It's pretty magical to see it transform from shaggy and crazy-looking to supple and silky, right before your eyes. And when you bake it, the puffed, golden, flaky results will blow minds and take names.

1 cup/128 g unbleached all-purpose flour, spooned and leveled, plus more for dusting

1 cup/128 g unbleached bread flour, spooned and leveled

3 tablespoons/38 g granulated sugar

2 teaspoons instant yeast

3/4 teaspoon fine sea salt

1 cup/225 g cold unsalted butter, cut into 1/2-inch/1.25 cm cubes

1/3 cup/75 g cold whole milk

1 large egg, cold

In the bowl of a food processor fitted with a steel S blade, combine the all-purpose and bread flour, sugar, yeast, and salt. Pulse several times to blend. Add the cold butter cubes and pulse 10 times, or until the butter chunks are broken down by about half.

In a medium bowl, whisk together the milk and egg. Dump the flour mixture into the bowl. Use a flexible spatula to gently stir the dough until nearly all the flour is moistened. Use your hand to quickly knead the dough just a few times in the bowl to bring it all together into a shaggy mass. There will lots of large chunks of butter still visible in the dough.

Line a work surface with plastic wrap. Turn out the dough onto the plastic and pat into a rectangle. Wrap the dough tightly. Refrigerate for at least 4 hours, or up to 2 days.

Lightly flour a work surface and rolling pin. Roll the dough out to a rough rectangle, 8 x 15 inches/20 x 38 cm. Fold the rectangle into thirds toward the center, like a letter. Rotate the dough 90 degrees. Roll it out again, 8 x 15 inches/20 x 38 cm. Fold into thirds. (This completes 2 turns of the dough. It will look a bit knobby and cracked at this stage, don't worry.) Wrap the dough in plastic wrap. Chill for at least 20 minutes. Repeat the rolling, folding, and chilling process twice more until you've completed 6 turns in all. After the last round of chilling, shape and bake according to your recipe, or wrap tightly in a double layer of clean plastic wrap and refrigerate for up to 3 days, or freeze for up to 2 months.

SEVEN SISTERS

Serves 7

IN DENMARK, THIS BREAKFAST PASTRY—MADE OF SEVEN INDIVIDUAL, FILLED DANISH pastry rolls nestled in a bed of luscious custard—is often known as *smørkage*, meaning "buttercake." It can be made with an enriched yeast dough like you'd use for cinnamon rolls, or with a flaky pastry. In Racine-area bakeries famous for their kringle, you'll find it made with the latter, and charmingly called Seven Sisters.

Since Denmark sits snugly between the North and Baltic Seas, the Danes have naturally always been a seafaring people. The star cluster known as Pleiades, or the Seven Sisters, is the brightest and closest to the Earth's Northern Hemisphere, especially in the winter months, when it can be seen with the naked eye from sunset to sunrise.

The Seven Sisters helped guide sailors' journeys, and this aptly named coffeecake guides cravings in the Midwest today. To manage the effort of creating this pastry centerpiece, I like to divide the tasks as a sailor would—make the pastry and fillings one day, and assemble the elements the next morning before baking.

CUSTARD FILLING:

³/₄ cup/168 g whole milk

3 tablespoons/38 g granulated sugar

1 large egg yolk

1 tablespoon plus 1 teaspoon cornstarch

Pinch of fine sea salt

¹/₂ teaspoon pure vanilla extract

¹/₂ teaspoon pure almond extract

ALMOND FILLING:

3 ounces/75 g almond paste

2 tablespoons light brown sugar

2 tablespoons unsalted butter, very soft

¹/₄ teaspoon pure almond extract

Pinch of fine sea salt

1 large egg white, lightly beaten

1 teaspoon ground cinnamon (optional)

DOUGH:

Nonstick cooking spray for pan

All-purpose flour, for dusting

1 batch Shortcut Danish Pastry (page 48), chilled

1 batch Five-Finger Icing (page 303)

Prepare the custard: In a 1- to 1½-quart/1 to 1.4 L saucepan, whisk together the milk, granulated sugar, egg yolk, cornstarch, and salt until well blended. Over medium heat, whisk often until the custard is very thick and just beginning to bubble, about 5 minutes. Whisk in the vanilla and almond extracts. Press the custard through a sieve into a small bowl. Cover the surface with a sheet of plastic wrap and refrigerate until cold and firm, at least 4 hours, or up to 2 days ahead.

Next, prepare the almond filling: In a small bowl, crumble the almond paste, then add the brown sugar, butter, almond extract, and salt. Mash with a fork to blend well. Add 1 tablespoon of the beaten egg white. Continue to mash and stir until a thick but spreadable paste forms. If necessary, drizzle in an extra teaspoon or two of egg white to reach a peanut butter–like consistency. Stir in the ground cinnamon (if using). Refrigerate until ready to use, up to 2 days ahead.

Prepare the dough: Spray an 8-inch/20 cm round cake pan with nonstick cooking spray.

On slightly floured work surface, cut off a third of the dough, crosswise. Roll out the smaller portion of dough to a rough 8-inch/20 cm square. Place the pastry in the prepared pan and press it thinly and evenly across the bottom and about 1 inch/2.5 cm up the sides. Set in the refrigerator to chill while you shape the rolls. Remove the almond filling and custard from the refrigerator.

Roll the other portion of dough to an 8 x 10-inch/20 x 25 cm rectangle, with the longer side facing you. Spread thinly and evenly with half the almond filling. Whisk the custard until smooth and spread about ¼ cup of it over the almond filling. Roll up into a tight log, pinching the seam together. Cut into 7 equal rolls.

Spread the remaining half of the almond filling evenly on the bottom of the chilled pastry shell. Top with the remaining custard. Place the rolls in the custard with the seams facing inward, first with 1 roll in the center, and the remaining 6 circling it. Cover loosely with plastic wrap and let rest in a warm place for about 30 minutes until slightly puffy (it will not rise as much as a bread dough).

Position a rack to the center of the oven and preheat it to 375°F/190°C. Bake for 40 to 45 minutes, until deeply golden and the custard is set on the edges—there may be a slight wobble toward the center. Set the pan on a wire rack to cool completely.

Drizzle with Five-Finger Icing. When the icing has set, cut and serve. Store any leftovers tightly covered at room temperature for up to 2 days.

DUTCH LETTERS

Makes 20 Dutch letters

THE FIRST SUMMER I BEGAN TRAVELING TO RESEARCH THIS BOOK WAS FULL OF hilarious people and stories, and many, many calories. One excursion was a four-day road trip across Iowa with my best friend, Sara, a native of the Hawkeye State. We stayed a couple of nights in the tiny village of Lynville, Iowa, where the owner of our rented apartment also ran the adjacent antique and coffee shop, providing Sara and me with new retirement goals. We could've made a documentary film with all the characters we met along the way and their opinions of what qualified as "must-haves" when trying to distill the state specialties.

One treat mentioned by all were the Dutch letters at Jaarsma Bakery in Pella, Iowa. We'd missed the town's famous Tulip Festival by just a couple of weeks, but remnants of Dutch pride still remained—the enormous windmill in the town square, rows of vibrant tulips, stacks of blue and white Delft tile and souvenirs in just about every shop, and of course, the famous Jaarsma Bakery, where we stood in the most cheerful line ever for a taste of its famous letters. We chowed down right outside the door on the sidewalk, shoulder to shoulder with other letter-eaters who couldn't wait to get back to their cars before tearing into waxed paper bags full of flaky almond pastries. When shaped into a few larger rolls rather than individual handheld pastries, this combination of pastry and almond filling is known in different parts of the region as almond banket.

PASTRY:

4½ cups/575 g unbleached all-purpose flour, spooned and leveled, plus more for dusting

1 teaspoon fine sea salt

2 cups/450 g unsalted butter, cut into ½-inch/1.25 cm cubes

1 cup/225 g cold water

1 large egg

FILLING:

8 ounces/225 g almond paste

2 large egg whites

½ cup/100 g granulated sugar, plus more for sprinkling

½ cup/113 g firmly packed dark brown sugar

⅛ teaspoon fine sea salt

1 teaspoon pure vanilla extract

FINISHING:

¼ cup/57 g whole milk for brushing

¼ cup/50 g granulated sugar for sprinkling

Prepare the pastry: In a large bowl, whisk together the flour and salt. Add the butter and toss with your fingertips until the butter pieces are all coated with flour.

In a small bowl, whisk together the cold water and the egg. Pour the egg mixture into the flour mixture. Stir with a wooden spoon to form a shaggy dough. Lightly flour a work surface and turn the dough out onto it. Knead until the dough just begins to come together, about 10 strokes. Roll out the dough into a 10 x 15-inch/25 x 38 cm rectangle. Fold the 2 short sides of rectangle toward the center so they meet in middle, and then fold the left side of the dough toward the right, closing it like a book. Rotate the rectangle 90 degrees; repeat the rolling and book-folding technique. Wrap the dough in plastic wrap and chill for 20 minutes. Unwrap the dough and repeat the rolling and folding technique twice more. Wrap the dough with plastic wrap again and chill for 1 hour more. Don't clean that work surface just yet!

Meanwhile, prepare the filling: In a medium bowl, combine the almond paste, egg whites, granulated and brown sugar, salt, and vanilla. Use a handheld mixer on medium-high speed to beat the filling until smooth, about 2 minutes.

Position racks to the upper and lower thirds of the oven and preheat it to 375°F/190°C. Line two 12 x 17-inch/30 x 43 cm baking sheets with parchment paper.

Lightly reflour your work surface. Divide the dough into 4 equal portions. Working with 1 portion of dough at a time (and keeping the remainder wrapped and chilled), roll each piece into a 10 x 12½-inch/25 x 32 cm rectangle. Using a pizza cutter or thin, sharp knife, divide the rectangle into 5 strips, each measuring 2½ x 10 inches/6.3 x 25 cm. Place 1 heaping tablespoon of the filling onto each strip. Slightly dampen your fingertips and use them to spread the filling in a long ribbon down the center of each strip.

Roll up each strip lengthwise into a thin tube, completely encasing the filling. Using a pastry brush, dampen the edges and ends of each with milk, and pinch the dough to seal tightly. Roll the tube back and forth a few times to ensure the seal and lengthen the tube by 1 inch/2.5 cm or so. Shape each tube into an S shape and place the pastries, seam-side down and evenly spaced, on the prepared baking sheets, 5 per sheet. Brush the tops lightly with milk and sprinkle liberally with granulated sugar.

Bake the pastries until golden, about 25 minutes, rotating the sheets from top to bottom and front to back halfway through the baking time. Transfer to a wire rack and let cool for 20 minutes before serving.

TIP › *Even though it's rare you'll find yourself needing 20 Dutch Letters, I urge you to make an entire batch while you're in the groove, shape them, bake half, and freeze the remainder. Bake them from frozen, tacking on a couple of extra minutes to the baking time.*

WHITE CHOCOLATE CREAM CHEESE DANISH

Serves 9

OFTEN WHEN WE WANT "A DANISH," AN INDIVIDUAL, HANDHELD FILLED PASTRY like this is what we're after. And once you've rolled and folded your Danish dough, just about any shape of pastry can be yours. After rolling the dough out and trimming it into neat squares, you can just dollop filling in the center of each square and leave as is to create lovely little pillows, or you can get crafty, folding in the corners to create flower shapes (as instructed below), pinwheels, twists, and more—the Internet boasts a bevy of shaping ideas.

To serve these pastries at their optimal freshness, make the dough the day before, and give it its final chill overnight. The filling can be made a day ahead as well—just allow it to soften at room temperature while you shape the pastries.

FILLING:

4 ounces/113 g full-fat cream cheese, at room temperature

1 large egg yolk

½ teaspoon pure vanilla extract

¼ teaspoon pure almond extract

3 ounces/75 g high-quality white chocolate, melted and cooled

⅓ cup/110 g all-fruit preserves, lemon curd, or Apricot and Orange Blossom Lekvar (page 302) (optional)

DOUGH:

All-purpose flour for dusting

1 batch Shortcut Danish Pastry (page 48), chilled

1 large egg

1 tablespoon water

Pinch of fine sea salt

ICING:

1 batch Five-Finger Icing (page 303)

Prepare the filling: Place the cream cheese in the bowl of an electric mixer fitted with the paddle attachment. Beat on medium speed until soft and creamy, about 30 seconds. Add the egg yolk, vanilla, and almond extract. Beat until smooth. Add the melted white chocolate and beat just until blended.

Prepare the dough: Line two 12 x 17-inch/30 x 43 cm baking sheets with parchment paper. Lightly flour your work surface. Roll out the dough to a rough 13-inch/33 cm square. Use a ruler to mark out a 12-inch/30 cm square, and trim the edges neatly with a pizza cutter or sharp knife. Divide the dough into nine 4-inch/10 cm squares.

In a small cup, whisk together the egg, water, and salt. Use a pastry brush to lightly brush the dough with the egg wash. Working with 1 square at a time, fold all 4 corners toward the center of each piece of dough, pressing them down firmly in the center (or skip this shaping step and leave them square). Place each pastry onto the prepared baking sheets, evenly spaced. Dollop the filling into the center of each pastry, a scant 2 tablespoons each. Dab a teaspoon of jam (if using) on top of the filling. Let rise in a warm spot until slightly puffy, about 1 hour.

Position a rack to the center of the oven and preheat it to 375°F/190°C. Postrise, give the pastries a second light brushing of egg wash.

Bake until they are puffed and golden brown all over, 15 to 20 minutes. Let cool for 15 minutes. Drizzle with Five-Finger Icing.

GLAZED APPLE SLICES

Makes 2 dozen slices

THERE'S A FINE LINE BETWEEN APPLE PIE AND THIS RECIPE. ACTUALLY, I'LL LEVEL with you—I'm not sure there's a line at all. What it comes down to is how this item is found in midwestern bakeries: on sheet pans the size of barn doors, slicked with icing, often called an apple slice or apple square, and eaten out of hand midday with no thought about it being dessert. So, this recipe being a pastry and not pie is a state of mind, is what I'm saying.

I was drawn to this recipe from a late 1970s University of Wisconsin–Madison cookbook because of its inclusion of crushed cornflakes, running a highly convincing campaign on the basis of kitsch and function. What you get here is a pastry dough that's more forgiving than typical pie crust, and the ideal ratio of apple filling to crisp pastry, totally sog-proof thanks to that brilliant layer of crushed cereal, which magically disappears during baking. It's the seventh wonder of the midwestern baking world.

PASTRY:

2¾ cups/352 g unbleached all-purpose flour, spooned and leveled, plus more for dusting

2 tablespoons granulated sugar

1 teaspoon fine sea salt

1 cup/225 g unsalted butter, cold and cut into cubes

½ cup/113 g whole milk

1 large egg yolk

FILLING:

2¾ pounds/1.25 kg Granny Smith apples, peeled, cored, and thinly sliced (about 8 cups prepared)

⅓ cup/75 g firmly packed brown sugar

⅓ cup/67 g granulated sugar

1 teaspoon ground cinnamon

½ teaspoon freshly grated nutmeg

⅛ teaspoon fine sea salt

ASSEMBLY AND ICING:

3 cups/85 g cornflake cereal, finely crushed (to equal 1 cup/85 g crumbs)

1 large egg white

Pinch of fine sea salt

1 batch Five-Finger Icing (page 303)

Prepare the crust: In the bowl of a food processor fitted with the steel S blade, combine the flour, granulated sugar, and salt. Pulse several times to blend. Add the butter cubes and pulse until the mixture appears crumbly.

In a small cup, whisk together the milk and egg yolk. With the processor running, pour in the milk mixture and blend until the dough comes together.

Turn out the dough onto a work surface and divide in half. Pat each portion into a disk, wrap each tightly in plastic wrap, and refrigerate.

Prepare the filling: In a large bowl, toss together the apples, brown and granulated sugar, cinnamon, nutmeg, and salt.

Position a rack to the center of the oven and preheat it to 400°F/200°C. Line a 12 x 17-inch/30 x 43 cm baking sheet with parchment paper.

Roll out 1 portion of dough into a rectangle slightly smaller than the pan. Place the dough on the parchment. Scatter the dough with the crushed cornflakes, leaving a 1-inch/2.5 cm bare border. Spread the apple filling over the cornflakes in an even layer, leaving the border bare.

Roll out the second portion of dough to the same size. Lay this dough sheet over the apples. Make a 1-inch/2.5 cm upward fold all around the perimeter, and crimp to seal.

In a small cup, beat together the egg white and salt until liquefied. Use a pastry brush to lightly slick the surface of the dough with egg white.

Bake until golden brown, 50 to 60 minutes. Let cool on the pan set over a wire rack for about 15 minutes. While still warm, glaze the top with Five-Finger Icing. Let cool completely before serving.

CANDY BAR BAKLAVA

Makes about 2¹/₂ dozen pieces

RIGHT OFF THE TOP, LET ME SAY THIS RECIPE IS A TOTAL ABOMINATION TO MY Greek ancestry, I'm certain of that. But in my defense, I'm only, like, one-eighth Greek. So, basically what that means is I'm just Greek enough that adorable, rotund old Greek men approach me in random places with their hairy forearms, chunky gold rings, and Old Spice-d collars, silently look at my face with slightly narrowed eyes for a solid six seconds, and then ask me what my last name is (it's actually my mother's maiden name—Foropoulos—which becomes the big revelation in these conversations). But I'm not so Greek that I can't do ridiculous things like bastardize baklava in dangerously Pinteresting ways.

The roots of baklava, or baklawa, run deep in the Midwest. Not only is there a rich history of Greek immigrants, especially in urban areas—by 1920, one of every three restaurants in Chicago was operated by a Greek—but there's also a wonderfully strong representation of the Middle East throughout the region, and the pastry shops prove it. Such as in Dearborn, Michigan, home of the nation's largest Arab American population and the famous Shatila Bakery. It turns out legendary baklawa in different varieties that will inspire you to put your own twist on the classic, like this one.

Nonstick cooking spray for pan

LAYERS:

10 tablespoons/140 g unsalted butter

¹/₄ teaspoon plus ¹/₈ teaspoon fine sea salt, divided

1 cup/300 g chocolate hazelnut spread

1 (16-ounce/453 g) box phyllo dough*

3¹/₂ cups/420 g salted cocktail-style peanuts, very finely chopped**

SYRUP:

1¹/₄ cups/281 g lukewarm water, divided

1 cup/200 g granulated sugar

1 tablespoon honey

¹/₄ teaspoon fine sea salt

¹/₂ teaspoon pure vanilla extract

*You'll need 40 sheets of phyllo for this recipe.

**You want a mixture of nearly ground and pebbly lentil-size pieces. A food processor is the easiest way to do this, with about 25 pulses.

Position a rack to the center of the oven and preheat it to 350°F/180°C. Spray a 9 x 13-inch/23 x 33 cm light-colored metal baking pan with nonstick cooking spray.

Prepare the layers: In a 1- to 1¹/₂-quart/1 to 1.4 L saucepan, combine the butter and ¹/₄ teaspoon of the salt. Brown the butter (see page 177). Pour into a clean bowl and set aside to cool.

In a small, microwave-safe bowl, combine the chocolate hazelnut spread and remaining ⅛ teaspoon of salt. Heat in a microwave for about 30 seconds on **HIGH**, or until somewhat fluid.

Get your layering station ready: Unroll the phyllo pastry into a stack on a work surface (if your phyllo comes in a box with 2 rolls, unwrap only 1 roll to start, and unwrap the other as you need it). If the dimensions of the phyllo sheets are larger than your pan, use kitchen scissors to trim the stack of phyllo so the sheets will fit neatly. Wet a tea towel and wring it out until it's just damp. Place the towel over the pastry to keep it from drying out. Have your bowls of browned butter, warm chocolate hazelnut spread, and a pastry brush at the ready.

Start the layering: Place 2 sheets of phyllo in the bottom of the prepared pan. Lightly brush with browned butter. Add 2 more sheets and butter them. Repeat 3 more times until you have 10 sheets in total. Sprinkle with one third of the peanuts, and drizzle 1/3 cup of chocolate hazelnut spread on top. Place 2 more sheets of phyllo on top and butter them. Repeat 2 more times for a total of 6 new sheets. Add half of the remaining peanuts and 1/3 cup more chocolate hazelnut spread.

Layer with another 6 sheets, buttering every 2 sheets. Add the remaining peanuts and chocolate hazelnut spread (if either the browned butter and/or chocolate begins to solidify, microwave for 10 to 15 seconds). Add 6 more sheets of phyllo, buttering every other sheet. For the last 4 sheets at the top, butter between every single sheet, and the very top.

Using a thin, sharp knife, cut the baklava into diamond-shaped portions, slicing all the way through to the bottom of the pan. Start with 3 straight cuts evenly spaced down the length of the pan. Then, make 8 or 9 diagonal cuts across the pan, evenly spacing them.

Bake until golden and crisp, about 45 minutes.

During the final 10 minutes of baking, prepare the syrup: Pour 1/4 cup/57 g of the lukewarm water into a 1- to 1½-quart/1 to 1.4 L saucepan. Gently pour the sugar over the water in an even layer. Add the honey and salt. Place the pan over medium heat and stir slowly in a figure-eight motion to help the sugar dissolve while the mixture heats up. Once the syrup is nearly clear, increase the heat to high and stop stirring. Boil, swirling the pan occasionally, until the sugar caramelizes and turns a deep amber with a few wisps of smoke, 7 to 8 minutes total.

Briefly remove the pan from the heat and carefully pour in the remaining 1 cup/225 g of lukewarm water. Swirl the pan to incorporate the water into the caramel. Place the pan back over high heat and boil to a thin syrup, reducing it to about 1¼ cups/285 ml, about 5 minutes.

When the pastry has finished its 45-minute bake, transfer the pan to a wire rack to cool for 10 minutes. Leave the oven on! As soon as the syrup has finished reducing, whisk in the vanilla, then slowly drizzle the hot syrup over the still-hot pastry. Return the pastry to the oven to bake for 5 more minutes. Let cool completely in the pan set on a wire rack and rest at room temperature for at least 4 hours before serving.

A SIMPLE BRAN MUFFIN

Makes 10 muffins

IF YOU WERE A CHILD OF THE LATE '70S AND EARLY '80S, YOU LIKELY WENT THROUGH the harrowing period of your mom taking a flamethrower to everything in the cabinets that actually tasted good, and then expecting you to pretend carob was chocolate. Perhaps you also then had to take new, weird vitamins from a pyramid scheme company. Or occasionally sit in a hot car during yet another trip to a food co-op that smelled so weird inside you opted for the hot car. (This was also obviously before people called the cops on parents for this sort of thing.) My informal research of people my age indicates my experience was far from isolated, and that we all remember this torture lasting for approximately six months.

A bright spot in this bleak era of eating was the Jiffy bran muffin mix that would sometimes appear in the cupboard. Perhaps it was the "bran" and inclusion of fossilized dates in the powdery mix that allowed it to make the cut? I didn't care about the logic, because after too many snacks of cardboardy sprouted wheat cracker things, a Jiffy bran muffin hit the palate like a Twinkie. And even after this phase of hippie culinary values passed, I continued to crave those box-mix muffins. I still love a simple bran muffin, in fact. Nubbly with a springy chew, not too sweet, great with a smear of butter. Sometimes I throw in raisins, dates, dried cherries or blueberries, *never carob*. But most often I just want a straightforward, simple bran muffin.

3 cups/135 g bran flake cereal, finely crushed

1¼ cups/160 g unbleached all-purpose flour, spooned and leveled

⅔ cup/148 g firmly packed light brown sugar

1½ teaspoons baking soda

½ teaspoon fine sea salt

½ teaspoon ground cinnamon

1 cup/225 g well-shaken buttermilk

⅓ cup/75 g vegetable oil

1 large egg

½ teaspoon pure vanilla extract

3 tablespoons/37 g turbinado sugar for sprinkling

Into a large bowl, combine the cereal, flour, brown sugar, baking soda, salt, and cinnamon. Mix again, breaking down any clumps of brown sugar.

In a separate bowl, whisk together the buttermilk, oil, egg, and vanilla. Pour the wet ingredients into the dry and stir to blend well. Cover the bowl tightly with plastic wrap and refrigerate for at least 4 hours, or up to 12 hours. The batter will become very thick.

Position a rack to the center of the oven and preheat it to 400°F/200°C. Line a 12-well muffin tin with 10 paper liners. Divide the batter equally among the cups, filling them completely. Sprinkle with the turbinado sugar. Bake until golden and a toothpick inserted into the center of a muffin comes out clean, about 20 minutes. Let cool in the tin for 2 minutes before transferring them to a wire rack to cool completely. Store in an airtight container for up to 3 days.

TIP › *This recipe makes a rather, shall we say, controversial yield of 10 muffins. You can stretch it to an even dozen by putting less batter in each cup, but I like a generous look to my muffins, so I fill the muffin cups right up to the top and just make 10. You can double the recipe and keep the batter in a big covered bowl, refrigerated for up 5 days, baking off muffins as you need them.*

SCONE-TOP BLUEBERRY MUFFINS

Makes 12 muffins

AS RELATED TO THE APPEARANCE OF THE HUMAN BODY, A MUFFIN TOP IS TYPICALLY something to avoid. But as far as satisfying the breakfast cravings of a human body goes, a great muffin top is one of life's greatest pleasures. Of course, too many muffin tops of the latter sort can lead to the development of the former, but that is neither here nor there. When I landed on a muffin formula and method resulting in a crunchy, nubbly top reminiscent of my absolute favorite scones—those at Big Sur Bakery in Big Sur, California—with the tender interior you'd expect from a classic dump-and-stir muffin your grandmother might make, I forgot about how my pants might fit the next day after eating half of the batch, for at least an hour.

While the jury is out on whether a muffin should count as a "pastry," I can tell you this: the mixing method here begins with a pastry-making sensibility, and its irresistible sconelike muffin top qualify it for a spot in this section.

Nonstick cooking spray for pan (optional)

2½ cups/320 g unbleached all-purpose flour, spooned and leveled

1 cup/200 g granulated sugar, divided

2 teaspoons baking powder

¾ teaspoon baking soda

½ teaspoon fine sea salt

½ cup/113 g cold unsalted butter, cut into ½-inch/ 1.25 cm cubes

1 cup plus 2 tablespoons/253 g cold, well-shaken buttermilk

2 large eggs

2 teaspoons finely grated lemon zest

2½ teaspoons pure vanilla extract

¾ teaspoon pure almond extract

1 (12-ounce/340 g) bag frozen blueberries*

Frozen berries make this muffin possible year-round, and also tend to bleed into the batter less than fresh, but if you've got fresh, just fold them in as gently as possible. For frozen berries, keep them in the freezer right up until the moment you stir them into the batter.

Position a rack to the center of the oven and preheat it to 425°F/220°C. Line a 12-well muffin tin with tulip-style paper liners for a loftier rise, or if you're using regular paper liners, spray the top of the muffin pan with nonstick cooking spray in case the muffins mushroom outward.

In the bowl of a food processor fitted with the steel S blade, combine the flour, ¾ cup/150 g of the sugar, baking powder, baking soda, and salt. Pulse several times to blend. Add the butter pieces and process until the mixture resembles cornmeal, with no discernible butter pieces.

In a large bowl, whisk together the buttermilk, eggs, lemon zest, vanilla, and almond extract. Dump the contents of the food processor into the wet ingredients. Use a large, flexible spatula to fold the batter until well blended with no dry pockets. Add the frozen blueberries straight from the freezer. Fold the berries into the batter with just 4 or 5 productive turns of the spatula, to avoid streaking the batter with berry juice.

Divide the batter equally among the prepared muffin wells—each should be mounded full with batter. Pour the remaining ¼ cup/50 g of sugar into a small cup. Dampen your fingertips with water and work them through the sugar to make it clump slightly, like snow. Top each muffin with a generous pinch of snowy sugar.

Bake the muffins for 10 minutes at 425°F/220°C. Without opening the oven door, reduce the oven temperature to 375°F/190°C. Continue to bake for another 15 to 20 minutes, or until the muffins are golden and a toothpick inserted in the center of each muffin comes out clean. Let the muffins cool in the pan for just 2 minutes before transferring them carefully to a wire rack to cool completely (you may need to use a thin offset spatula or knife to loosen the edges of each muffin top from the pan first, if you didn't use tulip-style liners). Allow the muffins to cool completely before serving.

CHAPTER 3

PIE

WHEN DECIDING ON THE CHAPTERS FOR THIS BOOK, I KNEW PIE
would be a stand-alone, having a deep connection to the great Midwest. But it was hard to put it into words exactly where that connection comes from, and why it's such an important part of our history here in the central states. So, like any good pie enthusiast, I went to the ultimate expert, Paula Haney of Hoosier Mama Pie Company in Chicago, who spoke to me in the back of her shop as she worked her way through a giant mountain of her famous all-butter pie dough, kneading huge handfuls into portions for crusts. And she broke it down for me as such:

"I often compare it to cheese. The English, they made incredible cheese. They'd make it in these huge fifty-pound blocks, so they could get through the winter. But it was still really great cheese. Then there's the French, who made little tiny cheese, in pretty shapes, with a little fern on it or something. And that's great cheese, too; it's just a different approach. People tend to celebrate the French stuff more because of all the froufrou bits, but I don't think that's fair." Tell 'em, girl.

She went on. "The point is, with food, the practical approach doesn't usually get recognized as much, but there's still a lot of craft there. And that's how I feel about midwesterners and pie. Like, why would you make a bunch of individual desserts when you could feed your whole farm family of nine kids with one giant pie? It's still delicious, and just makes more sense." Indeed.

In addition to its practicality, pie is true farm food, showcasing all the good stuff the Midwest has to offer. The building blocks of a good pie are the bounty of the land: flour from hearty wheat; fresh dairy in the form of butter, milk, and cream, lard, and/or butter; and a rainbow of seasonal fruits. When those things are working in harmony with good technique, pie manages to be both elemental and, quite possibly, the perfect dessert.

Above all that, pie personifies the Midwest. Pie is home food. It's not pretentious. Pie is designed to be shared, in a slowed-down moment, at a table, in a chair, with a fork. Not too many things you can say that about anymore, now can you?

BLUEBARB AND LIME CRUMBLE PIE

Serves 8

MY HIGHLY SCIENTIFIC FOCUS GROUP RESEARCH (READ: VERY INFORMAL SOCIAL media polling) on the subject of pie quickly revealed something shocking: when it comes to fruit pies, people really, really love crumble toppings. Like flipping the bird to glossy double crusts—impassioned responses, I'm telling you. I was surprised. I mean, what is more beloved and all-American than a double-crusted apple pie? Apparently, a crumble-topped option. You get more crunchy texture in every bite, more brown-buttery and brown sugary depth, and a nice salty-sweet finish if the crumble is done right. The bonus here is that a crumble-topped pie is so much simpler than a double crust—turns out we've all been overthinking pie! With a recipe like this one, you only have to roll out and crimp one crust, which saves all that bicep strength for shoveling pie into your face.

The combination of blueberries and rhubarb is a midwestern classic, and to me, exponentially more exciting than pairing rhubarb with strawberries. The sharp hit of lime and whisper of ginger here give this pie a nice little kick.

TOPPING:

3/4 cup/96 g unbleached all-purpose flour, spooned and leveled

5 tablespoons/70 g unsalted butter, at cool room temperature

1/4 cup/50 g granulated sugar

2 tablespoons turbinado sugar

1/4 teaspoon fine sea salt

CRUST:

1 single batch My Favorite Pie Crust (page 74), chilled

2 teaspoons granulated sugar

2 teaspoons unbleached all-purpose flour

FILLING:

1 cup plus 2 tablespoons/225 g granulated sugar

6 tablespoons/48 g cornstarch

1/4 teaspoon ground cinnamon

1/4 teaspoon ground ginger

1/8 teaspoon fine sea salt

3 cups/450 g fresh blueberries

3 cups/300 g rhubarb, cut into 1/2-inch/1.25 cm pieces*

1 teaspoon finely grated lime zest

1 tablespoon freshly squeezed lime juice

1 tablespoon unsalted butter, melted

If you're using frozen rhubarb, measure the rhubarb while still frozen, then thaw it completely. Drain it in a colander, but don't press out any excess liquid.

Position a rack to the lower third of the oven and preheat it to 425°F/220°C.

Prepare the crumb topping: In the bowl of an electric mixer fitted with the paddle attachment, combine the flour, butter, granulated and turbinado sugar, and salt. Mix on medium-low speed until well blended, then continue to mix until the crumble forms gravel-size pieces. Freeze until ready to use.

Prepare the crust: Roll out the dough into an 11-inch/28 cm circle. Transfer to a 9-inch/23 cm pie plate, tuck under the edges, and crimp decoratively. Combine the sugar and flour in a small bowl and set aside. Set the pie plate in the freezer and freeze for at least 15 minutes.

Prepare the filling: In a large bowl, whisk together the sugar, cornstarch, cinnamon, ginger, and salt. Add the blueberries, rhubarb, lime zest and juice, and melted butter. Use your hand to gently toss the mixture until the fruit is evenly coated and there are no dry pockets.

Set the frozen crust on a rimmed baking sheet. Scatter the reserved flour mixture over the bottom of the crust. Scrape in the filling and spread it out evenly. Take the crumble from the freezer and scatter evenly over the top of the pie, patting gently so the crumble stays in place.

Bake for 10 minutes at 425°F/220°C, then lower the oven temperature to 375°F/190°C. Bake for 1 hour more, or until the juices are bubbling up through the crumb topping, tenting the pie with foil at about 45 minutes into the total baking time, to prevent the topping from burning. Let cool completely before slicing and serving, at least 2 hours.

NOTE > *Crust Dust! One of my favorite tricks for avoiding soggy-bottomed fruit pies is to dust the bottom with 2 teaspoons each of flour and sugar.*

TIP > *Seek out vintage Pyrex pie plates! I am not saying this to be precious and seem more interesting. I honestly feel the older plates perform better, and they are a true 9-inch/23 cm diameter, so my pies are loftier and crimped edges prettier. I scour thrift stores for them and have become way too adept at figuring out how old they are based on the style of Pyrex logo they have.*

HOW TO BLIND BAKE

One of the things I love most about baking is there's always more to learn. A trick I've picked up over the years has greatly improved the beauty and success of my pie crusts, especially those prebaked, or blind baked, before filling. Essentially what I do is treat them like puff pastry. The gist is this: start with nearly frozen dough, blast it with high heat to quickly evaporate moisture from the dough and shock the structure of the crust into place, then lower the temperature to finish baking.

To blind bake a single crust, preheat the oven to 425°F/220°C. Roll out the crust in an 11-inch/28 cm circle, with thickness between 1/8 and 1/4 inch/3 to 6 mm. Tuck into a 9-inch/23 cm pie plate. Trim and crimp the edges. Freeze the crust for 15 to 20 minutes. Line the bottom and sides of the pie shell with parchment paper or aluminum foil, leaving the edges exposed, and fill with pie weights, dried beans, pennies, or uncooked rice. Bake for 10 to 15 minutes, or until the crust begins to look dry, blistered, and blond in color. Lower the oven temperature to 375°F/190°C. Remove the pie weights and liner and bake the crust until lightly golden and firm and dry to the touch, about 10 minutes more. Let cool completely in the pan set on a wire rack before filling.

MY FAVORITE PIE CRUST

PIE CRUST PURISTS WILL LIKELY OBJECT, BUT I'M A BIG BELIEVER IN USING A FOOD processor for pie crust making. If you don't overdo it, it just doesn't get any easier or faster.

We've all heard a thousand times that keeping the fat as cold as possible is the key to great pie crusts, and that's certainly a great tip. But I add a few pinches and splashes that I consider insurance, for when the kitchen is hot or I'm distracted by any number of children or things.

Vinegar is great for tenderness: I like red wine vinegar, but cider vinegar is good, too. A little pinch of baking powder makes a flakier crust a little more foolproof in case you happen to overwork the dough (happens to the best of us). For a crust with a savory filling, I include the smaller amounts of sugar as listed here for flavor and browning. For sweet pies, use 1 or 2 tablespoons, as you like.

single

MAKES: *1 (9- or 10-inch/23 or 25 cm) round bottom pie or tart crust*

1⅓ cups/170 g unbleached all-purpose flour, spooned and leveled

1 teaspoon to 1 tablespoon granulated sugar (see headnote)

½ teaspoon fine sea salt

⅛ teaspoon baking powder

½ cup/113 g very cold unsalted butter, cubed

¼ cup/57 g ice water

1½ teaspoons red wine vinegar

SPECIAL NOTES > *Pat the finished dough into a round disk before wrapping and chilling to make rolling it into a circle later much easier.*

double

MAKES: *1 (9- or 10-inch/ 23 or 25 cm) round double-crusted or lattice-topped pie*

2⅔ cups/340 g unbleached all-purpose flour, spooned and leveled

2 teaspoons to 2 tablespoons granulated sugar (see headnote)

1 teaspoon fine sea salt

¼ teaspoon baking powder

1 cup/225 g very cold unsalted butter, cubed

½ cup/113 g ice water

1 tablespoon red wine vinegar

SPECIAL NOTES > *Divide the dough in half before shaping and wrapping. For a lattice top, make one disk slightly larger for the bottom crust.*

slab

MAKES: *1 (10 x 15-inch/ 30 x 43 cm) slab pie*

5⅓ cups/680 g unbleached all-purpose flour, spooned and leveled

4 teaspoons to 4 tablespoons granulated sugar (see headnote)

2 teaspoons fine sea salt

½ teaspoon baking powder

2 cups/453 g very cold unsalted butter, cubed

1 cup/225 g ice water

2 tablespoons red wine vinegar

SPECIAL NOTES > *Make the dough in 2 batches (2 recipes of the doubled recipe, left), for the top and bottom crusts. Shape and wrap each batch separately.*

METHOD: In the bowl of a food processor, combine the flour, sugar, salt, and baking powder. Pulse a few times to blend. Sprinkle half of the butter pieces over the dry ingredients. Process until the mixture resembles cornmeal, about 15 seconds. Add the remaining cold butter and pulse about 10 times, until this batch of butter cubes is broken down by about half.

In a measuring cup, combine the water and vinegar. Add about three quarters of the liquid to the bowl. Pulse about 10 times, or until the dough begins to form a few small clumps. Test the dough by squeezing a small amount in the palm of your hand. If it easily holds together and your palm isn't dusty with floury bits, it's done. If not, add an additional ½ tablespoon of vinegared water and pulse 2 or 3 more times. Repeat this process as needed just until the dough holds together. Turn out the mixture onto a work surface. With a few quick kneads, gather the dough into a mass. For a single crust, pat the dough into a disk, wrapping tightly in plastic wrap. For double crust, divide the dough in half and shape into disks. For 2 slab crusts, shape each half of the dough into a 5 x 8-inch/12.5 x 20 cm rectangle. Refrigerate for at least 2 hours before rolling.

TIP › *The dough will keep tightly wrapped in the fridge for up to a week, and in the freezer for up to 6 months.*

SECRET-INGREDIENT SWEET CHERRY SLAB PIE

Serves 12 to 15

ALTHOUGH THE ORIGINS OF SLAB PIE ARE UNKNOWN, NOTHING SAYS "HEARTLAND hospitality" quite like a veritable swath of pie, baked far and wide in a rimmed sheet pan to serve a crowd with ease. Essentially what you're dealing with here is a giant Pop-Tart, a boon for crust-lovers, with only a modest amount of filling.

It also means the filling needs to be intensely flavored to stand up to all that buttery, flaky crust. My version of a cherry slab pie makes use of all the glossy, fresh sweet cherries that tumble into markets and roadside farm stands here in the summertime. This recipe also pumps up the fruit's flavor with a subtle hit of Chinese five-spice powder: with its combination of anise, star anise, cinnamon, ginger, and clove, it makes for an unlikely addition that doesn't hit you over the head with spice, but instead lifts the cherry flavor to an intensity reminding me a little bit of a cherry Jolly Rancher. Precooking the fruit with a light-bodied red wine builds the cherry flavor even further, while eliminating the risk of a soggy pie in the end.

FILLING:

3 pounds/1.4 kg sweet red cherries, stemmed and pitted (about 6 cups)

3/4 cup/170 g light-bodied red wine, such as pinot noir

3/4 cup/90 g confectioners' sugar

1/4 cup/57 g firmly packed light brown sugar

3 tablespoons/24 g unbleached all-purpose flour

1 teaspoon Chinese five-spice powder

1/4 teaspoon fine sea salt

2 tablespoons/28 g unsalted butter, melted and cooled

1 tablespoon freshly squeezed lemon juice

1/2 teaspoon pure vanilla extract

1/2 teaspoon pure almond extract

CRUST:

All-purpose flour for dusting

1 slab-shaped batch My Favorite Pie Crust (page 74), chilled

FINISHING:

1 large egg

1 tablespoon water

1/8 teaspoon fine sea salt

3 tablespoons/38 g granulated sugar

Prepare the filling: Place the cherries in a 12-inch/30 cm skillet. Add the wine. Bring to a boil over medium heat, then lower the heat to a simmer. Cook, gently stirring every few minutes, until the cherries are soft and the liquid has reduced to a thick syrup, about 10 minutes. Scrape the cherries into a heatproof bowl and chill until completely cooled.

In a large bowl, whisk together the confectioners' sugar, brown sugar, flour, Chinese five-spice powder, and salt. Add the cooled cherries. Pour in the melted butter, lemon juice, vanilla, and almond extract. Stir gently until well combined.

Position a rack to the center of the oven and preheat it to 375°F/190°C. Have ready a 10 x 15-inch/25 x 38 cm rimmed sheet pan (a.k.a. a jelly-roll pan).

Prepare the crust: Generously flour a work surface. Place 1 piece of the dough on the surface, and dust with flour. Roll out the dough to about 14 x 19 inches/26 x 48 cm. Carefully transfer it to the sheet pan. It can be tough to roll it all out flawlessly in a single go, so feel free to patch corners and thinner spots with trimmed bits of dough from thicker areas—it will all come out lovely in the end.

Scrape the filling into the crust and smooth it evenly. It may look a bit scant, but that's okay. (Remember slab pie isn't as generously filled as a traditional round.)

Reflour your work surface and roll out the second piece of dough to 12 x 17 inches/30 x 43 cm. Cut lengthwise into strips to create a lattice top, or carefully drape the entire sheet over the filling. Fold the overhanging edges over the top crust. Use a fork or your fingertips to gently crimp the top and bottom crusts together. Knife several vents in the top crust.

In a small cup, beat together the egg, water, and salt. Using a pastry brush, brush the entire pie with the egg wash. Finish by dusting with granulated sugar.

Bake until deeply golden and the filling is bubbling, 40 to 45 minutes, rotating the pie 180 degrees halfway through baking. Let cool completely before cutting into squares. Store any leftovers tightly covered at room temperature for up to 3 days.

FIND YOUR FOREVER PIN

When I first started pie-making, I made the mistake of buying what one of my favorite TV chefs used, a tapered French-style pin, thinking it would be the answer to all my pie crust–rolling woes. It didn't really help—I could never get the hang of this fancy pin. With a classic ball-bearing pin, I never feel like I'm one with the dough and estimating thickness correctly. I started to think rolling pie crust was like having a green thumb.

But what I realized is you've got to pick a pin that suits your hands, with a weight that works with the distribution of pressure your body naturally applies to the pin while rolling, and dealing with pie crust suddenly becomes easier and a lot more fun. I imagine it's a little like choosing a baseball bat or a golf club, if I had any sporting abilities whatsoever. I switched to a big, long, heavy maple dowel, and found my ultimate fit. You do you.

BROWNED BUTTER-SPECKLED SUGAR CREAM PIE

Serves 8 to 10

INDIANA SUGAR CREAM PIE IS A HOOSIER CLASSIC, AND FALLS INTO THE CATEGORY of "desperation pies," pulled together during lean times with few ingredients at a moment's notice. When done well, sugar cream pie is the kind of baking alchemy that takes a handful of questionable ingredients and turns them into something so divine, it's as though David Copperfield himself traded in all those hours of maintaining his coif for pie making.

This version of sugar cream pie is a winner: it takes a humble, traditional concept and builds in some modern techniques to make it seriously rich and flavorful, like a brown-sugared crème brûlée in a pie shell, I'm telling you. Don't be alarmed when the filling almost appears to still be completely liquid when you pull it from the oven—the last bit of magic happens as the pie cools and sets so creamy and firm that you can eat slices out of hand.

1 single batch My Favorite Pie Crust (page 74), blind baked and hot

3/4 cup/150 g granulated sugar

1/4 cup/57 g dark brown sugar

5 tablespoons/40 g unbleached all-purpose flour

Generous 1/4 teaspoon fine sea salt

1/8 teaspoon freshly grated nutmeg

2 tablespoons/28 g unsalted butter

1¼ cups/300 g heavy whipping cream

3/4 cup/170 g whole milk

1½ teaspoons pure vanilla extract

Confectioners' sugar for dusting

After blind baking the crust, increase the oven temperature to 400°F/200°C. Place the hot pie crust on a large, rimmed baking sheet.

In a large bowl, whisk together the granulated and brown sugar, flour, salt, and nutmeg, breaking up any clumps.

In a 1- to 1½-quart/1 to 1.4 L saucepan over medium-high heat, brown the butter (see page 177). Pour the hot browned butter into the flour mixture. Whisk until the mixture is uniform in texture, like slightly dampened sand.

Pour the cream and milk into the saucepan you used to brown the butter—no need to clean it. Place the pan over high heat and heat the mixture until hot to the touch, but don't let it simmer. Remove the pan from the heat and stir in the vanilla. Whisk half of the cream mixture into the flour mixture until smooth, then gently whisk in the remainder. Pour the warm filling into the warm crust. Bake the pie on the baking sheet for 20 minutes. Rotate the pan 180 degrees. Cover the edges of the pie with foil if it is already looking near done. Then, bake for 20 minutes more—the filling itself will still be quite liquidy; it will set as it cools. Let the pie cool on a wire rack until it reaches room temperature, then refrigerate for at least 4 hours, or until cold and set. Serve cool. Dust with confectioners' sugar before serving.

TIP › *Crust Spackle! If you've ever lovingly shaped and blind baked a pie crust, only to have it emerge from the oven with a crack that would surely lead to filling leakage, all is not lost. In a small cup, fork together 2 tablespoons of flour, 1 tablespoon of melted butter, and a pinch of sugar until a claylike substance forms. Gently pack and smooth the mixture into the cracks. Bake at 375°F/190°C until the patched area appears dry, about 5 minutes. Continue with your recipe as directed.*

PREPPING A PIE PLATE

We've all had that moment where you've baked an exquisite-looking pie, but can't get the first slice out without murdering the whole thing. My pie life changed completely when I learned this trick: Just as you carefully prep a cake pan, so should you with your pie plates. Why have we not always been doing this, you guys?

Spray the pie plate—bottom, sides, and rim—with nonstick cooking spray. Wipe away any pooling or beading oil with a paper towel. Deposit a handful of flour into the plate. Tap and rotate the plate to distribute the flour as evenly as possible. Invert and firmly tap out the excess flour, preferably into your kitchen sink to avoid a mess. You'll never have first slice woes again.

FRENCH SILK PIE

Serves 8 to 10

WHEN IT COMES TO ICONS OF THE 1980S, TO ME THE FRENCH SILK PIE IS RIGHT up there with the Walkman and Flock of Seagulls hairdos. During my elementary school years, any family gathering reached its peak when a Bakers' Square French silk pie emerged. Around the holidays, its peppermint-spiked Candy Cane Pie counterpart was equally as exciting. As it turns out, it couldn't be simpler to make at home.

There are a few secrets to making a French silk pie truly live up to its name, and allow the chocolate flavor to really sing. First, use a high-quality bittersweet chocolate you'd be happy to indulge in straight up—this is a great opportunity to play with the wide variety of artisanal chocolates available—and up that bold cocoa edge with a spoonful of cocoa powder. Second, beat in fridge-cold eggs one at a time, retrieving each from the refrigerator right before beating it into the filling, and speaking of beating time, give each egg a full five minutes of whipping to reach its maximum fluffy potential. Third, the final resting time of the finished pie is of utmost importance; it not only allows the chocolate flavor to really bloom, but also gives the sugar time to completely dissolve, resulting in an irresistibly silky, chocolaty, cloudlike quality.

FILLING:

3/4 cup/170 g unsalted butter, at cool room temperature

1 cup/200 g granulated sugar

1 tablespoon unsweetened Dutch-processed cocoa powder

1 tablespoon pure vanilla extract

1/2 teaspoon fine sea salt

33/4 ounces/107 g bittersweet chocolate (70% to 75% cacao), melted and cooled

3 large eggs, cold*

CRUST:

1 single batch My Favorite Pie Crust (page 74), baked and cooled

TOPPING:

1 batch Make-Ahead Whipped Cream (page 308)

1/4 ounce grated bittersweet chocolate (70% to 75% cacao)

The eggs aren't cooked in this recipe, so if that's a concern for you, seek out pasteurized eggs.

Prepare the filling: In the bowl of an electric mixer fitted with the paddle attachment, combine the butter, sugar, cocoa powder, vanilla, and salt. Beat on medium speed until light and fluffy, about 3 minutes. Add the melted chocolate and beat for 30 seconds, or until well blended. Add the cold eggs, 1 at a time, allowing each egg 5 full minutes of beating time (to ensure the eggs are truly cold, keep each in the refrigerator until it's time to add it).

Spoon the filling into the prepared crust and smooth the top. Dollop the whipped cream topping on top, leaving a 1-inch/2.5 cm border of chocolate filling showing around the perimeter.

Sprinkle with the grated chocolate. Refrigerate for at least 6 hours (overnight is even better) before serving.

GOLDEN RAISIN SOUR CREAM PIE
WITH OATMEAL COOKIE CRUST

Serves 8 to 10

FOR SOME FOLKS, ESPECIALLY IN THE DAKOTAS, KANSAS, OR THE VERY NORTHERN reaches of Minnesota or Wisconsin, sour cream raisin pie is the purest, simplest type of midwestern comfort food. Outside of that area, the combination usually sounds a bit too bizarre to be true, as though you must eat it in an old-school restaurant with yards of curving, fluorescent-lit pie cases like the iconic Carriage Crossing Restaurant in Yoder, Kansas, to really "get" this pie. It might be the very best definition of a "local favorite."

There seems to be as many recipes out there for sour cream raisin pie as there are grandmothers who make it. Sometimes it's lightly spiced with cinnamon, cloves, or nutmeg, but for the most part, it's a pretty simple combination of vanilla custard, raisins, and basic pie crust. Raisins became part of the recipe because they're a fruit that's available in the dead of winter when nothing else is growing. My version employs an oatmeal cookie-esque crust and golden raisins, for a sunnier take on the classic.

CRUST:

Nonstick cooking spray for pan

1½ cups/150 g old-fashioned rolled oats

6 tablespoons/85 g light brown sugar

¼ cup/32 g unbleached all-purpose flour

½ teaspoon ground cinnamon

¼ teaspoon fine sea salt

6 tablespoons/85 g unsalted butter, at room temperature

FILLING:

1 cup/160 g golden raisins

¼ cup freshly squeezed orange juice*

1½ cups/338 g whole milk

½ teaspoon orange zest*

4 large egg yolks

½ cup/100 g granulated sugar

4 tablespoons/32 g cornstarch

¼ teaspoon fine sea salt

1 teaspoon pure vanilla extract or pure vanilla bean paste

1 cup/240 g full-fat sour cream

TOPPING:

1 batch Make-Ahead Whipped Cream (page 308)

*From about ½ medium orange

Prepare the crust: Position a rack to the center of the oven and preheat it to 350°F/180°C. Spray a light-colored metal springform pan or 9-inch pie plate with nonstick cooking spray.

In the bowl of a food processor, combine the oats, brown sugar, flour, cinnamon, and salt. Process until the oats are broken down and tweedy looking, 10 to 15 seconds. Pour into a medium bowl and add the melted butter. Stir with a fork until evenly moistened. Turn into the prepared pan and press firmly about 1 1/2 inches up the sides of the pan, and evenly across the bottom. Freeze for 10 minutes.

Bake until golden and set, about 20 minutes. It will shrink a bit upon baking—gently reinforce the shape of the hot crust with a flat-bottomed glass or metal measuring cup. Let cool completely on a wire rack.

Prepare the filling: In a small, microwave-safe bowl, combine the raisins and orange juice. Cover the bowl tightly with plastic wrap. Microwave on **HIGH** for 1 minute. Leave the bowl covered and set aside.

Pour the milk into a 3- to 4-quart/2.8 to 3.75 L saucepan, add the orange zest, and set over medium-high heat. Bring the milk to a bare simmer, but don't let it boil. Meanwhile, in a large bowl, whisk together the egg yolks, sugar, cornstarch, and salt until paler in color, about 1 minute. Drizzle 2 tablespoons of the hot milk through a sieve into the egg mixture and whisk well. Pour the rest of the milk through the sieve into the bowl, to remove the zest. Whisk until well blended. Pour the mixture back into the saucepan. Set the pan over low heat and cook, whisking constantly, until the custard is just beginning to bubble and then becomes very thick, about 5 minutes. Whisk in the vanilla and sour cream. Set aside to cool until the crust is baked and cooled.

Assemble the pie: Drain any excess juice from the raisins. Fold them into the filling. Whisk the filling until smooth, then pour into the cooled crust. Cover the surface with a sheet of plastic wrap and chill until set, at least 2 hours. Top with lots of Make-Ahead Whipped Cream.

OHIO SHAKER LEMON PIE

Serves 8

SHAKERS ATE WHAT THEY COULD GROW THEMSELVES, AND THEY GREW AN ENORMOUS variety of produce. But one thing that wouldn't grow in the Midwest was lemons, so they became one of the few items Ohio Shakers would purchase. Therefore, there would be even more frugality when it came to lemons, not a single scrap wasted. The result is Shaker lemon pie, the ultimate in thrift and flavor. This pie uses whole lemons—zest, pith, pulp, and all. And in the spirit of the Shakers, the ingredient list here is minimal, but the process not rushed—I find macerating the lemon slices in sugar for a full 24 hours really gets the best out of them.

The type of lemons used really makes a difference between liking this pie and falling in love with it. Meyer lemons, the Elizabeth Taylor of citrus, are my top pick for this pie. If you make this pie in the winter months (and really you should, because can't we all use a little sunshine at the end of January?) you're more likely to find Meyers, which are sweeter than regular lemons, ambrosial, beautifully perfumed, and thin-skinned. A thin skin means less pith—the sort of wooly, fibrous, extremely bitter white layer between the zest and fruit—and the more pith in the pie, the more bitter it will be. (Ask your produce guy to cut one open for you so you can get a sense of what's in the lemon bin.)

FILLING:

½ pound/225 g unwaxed organic Meyer lemons

1½ cups/300 g granulated sugar

¼ cup/56 g light brown sugar

1 teaspoon pure vanilla extract

¼ teaspoon fine sea salt

4 large eggs

2 tablespoons cornstarch

3 tablespoons/42 g heavy whipping cream

CRUST:

Nonstick cooking spray for pan

All-purpose flour for dusting

1 double batch My Favorite Pie Crust (page 74)

FINISHING:

1 large egg

1 tablespoon water

Pinch of fine sea salt

1 tablespoon granulated sugar for sprinkling

Prepare the filling: Trim off the ends of each lemon. Cut them in half lengthwise, then into half-moons as thinly as possible—so thin they are almost translucent. You can do this with a thin, sharp knife and careful cuts, or a mandoline. Remove any seeds and place the lemon slices in a large, nonreactive bowl (glass is good). Add the granulated sugar, brown sugar, vanilla, and salt and stir to combine. Cover the bowl with plastic wrap and let sit at room temperature for 24 hours, stirring occasionally.

Position a rack to the center of the oven and pre-heat it to 425°F/220°C. Spray a 9-inch/23 cm glass pie plate with nonstick cooking spray and dust with flour, knocking out the excess.

On a lightly floured surface, roll out 1 dough disk into a 12-inch/30 cm circle. Place the dough in the prepared pie dish.

Complete preparing the filling: In a large bowl, whisk together the eggs and cornstarch. Whisk in the cream. Add the lemon mixture and stir to blend well. Pour the filling into the bottom crust.

Roll out the second dough disk to a 12-inch/30 cm circle. With your sharpest knife, slash 6 vents around the center of the top crust. Drape the dough over the filling. Press to seal the top and bottom crust edges together; trim to 1/2-inch/1.25 cm overhang. Fold overhang under; crimp decoratively.

In a small cup, whisk together the egg, water, and salt. Brush lightly over the top crust, and sprinkle with the sugar.

Line a rimmed baking sheet with aluminum foil. Place the pie on the prepared baking sheet.

Bake the pie at 425°F/220°C for 15 minutes, or until lightly golden. Rotate the pie 180 degrees. Lower the oven temperature to 350°F/180°C. Bake for another 30 to 35 minutes, or until deeply golden and the filling causes the top crust to puff up just a bit. If the pie's edges begin to get too brown at any point during baking, simply roll the foil from the lined baking sheet up over the pie's edges.

Allow the pie to cool completely at room tem-perature on a wire rack before slicing and serving, at least 3 hours.

LAYERED RHUBARB COBBLER PIE

Serves 12 to 15

COME SPRING, WE'VE GOT RHUBARB COMING OUT OF OUR EARS IN THE MIDWEST. It's exciting at first, but then rhubarb can quickly become a whole lot like a restless toddler—it's suddenly everywhere, in everyone's yard—did you even know you had a patch back there behind the garage?—and everyone's trying to hand it off to someone else.

But then, also just like the unruliest of toddlers, rhubarb is wildly vibrant and crazy-beautiful and even fun, when you can think of something new to do with it. And before you know it, you're saying to yourself, *Hey, maybe I should plant another rhubarb patch, to keep this other rhubarb company?* And then nine months later, you've got your hands full of rhubarb to a degree you never thought was possible and you're like, *Maybe this extra rhubarb patch wasn't such a good idea after all.* Am I right?

Anyway, if you're looking for a crowd-pleaser using a whopping 2½ pounds/1.2 kg of rhubarb in one go, here's your savior. It's like a nanny, for rhubarb.

CRUST:

1 double batch My Favorite Pie Crust (page 74)

Nonstick cooking spray for pan

All-purpose flour for dusting

FILLING:

2⅓ cups/466 g granulated sugar

⅔ cup/85 g unbleached all-purpose flour, spooned and leveled

2½ pounds/1.2 kg rimmed rhubarb, cut into ½-inch pieces (about 10 cups)

1½ tablespoons peach schnapps

½ teaspoon fine sea salt

½ teaspoon ground cinnamon

¼ teaspoon freshly grated nutmeg

ASSEMBLY AND FINISHING:

1 large egg, at room temperature

1 tablespoon water

Pinch of fine sea salt

2 tablespoons unsalted butter, cut into ¼-inch/6 mm cubes, chilled

2 tablespoons granulated sugar

Prepare the crust: Divide the dough into 3 equal pieces, and pat each portion into a rectangle. Wrap each piece tightly in plastic wrap and chill for at least 1 hour.

Position a rack to the center of the oven and preheat it to 375°F/190°C. Spray a 9 x 13-inch/23 x 33 cm glass baking dish with nonstick cooking spray.

Prepare the filling: In a large bowl, whisk together the sugar and flour. Transfer ½ cup/80 g of the mixture to a small bowl to be your "crust dust" and set aside. To the remaining flour mixture in the large bowl, add the rhubarb, peach schnapps, salt, cinnamon, and nutmeg. Toss to blend well and let sit for 15 to 20 minutes.

Meanwhile, in a small cup, whisk together the egg, water, and salt until liquefied.

Next, shape your crust layers: Lightly dust a work surface and rolling pin with flour. Have ready a baking sheet and 2 large sheets of parchment paper. Working with 1 portion of dough at a time, roll each into a rough 9 x 13-inch/23 x 33 rectangle—use your baking dish as a template to see exactly how large each layer should be to fit nicely in the pan. Place 2 of the layers on the baking sheet, separated by parchment paper, and place in the refrigerator or freezer. Place the remaining layer of dough in the bottom of the prepared pan. Prick all over with a fork and brush lightly with the egg wash. Bake until slightly firm and just beginning to turn golden at the edges, about 15 minutes. Remove the pan from the oven. Increase the oven temperature to 400°F/200°C.

Spread half of the reserved crust dust mixture over the baked crust. Top with half of the rhubarb filling, smoothing evenly. Sprinkle half of the chilled butter bits over the filling. Top with a second sheet of dough. Prick the dough all over with a fork and brush lightly with egg wash. Bake until the surface is firm and just turning golden in spots, about 20 minutes. Remove the pan from the oven.

Repeat the process of layering the crust dust, then the rhubarb filling, and the remaining butter bits. Place the third sheet of dough on top. Prick with a fork once more, brush with egg wash, and shower the top crust with the granulated sugar. Bake a final time until deeply golden and the filling is bubbling, about 40 minutes. Let cool in the pan set over a wire rack for at least an hour before serving.

BIG, BOLD BLUEBERRY PIE

Serves 8

AT THE HEIGHT OF SUMMER, WHEN OVERFLOWING PINTS OF DUSTY-INDIGO Michigan blueberries can be found at roadside stands, in stores, and at the farmers' market for just a couple of bucks a piece, I can't help but load up my basket. Baking with blueberries is always a joy, and few things mark midsummer quite like a slice of blueberry pie and cream, eaten on the porch.

The blueberry pie of my dreams is a thick, sturdy slice in a buttery pastry case, a stuffing of inky gloss suspending the fruit, with a notable proportion of berries holding their shape and then bursting in the mouth like deep violet caviar. Most important, I want my blueberry pie to taste deeply of berry. Cooking down some of the berries with pure maple syrup to a jammy goo concentrates the berry flavor and plays up its earthy sweetness. Folding in more raw berries just before filling the pie creates crave-worthy texture and powerhouse blueberry flavor.

FILLING:

7 cups/1.05 kg fresh blueberries, divided

1/3 cup/112 g pure maple syrup

1/2 cup/100 g granulated sugar

6 tablespoons/48 g cornstarch

1/4 teaspoon fine sea salt

2 tablespoons/28 g unsalted butter, melted

1 tablespoon freshly squeezed lemon juice

2 teaspoons finely grated lemon zest

1 teaspoon pure vanilla extract

CRUST AND ASSEMBLY:

Nonstick cooking spray and unbleached all-purpose flour for pan

1 double batch My Favorite Pie Crust (page 74), chilled

2 teaspoons unbleached all-purpose flour

2 tablespoons granulated sugar, divided

1 large egg

1 tablespoon water

Pinch of fine sea salt

In a 12-inch/30 cm skillet over high heat, combine 3 cups/450 g of the berries with the maple syrup and 1/4 cup/57 g of water. Bring to a boil, stirring often with a flexible heatproof spatula, until the berries have broken down and the juice is thick and syrupy, about 10 minutes—when you pull the spatula across the pan, it should leave a clean, dry track in the berries that takes 4 or 5 seconds to run back together. Remove the skillet from the heat and let the mixture cool to room temperature, about 30 minutes.

Position a rack to the center of the oven. Preheat the oven to 425°F/220°C. Line a 12 x 17-inch/30 x 43 cm baking sheet with aluminum foil. Spray a 9-inch/23 cm glass pie plate with nonstick cooking spray and dust with flour, knocking out the excess. Place the pie plate on the prepared baking sheet.

On a lightly floured surface, roll out 1 dough disk into a 12-inch/30 cm circle. Place the dough in prepared pie dish. In a small bowl, combine the flour and 2 teaspoons of the sugar. Scatter evenly across the bottom of the dough.

Complete preparing the filling: In a large bowl, whisk together the sugar, cornstarch, and salt until no lumps remain. Add the remaining fresh berries and the cooled berry mixture from the skillet. Add the butter, lemon juice, lemon zest, and vanilla. Fold gently to combine. Spoon the filling into the pie shell.

Roll out the second dough disk to a 12-inch/30 cm circle. Drape the dough over the filling. Press to seal the top and bottom crust edges together. Fold the overhang under; crimp decoratively. Slice a few vents in the top crust. Freeze the pie until the top crust is firm, about 15 minutes.

In a small cup, whisk together the egg, water, and salt. Brush lightly over the top crust, and sprinkle with the remaining 4 teaspoons of sugar.

Bake the pie at 425°F/220°C for 15 minutes. Rotate the pie 180 degrees. Lower the oven temperature to 375°F/190°C, then bake for another 50 to 60 minutes, until the filling is bubbling (this is the indicator that the starch has thickened the filling!) and the crust is deeply browned. If the pie's edges look as if they may burn at any point during the end of the baking time, simply roll the foil from the oven rack up over the pie's edges. Allow the pie to cool completely at room temperature on a wire rack before slicing and serving, at least 3 hours.

TIP > *If a pie filling contains a starch, such as cornstarch, tapioca, or flour, you must continue to bake the pie until the juices are bubbling out of any available vent, no matter what the recipe says, otherwise your filling will not set properly. If you're getting nervous about overbrowning of the crust at any point, you can always tent with foil.*

LEMON ANGEL PIE

Serves 8

FOR A REGION THAT DOESN'T FARE WELL WHEN IT COMES TO GROWING CITRUS, vintage cookbooks of the Midwest showcase an insane number of pies running on the puckering power of lemons. This book, however, has only two—the Ohio Shaker Lemon Pie (page 88) and this one, a pie that literally flips the script on a lemon meringue pie. With a crisp meringue shell, sharp lemon curd filling, and a cloud of vanilla bean whipped cream to finish everything off, this pie is a feather-light alternative to pies made with buttery pastry. It's even gluten-free, if that's your thing. Meyer lemons will make this pie extra special.

Nonstick cooking spray for pan

MERINGUE:

4 large egg whites, at room temperature

1/4 teaspoon cream of tartar

1/4 teaspoon fine sea salt

1 cup/200 g granulated sugar

1/2 teaspoon pure vanilla extract

1/4 teaspoon pure almond extract

FILLING AND TOPPING:

2/3 cup/150 g freshly squeezed lemon juice, divided

1 teaspoon unflavored gelatin

1 cup/200 g granulated sugar

6 large egg yolks

2 large eggs

2 tablespoons finely grated lemon zest

1/4 teaspoon fine sea salt

3 tablespoons/42 g cold unsalted butter, cut into small bits

1 cup/240 g heavy whipping cream, chilled

1/2 teaspoon pure vanilla bean paste

Position a rack to the center of the oven and preheat it to 275°F/135°C. Spray the bottom, sides, and rim a 9-inch/23 cm glass pie plate with nonstick cooking spray. Wipe away any excess oil with a paper towel.

Prepare the meringue shell: In the bowl of an electric mixer fitted with the whisk attachment, combine the egg whites, cream of tartar, and salt. Begin whipping the whites on medium speed until they start to become opaque and hold soft peaks, about 2 minutes. With the mixer running, spoon in the sugar, 1 tablespoon at a time—don't rush this stage, you want the sugar to dissolve as much as possible to yield a sturdy shell. When all the

sugar has been added, increase the mixer speed to medium-high and beat until the meringue reaches very stiff, glossy peaks, about 1 minute more. The meringue should ball up in the whisk and create an almost vertical peak when you lift the whisk from the bowl. Beat in the vanilla and almond extracts.

Pile the meringue into the prepared pie plate. Using the back of a small spoon, shape the cloud of meringue into a thick-bottomed pie shell, so it billows up the sides about an inch/2.5 cm and clings to the inner rim of the edge of the plate. Smooth the bottom evenly. Bake the shell until crisp, set, and ivory in color, about 1½ hours. Prop the oven door open with a wooden spoon and allow the crust to cool completely in the oven, about 1 hour more—don't worry if the shell falls or cracks a bit while cooling.

While baking the meringue, prepare the lemon filling: In a small cup, combine 2 tablespoons of the lemon juice with the gelatin and stir until any lumps disappear. Allow the gelatin to soften for 5 to 10 minutes. In a 2- to 2½-quart/1.9 to 2.4 L saucepan, whisk together the remaining lemon juice, sugar, egg yolks, eggs, lemon zest, and salt. Set the pan over medium heat. Whisking often, cook the curd until a few lavalike steam bubbles come to the surface, about 5 minutes. Whisk in the lump of softened gelatin until melted. Remove the pan from the heat and whisk in the butter. Pour the curd through a sieve into a clean bowl and cover the surface with plastic wrap. Allow the curd to cool at room temperature while the meringue shell is cooling.

When both have cooled completely, spoon the filling into the shell. Cover loosely with a sheet of plastic wrap. Chill the pie for at least 6 hours, or up to overnight. Just before serving, whip the cream with the vanilla bean paste to soft peaks, and pile on top of the curd.

PUMPKIN MERINGUE PIE

Serves 8 to 10

LIKE CILANTRO AND CIRCUS CLOWNS, PUMPKIN PIE CAN BE QUITE POLARIZING. Some take a hard pass, whereas others can't imagine cold-weather holidays without it. My earliest pumpkin pie memories involve trying not to stick my fingers in a store-bought Mrs. Smith's pie on Thanksgiving Day, baked from frozen that morning and cooling on the washing machine in the tiny laundry room off the kitchen at Gramma's house, while the rest of the Thanksgiving meal was prepared. By the time dinner was finished and the desserts rolled out, I was more interested in stealing spoonfuls from the Cool Whip tub next to the pie than I was in the pie itself. I became a late-in-life pumpkin pie convert, especially the homemade kind (no offense to Mrs. Smith), and have grown to love the simplicity and warming spices in an amber slice at the end of a celebratory meal.

A swooping, marshmallow-y Italian meringue topping manages to feel as luxurious as whipped cream but is free of fat, which balances nicely with a rich pumpkin custard. Italian meringue holds particularly well, so it can be made several hours ahead of time and transported easily if you find yourself on pumpkin pie duty for a gathering, and you get to wow the crowd as you torch it just before it hits the dessert buffet.

FILLING:

1 (15-ounce/425 g) can pure pumpkin purée

3 large eggs

1 large egg yolk

1 cup/240 g heavy whipping cream

2 tablespoons brandy

1/2 cup/113 g firmly packed dark muscovado or dark brown sugar

1 1/2 teaspoons ground cinnamon

1/4 teaspoon ground ginger

1/4 teaspoon Chinese five-spice powder or freshly grated nutmeg

1 teaspoon fine sea salt

CRUST:

1 single batch My Favorite Pie Crust (page 74), blind baked and cooled

TOPPING:

1 batch Italian Meringue (page 304)

Position an oven rack the center position and preheat the oven to 325°F/170°C.

Prepare the filling: In a large bowl, whisk together the pumpkin purée, eggs, egg yolk, cream, and brandy until well blended. In a small bowl, combine the brown sugar, spices, and salt. Whisk the spiced sugar into the pumpkin mixture.

Pour the filling into the prepared pie shell and bake until the filling is set but wobbles ever so slightly in the very center when jiggled, about 1 hour (the filling will set further as it cools). Turn off the oven and let the pie cool in the oven for 30 minutes. Let the pie cool completely on a wire rack. The untopped pie can be loosely covered and refrigerated for up to 2 days before serving.

To serve, use some paper towel to gently dab any excess moisture from the top of the pie. Pile the meringue atop the pie. Use a kitchen torch to toast the meringue to a deep golden brown.

MY FAVORITE DOUBLE-CRUST APPLE PIE

Serves 8

WHEN I WAS CONSIDERING INCLUDING A RELATIVELY STRAIGHTFORWARD APPLE pie recipe in this book, I thought, *Does the world really need another option for apple pie?* Even if every good midwesterner will make at least one orchard trip per autumn and pick way too many apples, which then demand pie making? So, I went back to that very informal social media pie polling I mentioned a few recipes back.

The consensus was clear: as with photos of babies and cats, people can't get enough good, classic apple pie recipes. I figure it's a bit like having extra blankets on hand for when the seasons suddenly shift but you can't be bothered to turn on the heat. It's just comforting to know you've got one accessible in the event it's required. So, whether you have a tried-and-true recipe and would never consider another, or you're the type of person who likes to try a different approach to apple pie every time you make one, I'm happy to share this one, my favorite, with you.

FILLING:

8 cups/950 g thinly sliced Honeycrisp apples (about 6 medium-size to large apples)*

1/2 cup/100 g granulated sugar

1/4 cup/57 g light brown sugar

1 teaspoon freshly squeezed lemon juice

1/2 teaspoon ground cinnamon

1/4 teaspoon freshly grated nutmeg

1/4 teaspoon fine sea salt

4 tablespoons/32 g cornstarch

CRUST AND ASSEMBLY:

Nonstick cooking spray for pan

All-purpose flour for dusting

1 double batch My Favorite Pie Crust (page 74), chilled

2 teaspoons unbleached all-purpose flour

2 tablespoons granulated sugar, divided

1 large egg

1 tablespoon water

Pinch of fine sea salt

Sometimes I swap out half of the apple slices for some thinly sliced Anjou pears, and that's never a bad idea, especially in the dreariest part of the winter, when apples and pears are the best fruits to be found.

Prepare the filling: In a large bowl, combine all the filling ingredients, except the cornstarch. Toss to mix well. Let sit at room temperature for 1 hour.

Drain the filling over a 2- to 2 1/2-quart/1.9 to 2.4 L saucepan, pressing down on the fruit gently and catching the liquid—you should have at least 1/2 cup/113 g of liquid. Return the apples their bowl. Set the pan over high heat and reduce the liquid to about ⅓ cup/75 g, which will take about 5 minutes. You can swirl the pan occasionally, but avoid stirring. Remove the pan from the heat and set aside to cool for 5 minutes.

Add the cornstarch to the apples and toss to coat. Pour the apple syrup over the fruit and stir gently to blend.

Position a rack to the center of the oven and preheat it to 425°F/220°C. Line a baking sheet with aluminum foil. Spray a 9-inch/23 cm glass pie plate with nonstick cooking spray and dust with flour, knocking out the excess. Place the pie plate on the lined baking sheet.

On a lightly floured surface, roll out 1 dough disk into a 12-inch/30 cm circle. Place the dough in the prepared pie dish. In a small bowl, combine the flour and 2 teaspoons of the sugar. Scatter evenly across the bottom of the dough. Scrape the filling into the crust. Roll out the second dough disk to a 12-inch/30 cm circle. Drape the dough over the filling. With a thin, sharp knife, slice a few vents around the center of the pie. Press to seal the top and bottom crust edges together. Fold the overhang under; crimp decoratively. Freeze the pie until the top crust is firm, about 15 minutes.

In a small cup, whisk together the egg, water, and salt. Brush lightly over the top crust, and sprinkle with remaining 4 teaspoons of sugar.

Bake the pie at 425°F/220°C for 15 minutes. Rotate the pie 180 degrees. Lower the oven temperature to 375°F/190°C. Bake for another 50 to 60 minutes, until the filling is bubbling (the bubbling is key to indicate that the starch has begun to thicken the filling!) and the crust is deeply browned. If the pie's edges look as if they may burn at any point during the end of the baking time, simply roll the foil from the pan up over the pie's edges.

Allow the pie to cool completely at room temperature on a wire rack before slicing and serving, at least 3 hours.

TIP > *Most double-crust pie recipes have you baking for about an hour in total. I like to take them quite a bit browner, as much as 20 minutes longer, to really develop color and the incredible flavor that comes from the marriage of deeply browned butter and flour. The pastry should be as much as part of a great pie as the filling, and you're missing out on a key component if your pastry isn't baked to its full potential. So, let your pies bake for a little longer than you think you should—I assure you it's really, really hard to actually overcook or burn a pie.*

NOTE > *Honeycrisps have become one of my favorite baking apples, and as it happens they're a midwestern invention, first cultivated at the University of Minnesota in 1974, and then finally released to the public in 1991 (hey, perfection takes time!).*

HONEYED RASPBERRY AND WHITE CHOCOLATE CREAM PIE

Serves 8 to 10

FROM THE OUTSET, THIS PIE APPEARS TO BE ONE OF THOSE FLOATY, FEMININE food things, because it's just so dang pretty. However! The fluff factor here—a cloud of white chocolate cream, bolstered by cream cheese—is quickly tempered by the thick raspberry layer beneath it, sharp and nubbly with all those nutty little berry seeds, which I happen to love. The mix of cooked and raw berries help to intensify the raspberry flavor, making you wonder: why there aren't more raspberry pies out there, anyway?

CRUST:

2 ounces/57 g high-quality white chocolate, chopped

1 tablespoon heavy whipping cream

1 single batch My Favorite Pie Crust (page 74), blind baked and cooled

FILLING:

2/3 cup/132 g granulated sugar

1/4 cup/32 g cornstarch

1/4 teaspoon fine sea salt

1 cup/225 g lukewarm water

3 tablespoons/63 g honey

1 teaspoon freshly squeezed lemon juice

4 cups/500 g fresh raspberries, divided

1 tablespoon unsalted butter

TOPPING:

1 cup/240 g heavy whipping cream, very cold

1 teaspoon pure vanilla extract

1/4 teaspoon pure almond extract

4 ounces/113 g full-fat cream cheese

4 ounces/113 g high-quality white chocolate, melted and cooled

Prepare the crust: Combine the white chocolate and cream in a small, microwave-safe bowl. Microwave with 20-second bursts on **MEDIUM**, stirring until smooth. Spread evenly over the bottom of the cooled crust. Allow to set at room temperature.

In a 3- to 4-quart/2.8 to 3.75 L saucepan, whisk together the sugar, cornstarch, and salt until lump-free. Whisk in the lukewarm water, honey, and lemon juice. Add 2 cups/250 g of the raspberries. Cover and set the pan over high heat. Bring to a boil, stirring occasionally. Once the berries begin to break down and the mixture is slowly bubbling all over the surface like lava, cook for 2 timed minutes, stirring often. Stir in the butter. Remove the pan from the heat and let cool completely, about 1 hour.

Prepare the topping: In the bowl of an electric mixer fitted with the whisk attachment, whip the cream with the vanilla and almond extract until stiff peaks form. Transfer the whipped cream to a clean bowl. Swap out the whisk attachment for the paddle. Add the cream cheese and melted white chocolate to the mixer bowl (no need to clean it). Beat on medium speed until smooth and creamy. Gently stir about a third of the whipped cream into the cream cheese mixture to lighten it, then carefully fold in the remaining whipped cream.

Assemble the pie: Scatter 1 cup of the remaining berries over the bottom of the crust. Spoon the raspberry filling over them, then add the remaining berries on top. Pipe or dollop the white chocolate cream topping over the pie, leaving a 1-inch/2.5 cm border of the ruby red filling all around the edges. Refrigerate for at least 3 hours to set. Let soften at room temperature for about 20 minutes before serving.

CHAPTER 4

COOKIE JAR CONTENDERS

COOKIE JAR COOKIES ARE THE HUB OF ANY HOME BAKER'S RECIPE box. In the Midwest, they're especially key during those long, cold months when it just feels right to fire up the oven on a weekday afternoon, and for those days year-round when you just have the urge to bake but don't want a long-term commitment or an unholy mess. These cookies are happy baking of the highest order.

Cookies destined for the jar have several defining characteristics. We want scooping or slicing or maybe a bit of patting into their final form, but no pains-taking shaping, filling, or sandwiching. Minimal dishes, please. They need to be sturdy enough to stack, with ingredients allowing for casual counter storage over several days.

The very best cookie jar cookies start life as a recipe destined for one's own in-house consumption, and then soon must be made again and again for sharing and bringing along to locations far from home. And of course, making it generally impossible to have just one.

MONSTER COOKIES

Makes about 5 dozen cookies

THE ORIGINAL MONSTER COOKIE WAS CREATED BACK IN 1971 BY A MAN WHO JUST might be America's Ultimate Dad. Meet Dick Wesley—University of Michigan photographer, father of six, inventive Cub Scout leader who regularly baked peanut butter cookies to feed the juvenile masses (knock it off, Dick, you're making us all look lazy). During one baking session, he found himself out of flour, but improvised wildly using oatmeal and other odds and ends from his cabinets, and the flourless Monster Cookie was born.

Due to high demand, the yield grew and grew to include such modest portions as 12 eggs and 18 cups of oatmeal. Dick burned out two electric mixers making his famous cookies, and eventually switched to an electric drill, which he craftily fitted with a beater attachment. (Because of course he did.) The cookies became so well known, the *Lansing State Journal* ran a feature on Dick's recipe with the amazing headline "Local Man Doesn't Skimp—Monster Cookies a Real Challenge." *Legend*.

My scaled-down Monster Cookie recipe plays up the peanut butter with Reese's Pieces candy instead of the usual M&M's. I should also note I use a regular electric mixer without the aid of other power tools because, let's face it, we're all a lot more uninteresting than Dick Wesley.

10 tablespoons/140 g unsalted butter, melted and cooled

1 cup/225 g dark brown sugar

1 cup/200 g granulated sugar

2 teaspoons light corn syrup or mild clover honey*

1½ teaspoons pure vanilla extract

4 large eggs

1⅓ cups/340 g creamy peanut butter, such as Skippy brand

4½ cups/450 g old-fashioned rolled oats

6 tablespoons/48 g unbleached all-purpose flour

2¼ teaspoons baking soda

¼ teaspoon fine sea salt

1 cup/225 g Reese's Pieces candy

1 cup/170 g semisweet chocolate chips

If you go with honey, you may get a little more browning than with corn syrup, so keep an eye on the cookies to prevent burned bits.

In the bowl of an electric mixer fitted with the paddle attachment, combine the melted butter, brown and granulated sugar, corn syrup, and vanilla. Beat just until thick and smooth, about 1 minute. Beat in the eggs, 1 at a time. Reduce the mixer speed to low and stir in the peanut butter. Add the oats, flour, baking soda, and salt. Mix on low speed until well blended. Stir in the Reese's pieces and chocolate chips.

Cover the bowl tightly and refrigerate for at least 4 hours, or overnight—the oats will soften and swell a bit during this rest, so it's important to not skimp on the resting time.

Position racks to the upper and lower thirds of the oven and preheat it to 350°F/180°C. Line two 12 x 17-inch/30 x 43 cm baking sheets with parchment paper. Use a small scoop or 2 spoons to portion the dough into balls (about 3 tablespoons each) and place them about 2½ inches/6.4 cm apart on the prepared baking sheets.

Bake just until the edges are set and golden, 12 minutes tops. Set the pans on wire racks and allow the cookies to cool on the sheets for about 10 minutes before transferring them to the racks to cool completely. Repeat the shaping and baking process with the remaining dough. Store for up to 5 days in an airtight container at room temperature.

(THE ORIGINAL) MRS. BRAUN'S OATMEAL COOKIES

Makes 4 dozen cookies

A VERSION OF THIS COOKIE APPEARED IN MY BOOK *REAL SWEET*, MADE WITH A few different ingredients to fit the spirit of that title, but this recipe is the original article, my Gramma's oatmeal cookie, responsible for all my homemade oatmeal cookie memories.

If you are one of those people who thinks you don't like raisins in cookies, I have to ask, have you tried an oatmeal cookie with golden raisins? Because it's really a script-flipper, especially when combined with toasty walnuts. As long as I've made these cookies, I've always wondered why Mrs. Braun (pronounced "Brown," God bless those sturdy German last names) chose golden over dark raisins, because it's a pretty dang inspired choice. One request: Don't be tempted to swap out the shortening to make an all-butter cookie. Of course you *can*, and I have, but the combination of the two creates the stuff of bendy-cookie-lover dreams.

3 cups/300 g old-fashioned rolled oats

1½ cups/192 g unbleached all-purpose flour, spooned and leveled

1 teaspoon fine sea salt

1 teaspoon baking soda

½ teaspoon ground cinnamon

½ cup/92 g vegetable shortening

½ cup/113 g unsalted butter, at room temperature

1 cup/225 g dark brown sugar

1 cup/200 g granulated sugar

2 large eggs

1 teaspoon pure vanilla extract

1 cup/120 g golden raisins

3/4 cup/100 g chopped walnuts

Position an oven rack in the center of the oven. Preheat the oven to 350°F/180°C. Line two 12 x 17-inch/30 x 43 cm baking sheets with parchment paper.

In a large bowl, whisk together the oats, flour, salt, baking soda, and cinnamon.

In the bowl of an electric mixer fitted with the paddle attachment, cream together the shortening, butter, and brown and granulated sugar on medium speed until light and fluffy, about 2 minutes. Scrape down the bowl and beat in the eggs, 1 at a time, followed by the vanilla. Reduce the mixer speed to low and stir in the dry ingredients until almost fully incorporated. Stir in the raisins and walnuts.

Using a 2-tablespoon scoop, drop the batter in mounds, evenly spaced about 2 inches/5 cm apart, onto the baking sheets. Bake 1 sheet at a time, rotating the pan halfway through baking, until the edges are golden brown and can be lifted with a fingertip, but the cookies are still soft in their centers, about 12 minutes. Let cool for 1 minute on the baking sheet before transferring the cookies to a wire rack to cool completely. Store in an airtight container for up to 1 week.

MY GO-TO CHOCOLATE CHIP COOKIES

Makes about 3 dozen cookies

GRAMMA LITERALLY HAD THE BAKER'S TOUCH, WITH TEXTBOOK PASTRY HANDS— elegant, organ-playing fingers and smooth, cool palms, ideal for mixing batters and handling doughs. But only occasionally did I catch glimpses of her skills and how much she liked to bake, mostly surrounding birthdays and holidays, or when I would come over on a regular day and basically wear her down until we baked the Toll House recipe from the back of the crinkly yellow bag, double and triple batches. We lined the kitchen table with brown paper grocery bags, which served as the cooling station at the sheets came parading out of the oven.

Although the roots of the chocolate chip cookie belong in Massachusetts, I don't know how any American baking book could go without a great recipe for them. I think European-style butter really makes this cookie special, as does that fancy vanilla extract you've been saving, and bittersweet chocolate instead of semisweet, because I go for more sugar in the dough than the recipe on the yellow bag.

3 cups/384 g unbleached all-purpose flour, spooned and leveled

1¼ teaspoons fine sea salt

1 teaspoon baking soda

8 ounces/225 g unsalted European-style butter, at room temperature

1 cup/225 g firmly packed dark brown sugar

1 cup/200 g granulated sugar

2 teaspoons pure vanilla extract

1 large egg, at room temperature

2 large egg yolks, at room temperature

2 cups/340 g bittersweet chocolate chips (60% to 70% cacao)

Sift together the flour, salt, and baking soda into a large bowl.

In the bowl of an electric mixer fitted with the paddle attachment, beat together the butter, brown and granulated sugar, and vanilla on medium speed until light and fluffy, about 3 minutes. Beat in the egg and egg yolks, 1 at a time. On low speed, stir in the dry ingredients, then the chocolate chips.

Line a large rimmed baking sheet with parchment paper. Using a 2-tablespoon scoop, portion the dough into balls. Wrap the sheet tightly in plastic wrap. Chill for at least 1 hour, or up to 2 days ahead.

Position oven racks to the upper and lower thirds of the oven and preheat it to 350°F/180°C. Line two 17 x 12-inch/43 x 30 cm baking sheets with parchment paper.

Place 12 dough balls on each sheet, evenly spaced about 2 inches/5 cm apart. Bake until golden brown at the edges and slightly soft in the centers, about 13 minutes. Cool on the baking sheets (just a few minutes before transferring to a wire rack if you like crisp edges, or let them cool completely on the sheets for softer/chewier cookies). Store in an airtight container at room temperature for up to 5 days.

AFTER-SCHOOL SPECIALS

Makes about 40 cookies

CAN THERE POSSIBLY BE A COOKIE TO PLEASE EVERYONE? EVERY AFTER-SCHOOL cookie jar favorite—chocolate chip, oatmeal, snickerdoodle—all rolled into one recipe.

DOUGH:

1 cup/225 g unsalted butter, at room temperature

1½ cups/300 g granulated sugar

¼ cup/57 g firmly packed light brown sugar

1½ teaspoons pure vanilla extract

2 large eggs, at room temperature

2½ cups/250 g old-fashioned rolled oats

2 cups/256 g unbleached all-purpose flour, spooned and leveled

2 teaspoons cream of tartar

1 teaspoon baking soda

1 teaspoon fine sea salt

½ teaspoon flaky sea salt, such as Maldon

1½ cups/256 g bittersweet chocolate chips (60% cacao)

COATING:

½ cup/100 g granulated sugar

2 teaspoons ground cinnamon

⅛ teaspoon fine sea salt

Prepare the dough: In the bowl of an electric mixer fitted with the paddle attachment, beat the butter on medium speed until creamy, about 1 minute. Add the granulated and brown sugar and vanilla and beat on medium-high speed until aerated and notice-ably fluffy, 3 to 4 minutes. Add the eggs, 1 at a time, giving each about 30 seconds of beating time to incorporate fully.

Meanwhile, in a large bowl, whisk together the oats, flour, cream of tartar, baking soda, and fine and flaky salt. Reduce the mixer speed to low and slowly stir in the dry ingredients. Stir in the chocolate chips. Cover the bowl

tightly and refrigerate for 1 hour, or up to 2 days.

Position 2 oven racks to the upper and lower thirds of the oven and preheat it to 350°F/180°C. Line 2 baking sheets with parchment paper. In a shallow bowl, whisk together the sugar, cinnamon, and salt for the coating.

Using a 2-tablespoon scoop, form the dough into balls, dropping each dough ball into the cinnamon sugar and rolling to coat completely. Evenly space the dough balls about 2 inches/5 cm apart on the prepared baking sheets. Bake until golden and puffed, about 12 minutes, rotating the sheets halfway through the baking time. Let the cookies cool on the sheets for 5 minutes before transferring them to a wire rack to cool completely. Store in an airtight container at room temperature for up to 5 days.

ON COOKIE TABLES

Of all the great baking traditions of the Midwest, there's one lesser-known, but rich in the Heartland spirit of abundance and preserving heritage. The term *cookie table* sounds simple from the outset, but if you've ever been to a wedding in a relatively small pocket of northeastern Ohio surrounding Youngstown (or over the border into Pittsburgh, which also claims to own the tradition), you know there is absolutely nothing small about a matrimonial cookie table done right. In fact, the cookie table couldn't be more in line with the five baking tenets of the Midwest—Bake Big, Bake Easy, Bake with Purpose, Bake from the Past, Bake from the Present.

The tradition of the cookie table first came into fashion in Depression-era Youngstown in the 1930s. In this blue-collar town, it started as a way to create a celebratory dessert experience that was beautiful to look at without needing to spend money on expensive wedding cakes, and both the bride and groom's families could easily share the cost and the effort in creating the display, while showing off family recipes from each side. As the trend caught on, the displays expanded to become a collection of international favorites, showcasing goodies from a wide variety of immigrants who helped shape the cultural landscape of the town. These days, the tradition of the cookie table remains and is as important to a Youngstown wedding as the groom's showing up.

There's no doubt a Youngstown cookie table is all about baking big and baking with purpose—the point of a cookie table is simple: blow minds and take names with the sheer volume and array of cookies available, presented in a stunning display, like a holiday cookie tin on steroids. It's customary for female friends and family members of the bride to churn out thousands of cookies in hundreds of varieties. If you ask around, you'll hear legendary cookie table stories, ranging from area weddings with entire cookie *rooms*, to the cursed weddings opting for—gasp!!—no cookie table at all. In Youngstown, you do *not* want your wedding to be remembered for such a thing.

The layout of the display is intricately planned and is as important as the cookies that are part of it, since the spreads are usually used as a visually impressive way to draw guests into the reception. The tables are usually lavishly decorated around the platters of various heights, creating the look of cookies spilling out from all corners of the display, and often covered with tulle until serving time, so guests can look and admire, but not touch.

As far as "baking easy," well, maybe that's a tenet up for debate, as there's nothing simple about churning out thousands of cookies, and the rule is the cookies must always be scratch-made, never store-bought or from a bakery. But these days, cookie tables enjoy the luxury of modern refrigeration and freezing, which allow the dedicated cookie bakers to begin baking for a wedding several months in advance. Most cookies have a range of types to balance out the efforts; for example, lots of simple shortbread, or Italian *pizzelles* to help create volume; a lesser amount of shaped and filled cookies like *kolacky* or "ladylocks" (small pastry tubes shaped around clothespins, then cream-filled); and then perhaps only a few dozen intricately decorated cookies, such as *pesche con crema,* two round Italian butter cookies hollowed out, sandwiched together with lemon curd or buttercream, and covered with peach liqueur and colored sugar and topped with a mint leaf to resemble peaches.

Aside from their visual impact, looking a little closer at a cookie table is like a flowchart for immigrant influences in the area, blended with a few updated tastes. The foundation of Youngstown, and the tradition of the cookie table, runs on the power and influence of immigrants who settled in the area in the late 1800s. The first wave of Germans, Irish, and Welsh came for the exploding coal industry, and soon after, the rise of the steel mills made Youngstown a popular destination for people from Greece, Italy, and Eastern Europe (note: all cultures with strong cookie game). By the early twentieth century, African Americans were well represented, bringing southern traditions into the mix, and immigrants from Middle Eastern countries began settling in the area as well. The unique blend of cultures and family recipes has had a lasting impact in the form of wide-ranging selections on a cookie table menu, just one more thing to love about this quirky and delicious tradition.

CHOCOLATE CHIP COOKIE BRITTLE

Serves 12 to 15

THIS RECIPE HAS MADE THE ROUNDS, AND NEVER FAILS TO IMPRESS. IT'S ALL THE satisfaction of crisp, sugary, brown-buttery chocolate chip cookies for very little time and effort. Perfect for weekday baking, gifting, compulsive snacking, and making friends and influencing people.

Try a variety of chip and nut combinations in the mix—I love bittersweet chocolate chips and pecans, but consider cashews and butterscotch chips, shredded coconut, salted peanuts, and more—this workhorse of a recipe can take it.

1 cup/225 g unsalted butter, melted and cooled

2 teaspoons pure vanilla extract

1 cup/200 g granulated sugar

1 teaspoon fine sea salt

2 cups/256 g all-purpose flour, spooned and leveled

1 cup/170 g chopped pecans, lightly toasted

1 cup/170 g bittersweet chocolate chips (60% cacao)

Position a rack to the center of the oven and preheat it to 350°F/180°C. Have ready a 12 x 17-inch/30 x 43 cm rimmed baking sheet.

In a large bowl, whisk together the melted butter and vanilla. Add the sugar and salt and continue to whisk until the mixture thickens and appears pastelike. Switch to a wooden spoon or spatula and mix in the flour. Stir in the nuts and chocolate chips. Press the mixture into the ungreased pan in a thin, even layer (use the chocolate chips as your guide—try to get them in as close to a single layer as possible throughout the dough, and you'll have the right thickness).

Bake for 23 to 25 minutes, or until light golden brown (the edges will be a bit darker than the center), rotating the pan 180 degrees every 7 to 8 minutes during baking. Let cool completely before breaking into charmingly irregular pieces. Store in an airtight container at room temperature for up to 1 week.

CRISPY ICED OATMEAL FLATS

Makes 2 dozen flats

THERE ARE ONLY A SCANT FEW PACKAGED COOKIES I HOLD IN HIGH REGARD. One is the inimitable Matt's Chocolate Chip Cookie, a Midwest specialty out of Wheeling, Illinois, that I special-ordered by the case during my first pregnancy in San Francisco. When I bought them right after our move back to Chicago, the first thing my daughter said upon trying one was, "Why does this taste so familiar?" (Probably because Mommy ate 180 of them during the week your senses were developing and the Internet said you were the size of an heirloom tomato.)

My second most-revered packaged cookie is the Oreo (obviously—I'm not an animal!), and the last is the completely superb Archway Crispy Iced Oatmeal Cookie: thin, crisp, tweedy with minced oats, with a snowy, matte slick of icing. My version of this cookie, dare I say it, manages to be even better than the store-bought version. With a punch of nutmeg and an unbeatable crunch, this slice-and-bake dough comes together in a snap in the food processor. Plus, it's so fun to ice these puppies with their neat dipping method, and I'm pretty in love with the way the icing settles on the topography-like surface of each cookie.

DOUGH:

1½ cups/150 g old-fashioned rolled oats

¾ cup/170 g firmly packed dark brown sugar

½ cup/64 g unbleached all-purpose flour, spooned and leveled

½ teaspoon fine sea salt

½ teaspoon baking soda

¼ teaspoon baking powder

½ teaspoon ground cinnamon

¼ teaspoon freshly grated nutmeg

½ cup/113 g cold unsalted butter, cut into cubes

1 large egg yolk

ICING:

1 large egg white

1¼ cups/150 g confectioners' sugar

¼ teaspoon pure vanilla extract

⅛ teaspoon fine sea salt

Prepare the dough: In the bowl of a food processor fitted with the steel S blade, grind the oats to a flour. Add the brown sugar, flour, salt, baking soda, baking powder, cinnamon, and nutmeg and process briefly to blend. Toss in the butter cubes and process until the butter is well incorporated and the dough begins to clump and pull off the sides of the bowl. Add the egg yolk and pulse until the dough comes together with no dry pockets.

Line a work surface with a large sheet of plastic wrap. Turn out the dough onto the plastic wrap and form it into log about 10 inches/25 cm long and 1½ inches/3.8 cm in diameter. Wrap the dough tightly. Chill the dough until firm, about 3 hours in the refrigerator.

Position a rack to the center of the oven and preheat it to 350°F/180°C. Line 2 baking sheets with parchment paper. Use a thin, sharp knife to slice the dough log into 2 dozen rounds, each just shy of ½-inch/1.25 cm thick. Transfer the rounds, evenly spaced about 2 inches/5 cm apart, to the prepared baking sheets. Bake until golden and firm on the edges with a bit of give in the centers, about 12 minutes. Transfer the cookies to a wire rack to cool completely—they will crisp all the way through as they cool.

Prepare the icing: In a small bowl, combine the egg white, confectioners' sugar, vanilla, and salt. Mix with a handheld electric mixer until smooth and thick. Blend in 2 teaspoons of water until smooth. To ice the cookies, working 1 at a time, kiss the tops lightly to the surface of the icing—you want to just show the cookie to the icing, not submerge it. Let the excess icing drip off for a moment, and then set the iced cookie on a wire rack. If the icing begins to firm while you're dipping, loosen it with a few drops of water. Allow the icing to dry completely before serving, about 1 hour. Store in an airtight container for up to 1 week.

GOLDEN ALMOND COOKIES

Makes 4 to 5 dozen cookies

NOW, DON'T GET ME WRONG—THE CONCEPT OF A CHINESE ALMOND COOKIE IS no way a "Midwest thing." But! I do find it fascinating that midwesterners, specifically Chicagoans, are particularly familiar with these golden, crisp, nutty cookies that accompany their takeout from highly Americanized Chinese food restaurants. As it turns out, one of America's top almond (and fortune) cookie producers is Golden Dragon, a small factory on the south side of Chicago, where you can walk in off the street and buy insane amounts of fresh cookies directly from them (10 almond cookies in a sleeve for $1!).

You'll notice this recipe contains shortening, only one of two recipes in this book that does. I rarely use shortening in my baking, but here it's the necessary ingredient to get the texture just right. In fact, if you want to be very traditional, you'll use lard.

4 ounces/113 g blanched slivered almonds, lightly toasted*

1¼ cups/250 g granulated sugar, plus more for flattening cookies, divided

2½ cups/384 g unbleached all-purpose flour, spooned and leveled

1 teaspoon baking soda

¾ teaspoon fine sea salt

¼ teaspoon baking powder

1 cup/185 g vegetable shortening

2 large eggs

2 teaspoons pure almond extract

1 large egg yolk, beaten

If you have almond meal or almond flour, you can skip the food processor and throw everything into a mixer instead.

Position oven racks to the upper and lower thirds of the oven and preheat the oven to 350°F/180°C. Line 2 baking sheets with parchment paper.

In the bowl of a food processor fitted with the steel S blade, combine the almonds and ¼ cup/50 g of the sugar. Grind the almonds until very fine, at least 1 continuous minute. Add the flour, remaining 1 cup/200 g of sugar, and the baking soda, salt, and baking powder and mix until well blended, being sure to scrape down into the corners of the processor bowl occasionally. Add the shortening and process until the mixture begins to clump together. In a small bowl, beat together the eggs and almond extract. With the processor running, pour in the egg mixture, and blend until the dough comes together and clears the sides of the bowl. If the dough appears dry, pulse in 1 to 2 teaspoons of water until the dough comes together.

Using a 2-tablespoon scoop, portion the dough, evenly spaced about 2 inches/5 cm apart, onto the prepared baking sheets. Spoon a few tablespoons of sugar onto a plate. Using a jar or large glass with a flat bottom, dampen the bottom of the glass and dip into the sugar. Lightly press each cookie to a ¼-inch/6 mm thickness, resugaring the glass with each press. Brush the cookies lightly with the beaten egg yolk. Bake the cookies until golden brown on the edges and bottoms, 16 to 18 minutes. Let cool on the baking sheets for 2 minutes before transferring to a wire rack to cool completely—they will crisp as they cool. Repeat the scooping, flattening, and baking process with the remaining dough. Store in an airtight container at room temperature for up to 1 week.

POTATO CHIP-CHIP SHORTBREAD

Makes 4 dozen cookies

EVERY REGION OF THE COUNTRY SEEMS TO HAVE THEIR FAVORITE HYPER-LOCAL potato chip producers, and the Midwest is a hotbed of opinions on the matter. My earliest potato chip memories in the Chicago area involve a crinkly bag of Jay's (Al Capone stocked them in his speakeasies; what more could you want?), double-dipped into a plastic tub of Dean's French Onion Dip. But if you're from a little farther east, particularly Ohio or Indiana, you might be partial to Mike-Sell's chips, a century-old company touted as America's first mass potato chip producer. Or maybe Sterzing's, Ballreich's, Better Made, or Grippo's are your Heartland chip of choice.

Going through vintage recipes, it's obvious potato chips had a moment. Potato chip cookies became popular in the 1940s, likely a promotional effort spawned by so many chip-producing companies, a unique way to repurpose a popular snack food. But as it turns out, when finely crushed, potato chips in a cookie dough are more than just a quirky add-in; they actually lend themselves to a making a good shortbread formula even "shorter"—pleasantly crumbly, buttery, and melting. Throw some chocolate into the mix, and, well, you've really done it now, haven't you?

8 ounces/225 g unsalted European-style butter, at room temperature

1 teaspoon pure vanilla extract

1/4 teaspoon fine sea salt

1/2 cup/113 g firmly packed light brown sugar

1/4 cup/30 g confectioners' sugar

2 cups/256 g unbleached all-purpose flour, spooned and leveled

2 cups/190 g finely crushed salted potato chips*

1 cup/170 g semisweet chocolate chips

1 large egg

1 tablespoon water

A few pinches of granulated sugar

Use a really thin, delicate chip for these cookies, such as Lay's Classic, which can be found nationwide. This variety is very salty, so I only add 1/4 teaspoon of salt to the dough itself. The key to these cookies is their salt level, so if you use a lightly salted chip or another brand, taste the dough for salt and see if you'd like a bit more (1/8 teaspoon or a couple of pinches) to achieve the level of salty-sweetness you like. It's easiest to weigh the amount of whole chips you need, and then crush them in a resealable plastic bag with a rolling pin.

Position a rack to the center of the oven and pre-heat it to 375°F/190°C. Line 2 baking sheets with parchment paper.

In the bowl of an electric mixer fitted with the paddle attachment, beat the butter, vanilla, and salt together on medium-high speed until creamy, about 1 minute. Add the brown and confectioners' sugar and continue to beat until very fluffy, 2 minutes more. Scrape down the bowl well and add the flour. Mix on low speed until a smooth dough forms. Stir in 1 cup/95 g of the crushed potato chips and the chocolate chips.

To form the cookies, sprinkle about ½ cup/48 g of the remaining crushed potato chips onto a work surface in small area, about 10 x 12 inches/25 x 31 cm. Turn out the dough onto the crushed potato chips and pat it into a rough rectangle. Cover the surface of the dough with parchment paper or plastic wrap. Roll the rectangle to a ½-inch/1.25 cm thickness, about 7 x 11 inches/18 x 28 cm. Remove the parchment or plastic wrap.

In a small cup, beat the egg vigorously with the water and granulated sugar until smooth. Brush the surface of the dough lightly with the egg wash, then scatter the remaining crushed potato chips over the dough. Lightly roll over the dough with a rolling pin to encourage the chips to adhere. Use a bench scraper or large, sharp knife to cut the rectangle into 4 dozen 1¼-inch/3.2 cm squares. Transfer the cookies to the prepared baking sheets with a bench scraper or small offset spatula, spacing the cookies about 2 inches/5 cm apart on the cookie sheet.

Bake 1 sheet at a time until set and golden in color, about 13 minutes. Let the cookies cool on the baking sheets for 2 minutes before transferring them to a wire rack to cool completely—they will crisp as they cool. Store in an airtight container for 3 to 4 days. They taste even better after an overnight rest.

GINGER MOLASSES SOFTIES

Makes about 30 cookies

IN MY MIND, SPICE COOKIES HAVE ALWAYS BEEN FOR COOLER WEATHER AND winter holidays, but my conversations with passionate ginger cookie lovers tell a different story. Apparently, I've been doing it all wrong and missing out on the glory of a great big, soft ginger cookie the other ten months of the year, with a chewy center and lots of sparkling, crunchy sugar. I've been changed.

As far as cookie jar cookies go, this one is a must-have—it only gets better, chewier and more flavorful, in the days after baking. Keep in mind the spices here are potent, so any other cookie going into a cookie jar with these will taste like a ginger cookie.

3 cups/384 g unbleached all-purpose flour, spooned and leveled

1½ teaspoons baking soda

¾ teaspoon fine sea salt

1 teaspoon ground ginger

½ teaspoon ground cinnamon

⅛ teaspoon ground cloves

½ cup/170 unsulfured black-strap molasses

½ cup/120 g full-fat sour cream, at room temperature

1 large egg yolk

10 tablespoons/140 g unsalted butter, at room temperature

¾ cup/170 g firmly dark brown sugar

1 teaspoon pure vanilla extract

¾ cup/150 g turbinado sugar for coating cookies

In a medium bowl, whisk together the flour, baking soda, salt, ginger, cinnamon, and cloves.

In a separate bowl, whisk together the molasses, sour cream, and egg yolk until smooth.

In the bowl of an electric mixer fitted with the paddle attachment, on medium-high speed, beat the butter until creamy, about 30 seconds. Add the brown sugar and vanilla and beat until light and fluffy, about 3 minutes. Slowly pour in the molasses mixture and beat until

well mixed—the mixture will curdle. Reduce the mixer speed to low. Gradually add the flour mixture and mix until the dough is smooth. Cover the bowl and refrigerate until the dough is firm, about 1 hour.

Position a rack to the center of the oven and preheat the oven to 350°F/180°C. Line 2 baking sheets with parchment paper.

Pour the turbinado sugar into a shallow bowl. Using a cookie scoop or 2 spoons, portion the dough into generous 2-tablespoon portions. Working a few portions at a time, gently roll the dough portions into balls and roll in the turbinado sugar to coat completely. Evenly space the dough balls on the prepared baking sheets, about 2 inches/5 cm apart.

Bake until the edges of the cookies are set and can be lifted off the sheets with a fingertip, but are still quite soft in the centers, about 12 minutes, rotating the sheets from top to bottom and front to back halfway through the baking time. Let the cookies cool on the sheets for several minutes before transferring to wire racks to cool completely.

The cookies keep sealed in an airtight container for up to 1 week, and they only get better as they rest.

GIANT, AWESOME PEANUT BUTTER COOKIES

Makes about 14 cookies

I OFTEN BELIEVE I'M A MISPLACED MINNESOTAN. EVERY TIME I AM ABLE TO VISIT, I end up looking at real estate while waiting to board my flight home. It's simply unlike any other place in the Midwest. For starters, "Minnesota Nice" is a very real phenomenon. And the eclectic food history of the state—rich with Scandinavian influences, Native American roots, and religious traditions (long live the Lutheran church basement potluck!)—is one I can dig through for hours.

One of my must-stops for sweet treats in Minneapolis is Rose Street Patisserie. It's at once cozy, familiar, edgy, and elegant, with an irresistible mix of gorgeous, high-end pastries and cookies and breads that immediately remind you of homey favorites that just look much, much more beautiful. One trip had me buying a pastry and coffee for eating immediately, and a peanut butter cookie the size of my outstretched hand for the airport, assuming a pending blizzard would extend my wait time. As it happened, I ate that enormous, soft, heavenly peanut butter cookie in a pristine hotel bed upon learning my flight was canceled altogether. But when I finally landed at home the next day, I headed straight to the kitchen to try and re-create that cookie.

2 cups/500 g creamy peanut butter, such as Skippy brand*

1¼ cups/280 g firmly packed light brown sugar

4 tablespoons/57 g unsalted butter, melted and cooled

¼ teaspoon fine sea salt

2 large eggs, cold

1 teaspoon pure vanilla extract

2 tablespoons/16 g cornstarch

1 teaspoon baking soda

½ cup/100 g granulated sugar for coating

As much as I love the huge peanut flavor of natural-style peanut butter (such as in the Peanut Better Blossoms, page 279) for an old-school, even-textured, soft and chewy peanut butter cookie, for this cookie, I reach for commercially produced, creamy peanut butter.

Position the oven racks to the upper and lower thirds of the oven and preheat it to 350°F/180°C. Line 2 baking sheets with parchment paper.

In the bowl of an electric mixer fitted with the paddle attachment, beat together the peanut butter, brown sugar, melted butter, and salt on medium speed until well blended, about 1 minute. Beat in the eggs, 1 at a time, then the vanilla, just until incorporated. Reduce the mixer speed to low and stir in the cornstarch and baking soda. Mix until the dough comes together and begins to come off the sides of the bowl.

Using a standard ice-cream scoop, portion out the dough into ¼-cup balls. Roll each ball in granulated sugar to coat completely. Place them, evenly spaced about 2 inches/5 cm apart, on the prepared baking sheets. Use an old-school grid-style potato masher or large serving fork to flatten the cookies into ½-inch/1.25 cm thick disks. Sprinkle the tops with a little extra granulated sugar.

Bake the cookies for 12 minutes, rotating the sheets from top to bottom and front to back halfway through the baking time. The cookies will seem underdone, and the edges just barely set. Set the pans on wire racks and let the cookies cool completely on the pans—they will continue to bake and set as they cool. Store in an airtight container at room temperature for up to 3 days.

TIP > *If you want to make the cookies smaller, use a 2-tablespoon scoop and reduce the bake time to 8 minutes.*

SALTED DOUBLE CHOCOLATE CHEWIES

Makes about 40 cookies

THE FIRST CHRISTMAS I WAS A MARRIED LADY, I STARTED MAKING A VERSION OF these cookies, with the intention of them becoming a tradition for our new little family. By the next year, with some tweaks and an extra hit of salt to make them even more crave-worthy, they'd broken out of the holiday cookie tin and become a year-round fixture in my cookie-baking rotation. Especially when I discovered they make a splendid enclosure for a summertime ice-cream sandwich.

2 cups/256 g unbleached all-purpose flour, spooned and leveled

3/4 cup/72 g unsweetened Dutch-processed cocoa powder

1 teaspoon baking soda

1 teaspoon flaky sea salt, such as Maldon

1/2 teaspoon fine sea salt

1 cup plus 4 tablespoons/282 g unsalted butter, at room temperature

1 cup/225 g dark brown sugar

1 cup/200 g granulated sugar, plus 1/2 cup for coating cookies

2 teaspoons pure vanilla extract

2 large eggs

8 ounces/225 g bittersweet chocolate (60% to 70% cacao), finely chopped

In a medium bowl, whisk together the flour, cocoa powder, baking soda, and flaky and fine salt.

In the bowl of an electric mixer fitted with the paddle attachment, beat the butter on medium speed until creamy, about 30 seconds. Add the brown and granulated sugar and the vanilla. Beat until light and fluffy, about 2 minutes. Beat in the eggs, 1 at a time. Reduce the mixer speed to low and gradually add the flour mixture. Stir in the chopped chocolate.

Cover the bowl and chill until firm, about 1 hour.

Position racks to the upper and lower thirds of the oven and pre-heat it to 350°F/180°C. Line 2 baking sheets with parchment paper.

Pour the remaining 1/2 cup of granulated sugar into a shallow bowl. Using a cookie scoop or 2 spoons, portion the dough into rounded tablespoons. Gently roll the dough portions into balls and roll in the sugar to coat completely. Evenly space the dough balls about 2 inches/5 cm apart on the prepared baking sheets.

Bake until the edges of the cookies are set and can be lifted off the sheets with a fingertip, but are still quite soft in the centers, about 12 minutes, rotating the sheets from top to bottom and front to back halfway through the baking time. Cool on the sheets for several minutes before transferring to wire racks to cool completely. The cookies keep sealed in an airtight container for up to 1 week.

CHAPTER 5

COUNTER CAKES

I CAN'T THINK OF A TIME GROWING UP WHEN THERE WASN'T AT least an Entenmann's cake on Gramma's counter, in its thin white paperboard box and a flimsy foil tin, and the coffee pot always seemed to be on, just in case someone dropped in. While it might not make sense every single day in our current lives to have these elements at the ready (you know, with gluten, sugar, processed foods, and excessive energy consumption being Code Red), it's such a beautiful part of midwestern life, the concept of what I like to call the "counter cake," especially one that's homemade.

Ready to be shared at a moment's notice, the ideal counter cake is dense, moist, and a no-frosting-required affair. Drizzly glazes are acceptable, but there's nothing about these casual cakes needing fussy decoration or extra steps. The real beauty here is in the cake part, all on its own. These are cakes that only get better with time, as they rest in a cake dome. The kind of cakes that beckon to you from the countertop so often you eventually succumb to just leaving the knife inside said cake dome. And then nearly wearing a shallow groove in the floor as you go back and forth toward the cake over several days, shaving off a portion every time you pass through the kitchen. We've all been there.

DONUT LOAF

Serves 8 to 10

ASIDE FROM BEING A REALLY FUN PHRASE TO SAY ALOUD OVER AND OVER AGAIN, this loaf is the sort of taste sensation belying its appearance. I wish I had a dollar for every time someone has eaten this modest-looking cake and exclaimed with wonder that it indeed tastes like a giant powdered sugar donut. And as my friend, the brilliant cookbook writer Kate Leahy, noted while testing it, "I completely underestimated the role nutmeg plays in making something donut-flavored."

Nonstick cooking spray for pan

2¾ cups/352 g unbleached all-purpose flour, spooned and leveled

2½ teaspoons baking powder

½ teaspoon baking soda

1 teaspoon fine sea salt

2 teaspoons freshly grated nutmeg*

14 tablespoons/197 g unsalted butter, at room temperature

¾ cup plus 2 tablespoons/175 g granulated sugar

1 teaspoon pure vanilla extract

3 large eggs, at room temperature

1 cup/225 g well-shaken buttermilk, at room temperature

FINISHING:

1 cup/120 g confectioners' sugar, sifted, plus more as needed

2 tablespoons/28 g unsalted butter, melted

Freshly grated makes all the difference here.

Position a rack to the lower third of the oven and preheat it to 325°F/170°C. Spray a 9 x 5-inch/23 x 12.7 cm light-colored metal loaf pan with nonstick cooking spray and line it with 2 perpendicular strips of parchment paper—1 cut skinnier to fit lengthwise across the bottom and up the 2 short sides, 1 to fit crosswise and up the 2 longer sides. Cut the strips long enough to have a few inches/cm of overhang on all sides.

In a medium bowl, whisk together the flour, baking powder, baking soda, salt, and nutmeg.

In the bowl of an electric mixer fitted with the paddle attachment, beat the butter on medium-high speed until creamy. Add the sugar and vanilla and beat until light and fluffy, about 3 minutes. Beat in ¼ cup/57 g of the flour mixture. Beat in the eggs, 1 at a time. Reduce the mixer speed to low, and stir in the remaining flour mixture and buttermilk in 5 alternating additions, beginning and ending with the flour mixture. Finish folding the batter by hand to make sure everything is incorporated—the batter will be very thick.

Scrape the batter into the prepared pan and smooth the top. Bake until the loaf is golden with a couple of cracks on top, and a toothpick inserted into the center comes out clean, 60 to 75 minutes. Let cool in the pan set over a wire rack for 15 minutes. Use the parchment paper to lift the loaf from the pan. Let rest for another 30 minutes.

When the loaf is cool and firm enough to handle, but still slightly warm, sift the confectioners' sugar all over a large rimmed baking sheet (keep the sieve handy). Peel the parchment from the cake. Gently turn the loaf over in 1 hand, using part of your forearm to support it. Using a pastry brush, brush the bottom of the cake with some of the melted butter. Carefully set the loaf, right-side up, in the confectioners' sugar. From there, brush the long sides with the butter, turning the cake from side to side to coat in sugar, then brush and coat the short sides. Lastly, brush the top with the butter, grab a handful or two of sugar from the tray, deposit into the sieve, and sift sugar generously over the top of the loaf. Roll the entire loaf in sugar once more so that it resembles a giant powdered sugar donut. Carefully transfer the cake to a wire rack to cool completely before slicing and serving, touching up the loaf with a quick sifting of sugar as needed.

CINNAMON-SUGARED PUMPKIN CHIP SNACK CAKE

Serves 12

THOSE IN THE MIDWEST KNOW THE DAY WELL: WE OPEN OUR EYES ONE MORNING to find the sticky, seemingly endless dog days of August have made an abrupt exit overnight, and think maybe we shouldn't have left the windows open because *brrrrrr*. Suddenly a plaid flannel, light sweater, and/or closed-toed shoes suddenly feel highly appropriate. Maybe we won't need two showers today! Maybe we'll even go apple picking this weekend! Glory be!

For much-welcomed early autumn mornings like these, this is the first fall-feeling recipe for which I fire up the oven, hoping the poor thing doesn't sputter and cough upon igniting, having been neglected for many weeks in exchange for outdoor grilling. If you can find roasted, salted pumpkin seed kernels, throw a few handfuls in the batter and sprinkle on top for extra crunch. It's October in an 8 x 8, I'm telling you.

CAKE:

Nonstick cooking spray for pan

1¾ cups/224 g unbleached all-purpose flour, spooned and leveled

2 teaspoons ground cinnamon

½ teaspoon freshly grated ground nutmeg

¼ teaspoon ground ginger

¼ teaspoon ground allspice

1 teaspoon baking soda

1 teaspoon baking powder

1¼ teaspoons fine sea salt

1½ cups/200 g canned pure pumpkin purée

½ cup/113 g vegetable oil

1¼ cups/250 g granulated sugar

2 large eggs

1 teaspoon pure vanilla extract

⅓ cup/75 g cold water

1 cup/170 g bittersweet chocolate chips (60% cacao)

TOPPING:

3 tablespoons granulated sugar

½ teaspoon ground cinnamon

Prepare the cake: Position a rack to the lower third of the oven and preheat it to 350°F/180°C.

Spray an 8-inch/20 cm square light-colored metal baking pan with nonstick cooking spray and line it with parchment paper.

In a large bowl, whisk together the flour, cinnamon, nutmeg, ginger, allspice, baking soda, baking powder, and salt.

In another large bowl, whisk together the pumpkin purée, oil, and sugar until well blended. Whisk in the eggs and the vanilla until combined, then whisk in the cold water. Fold in the chocolate chips.

Fold the dry ingredients into the wet, being careful not to overmix the batter. Spread the batter into the prepared pan, and gently knock the bottom of the pan on the countertop to even out the batter. Use a spatula to smooth the top.

Prepare the topping: Combine the sugar and cinnamon in a small bowl. Dampen your fingertips with water and work them into the sugar until it just begins to clump up a bit. Scatter over the batter.

Bake in the center of the oven until a toothpick inserted in a chocolate chip–free area comes out clean, 60 to 70 minutes. Let cool completely before slicing and serving. Store any leftovers wrapped tightly in plastic wrap for up to 5 days.

THE ONLY BANANA BREAD
YOU'LL EVER NEED

Serves 8 to 10

SOMETIMES RECIPES ARE SO UBIQUITOUS, SO DEEPLY EMBEDDED IN OUR CULTURE, it's hard to believe there was a time when that recipe didn't exist in the home baker's canon. The ultimate example of this is banana bread. I mean, how many of us have eaten banana bread, experienced it as the first recipe we ever baked, or christened a new kitchen by firing up the oven and baking a loaf to create an instant feeling of home? We have legendary home economist Mary Ellis Ames to thank for this ever-present American classic, a Minnesotan who reached celebrity status in the 1930s–'50s as a veritable prototype for Martha Stewart. Her recipe for banana bread was the first-ever published for it, printed in a 1933 edition of *Pillsbury's Balanced Recipes* cookbook.

The appearance of banana bread also has a fascinating connection to the time period: Quick breads were still relatively young in terms of food history, with the invention of the first double-acting baking powder coming out of Calumet City, Illinois, in 1889. Faster and easier than yeasted breads, new ideas for quick breads caught a lot of attention from harried housewives. Keep in mind the Great Depression had made it essential to not waste any scrap of food, and we all know that the more overripe bananas become, the better they are in banana bread. The timing of Mary Ellis Ames's brainstorm couldn't have been more on-target for creating an American classic. She basically out-Martha'd Martha with this one, is what I'm saying.

Nonstick cooking spray for pan

1¾ cups/400 g mashed, very ripe bananas*

¾ cup plus 2 tablespoons/196 g firmly packed dark brown sugar

½ cup/112 g vegetable oil

⅓ cup/75 g well-shaken buttermilk, at room temperature

2 large eggs

1 tablespoon dark rum (optional)

1 teaspoon pure vanilla extract

2 cups plus 2 tablespoons/272 g unbleached all-purpose flour, spooned and leveled

1 teaspoon baking powder

1 teaspoon baking soda

½ teaspoon fine sea salt

3 tablespoons/38 g granulated sugar for sprinkling

If you like to freeze bananas for bread-making purposes, just make sure you thaw them to room temperature, and then drain them for several minutes in a sieve to avoid adding too much liquid to the batter.

Position a rack to the lower third of the oven and preheat it to 325°F/170°C. Spray a 9 x 5-inch/23 x 12.7 cm loaf pan with nonstick cooking spray and line it with parchment paper with a couple of inches of overhang on 2 opposite sides.

In a large bowl, stir together the mashed bananas, brown sugar, oil, buttermilk, eggs, rum (if using), and vanilla.

In a medium bowl, whisk together the flour, baking powder, baking soda, and salt.

Pour the dry ingredients into the wet and fold until just blended. Pour the batter into the prepared pan.

Place the granulated sugar in a small bowl. Dampen your fingertips with water and work them into the sugar until it just begins to look like snow—if you pinch some, it should just barely hold together. Sprinkle the dampened sugar over the batter, aiming to get it clumped up together in spots.

Bake until a toothpick inserted into the center of the cake comes out clean, 60 to 70 minutes. Let cool for 20 minutes in the pan, then use the parchment paper to help lift the loaf out of the pan and cool completely on a wire rack. Store any leftovers in an airtight container for up to 5 days.

MARY AND ME ALMOND BUNDT CAKE

Serves 10 to 12

MARY TODD LINCOLN WAS A FORCE IN HER DAY, BOTH DURING HER TIME IN Springfield, Illinois, and in the White House. She was as devoted to social domesticity as she was to promoting her husband's career, and later, to her position as First Lady. It's well known that MTL loved to bake, once famously going through 13 pounds of sugar in one week (what, like it's hard?), at a time when that amount of sugar would've cost the equivalent of a week's pay for many women in Illinois. She often combined her obsession with baking with her duties as a politician's wife.

Along the way, she became known for a number of recipes, many of them inspired by her Kentucky upbringing. The most famous of her recipes is probably a simple almond cake, said to have been Abraham Lincoln's favorite dessert. I've reworked the original recipe to boost the flavor and moisture, and I hope Mary doesn't mind—I'd like to think we worked on this one together. The ingredients and prep here lean a little more toward weekend baking, but the velvety result is casual luxury, any day of the week.

Nonstick cooking spray for pan

1¼ cups plus 1 tablespoon/262 g granulated sugar, divided

1 cup/120 g blanched slivered almonds, lightly toasted and cooled

2⅔ cups/340 g unbleached all-purpose flour, spooned and leveled

1 tablespoon baking powder

¾ teaspoon fine sea salt

1 cup/225 g unsalted butter, at room temperature

2 teaspoons pure vanilla extract

½ teaspoon pure almond extract

8 ounces/225 g white chocolate, melted and cooled

1 cup/225 g full-fat coconut milk, well shaken, at room temperature

6 large egg whites, at room temperature

Position a rack to the lower third of the oven and preheat it to 325°F/170°C. Coat a 12- to 15-cup/2.8 to 3.6 L, light-colored metal Bundt pan with nonstick cooking spray, being sure to hit every pleat and pocket with spray. Invert the pan onto paper towels to prevent pooling in the bottom of the pan.

In a bowl of a food processor fitted with the steel S blade, combine 1 tablespoon of the sugar and the toasted almonds. Grind to a coarse meal. Add the flour, baking powder, and salt and pulse several times to blend.

In the bowl of an electric mixer fitted with the paddle attachment, beat the butter on medium speed until creamy. Add the remaining 1¼ cups/250 g of sugar, vanilla, and almond extract, and beat on medium-high speed until very light and fluffy, about 4 minutes. Reduce the speed to low and stir in the melted white chocolate. In 5 additions, alternate the dry ingredients and the coconut milk, beginning and ending with the flour mixture.

In a clean bowl with clean beaters, whip the egg whites to stiff peaks. Using a flexible large spatula, stir a third of the whipped whites into the batter to loosen it up a bit. Carefully fold in the remaining whites. Scrape the batter into the prepared pan and smooth the top.

Bake until the cake is golden and a toothpick inserted into the center of the cake comes out mostly clean with a few moist crumbs, 50 to 60 minutes. Let cool in the pan set on a wire rack for 20 minutes. Invert the cake onto the rack and let cool completely before slicing and serving. Store leftovers in an airtight container for up to 4 days.

CARAMEL APPLE DAPPLE CAKE

Serves 12 to 15

APPLE DAPPLE CAKES APPEAR IN MANY MIDCENTURY COMMUNITY COOKBOOKS, and they all seem to offer some little interesting riff on the concept of a cake so moist it's basically damp, baked in a 9 x 13 and packed with enough apple chunks to create a rippled effect on the surface of the cake, all the better to catch puddles of a simple confectioners' sugar icing. This version with the addition of coffee in the batter and a buttery brown sugar glaze, tempers the sweetness of both the cake and the fruit, and makes it awfully hard to stop at just one square.

CAKE:

Nonstick cooking spray for pan

2½ cups/320 g unbleached all-purpose flour, spooned and leveled

1 teaspoon baking soda

1 teaspoon fine sea salt

1 teaspoon ground cinnamon

½ teaspoon freshly grated nutmeg

½ cup/113 g unsalted butter, at room temperature

¾ cup/150 g granulated sugar

¾ cup/170 g firmly packed light brown sugar

2 teaspoons pure vanilla extract

¼ cup/57 g vegetable or canola oil

2 large eggs, cold

¾ cup/170 g lukewarm brewed coffee

4 cups peeled, cored, and chopped Honeycrisp apples (about 3 medium-large apples, cut into ½-inch/1.25 cm pieces)

GLAZE:

¾ cup/170 g firmly packed light brown sugar

4 tablespoons/57 g unsalted butter, cut into small pieces

¼ cup/57 g whole milk

¼ teaspoon fine sea salt

½ teaspoon pure vanilla extract

Prepare the cake: Position a rack to the center of the oven and preheat the oven to 350°F/180°C. Spray a 9 x 13-inch/23 x 33 cm light-colored metal baking pan with nonstick cooking spray and line it with parchment paper.

In a medium bowl, whisk together the flour, baking soda, salt, cinnamon, and nutmeg.

In the bowl of an electric mixer fitted with the paddle attachment, beat the butter on medium-high speed until creamy. Add the granulated and brown sugar and vanilla and beat until light and fluffy, about 3 minutes. Reduce the speed to medium-low and slowly stream in the oil until well blended. Beat in the eggs, 1 at a time. On low speed, spoon in half of the flour mixture. Slowly pour in the coffee. Stir in the remaining flour until the batter is smooth. Fold

in the apples by hand. Scrape the batter into the prepared pan and smooth evenly. Bake until the cake is deeply golden all over, begins to pull away from the sides of the pan, and a toothpick inserted into the center comes out clean, 45 to 50 minutes. Let cool slightly in the pan, set on a wire rack.

Prepare the glaze: In a 1- to 1½-quart/1 to 1.4 L saucepan over high heat, combine the brown sugar, butter, milk, and salt. Bring to a full rolling boil, stirring often, and boil until you can see it has thickened slightly, 2 to 3 minutes depending on your pan. Remove the pan from the heat. Stir in the vanilla. Let the glaze cool just until it stops bubbling. Pour the hot glaze over the still-warm cake. Working quickly, use a spatula to spread the glaze so it thinly and evenly covers the entire surface of the cake. Let the cake cool completely, uncovered, on the rack. Store any leftovers loosely covered at room temperature for up to 3 days.

DOUBLE CHOCOLATE ZUCCHINI LOAF

Serves 8 to 10

ZUCCHINI TENDS TO COME OUT OF EVERY MIDWESTERNER'S EARS IN THE SUMMER-time, whether or not you actually grow it in your own garden. Because even if you're not trying to unload some of your own crop onto someone else, there will always be neighbors or friends who are trying to unload theirs onto you. The good news is there are a million ways to use this mild vegetable, even in sweet baking. Zucchini bread is always a great way to chip away at any zucchini haul, and can even be relatively healthy with whole-grain flour and unrefined sugars.

But this is not that. This is a recipe that smothers that neutral, nutritious squash with loads of chocolate, nearly making it disappear in the loaf, and uses it only for the wonderful moisture it imparts. There's plenty of supply for a more virtuous zucchini preparation tomorrow.

Nonstick cooking spray for pan

3/4 cup plus 2 tablespoons/ 175 g granulated sugar

1/2 cup/113 g unsalted butter, melted and cooled

3 large eggs, at room temperature

1 tablespoon vegetable oil

1 teaspoon pure vanilla extract

1¼ cups/160 g unbleached all-purpose flour, spooned and leveled

1/2 cup/48 g unsweetened Dutch-processed cocoa powder

1 teaspoon baking powder

3/4 teaspoon fine sea salt

1/4 teaspoon baking soda

2 cups/225 g loosely packed grated zucchini (about 1 medium-size)*

1 cup/170 g semisweet chocolate chips, divided

Trim off the very ends, and use the large holes of a box grater.

Position a rack to the center of the oven and preheat the oven to 350°F/180°C. Spray a 9 x 5-inch/23 x 12.7 cm light-colored metal loaf pan with nonstick cooking spray and line it with parchment paper.

In a large bowl, whisk together the sugar, melted butter, eggs, oil, and vanilla. Place a large sieve over the bowl, and add the flour, cocoa powder, baking powder, salt, and baking soda. Sift the ingredients into the bowl. Whisk to combine—it will be quite thick. Switch to a flexible spatula and fold in the zucchini just until the batter begins to loosen a bit. Fold in three-quarters of the chocolate chips. Scrape the batter into the prepared pan and smooth the top. Sprinkle the remaining chocolate chips over the batter. Bake until a toothpick inserted deeply into the center comes out mostly clean, with just a few moist crumbs, about 1 hour. Let cool in the pan for about 20 minutes before transferring the loaf to a wire rack to cool completely. Store any leftovers tightly wrapped for up to 3 days.

EVERYDAY FUDGY CHOCOLATE SHEET CAKE

Serves 15 to 20

WHEN YOU HAVE A CASE OF THE MONDAYS AND JUST NEED SOME DANG CAKE, this is the recipe to have on hand, made with all fridge and pantry staples. This cake gets especially fudgy after a rest in the fridge, is a great building-block recipe for all manner of frostings and toppings, and can be also be baked in round pans and layered. But to keep it simple on a regular day that could use a little lift, I go for a 9 x 13, dust it with a little confectioners' sugar, and call it a (much better) day.

Nonstick cooking spray for pan

2⅓ cups/298 g unbleached all-purpose flour, spooned and leveled

2 cups/400 g granulated sugar

1½ teaspoons baking powder

½ teaspoon baking soda

1 teaspoon fine sea salt

1⅓ cups/300 g lukewarm water

1 cup/225 g unsalted butter

½ cup/48 g unsweetened Dutch-processed cocoa powder*

½ cup/113 g cold whole or low-fat milk

2 large eggs

1 teaspoon pure vanilla extract

Use half regular Dutch-processed and half black cocoa for the deepest chocolate flavor and color. Natural cocoa will work in a pinch.

Position a rack to the center of the oven and preheat it to 350°F/180°C. Spray a 9 x 13 inch/23 x 33 cm light colored metal baking pan or two 8-inch/20 cm round pans with nonstick cooking spray.

In a large bowl, whisk together the flour, sugar, baking powder, baking soda, and salt.

In a medium saucepan, combine the lukewarm water, butter, and cocoa powder. Set the pan over medium-high heat. Whisking often, bring the mixture to a boil. Pour the cocoa mixture over the flour mixture.

Using a handheld electric mixer, beat on medium-high speed until thick and smooth. Mix in the milk. Beat in the eggs, 1 at a time, then the vanilla. Scrape the batter into the prepared pan(s). Bake until a toothpick inserted into the center of the cake comes out with fudgy crumbs, 30 to 35 minutes—do not overbake. Set the pan on a wire rack to cool completely. The cake will keep covered in the refrigerator for up to 1 week.

ICED BUTTERY LEMON BUNDT CAKE

Serves 10 to 12

IF YOU HAVE HAD TO MUSCLE YOUR WAY AWAY FROM THE PASTRY CASE AT THE world's most recognizable coffee shop (ahem, green mermaid creature, ahem), I completely understand the pull of it, especially that thick slab of lemony yellow loaf cake it has, the one with the cap of bleached white icing. Particularly at three p.m. when morale is low, you're far from bedtime, and you're grabbing a coffee but would rather it were a cocktail. There's something undeniably attractive about that hunk of cottony iced lemon cake when you're just trying to get over the hump. I feel you. Desperate times, and all of that.

But I'll make you a deal. The next time that happens, if you can crowbar your face off the glass, pay for only a latte, and hightail your way home, I'll give you my recipe for this thickly iced, buttery lemon Bundt. A cake you can feel good about making, and falling into face first, during your next midday slump.

CAKE:

Nonstick cooking spray for pan

3/4 cup plus 3 tablespoons/211 g whole milk, at room temperature

1 tablespoon freshly squeezed lemon juice

5 large eggs, at room temperature

1 tablespoon pure vanilla extract

2 teaspoons pure lemon extract

3 1/4 cups/390 g cake flour, spooned and leveled, plus more for dusting

2 1/4 cups/450 g granulated sugar

1 heaping tablespoon finely grated lemon zest

2 teaspoons baking powder

1/2 teaspoon baking soda

1 teaspoon fine sea salt

1 1/4 cups/282 g unsalted butter, at very soft room temperature

Yellow food coloring (optional)

DRIZZLE:

1/2 cup/100 g granulated sugar

1 tablespoon unsalted butter

3 tablespoons/42 g freshly squeezed lemon juice

ICING:

1 cup/120 g confectioners' sugar

2 to 3 tablespoons half-and-half or heavy whipping cream*

1/4 teaspoon pure vanilla extract

1/8 teaspoon fine sea salt

*The lesser amount will give you a fondantlike icing that sets atop the cake in a thicker layer; more liquid will yield a thinner icing that cascades down the sides.

Prepare the cake: Position a rack to the lower third of the oven and preheat the oven to 325°F/170°C. Coat a 12- to 15-cup/2.8 to 3.6 L light-colored metal Bundt pan with nonstick cooking spray. Invert onto paper towels to prevent pooling in the bottom of the pan.

In a large measuring cup, whisk together the milk, lemon juice, eggs, vanilla, and lemon extract.

In the bowl of an electric mixer fitted with the whisk attachment, combine the cake flour, granulated sugar, lemon zest, baking powder, baking soda, and salt. Stir together on low speed and keep the mixer running. Add the butter pieces, 1 at a time, mixing until the mixture resembles chunky crumbs, like shortbread dough. Pour in three quarters of the milk mixture. Increase the mixer speed to medium and beat until pale and fluffy, 1½ minutes. Reduce the mixer speed to low. Slowly pour in the rest of the milk mixture. Increase the mixer speed to high and beat for 30 seconds more. Scrape down the bowl well and beat for 30 seconds to finish. Beat in a few drops of yellow food coloring, if you wish.

Lightly flour the sprayed pan and tap out the excess.

Scrape the batter into the prepared pan and smooth the top. Bake until golden and a toothpick sunk deep into the center comes out with just a few moist crumbs, 60 to 70 minutes. Let cool for 20 minutes in the pan set on a wire rack. Loosen the edges and invert the cake onto a wire rack set over a baking sheet.

Prepare the drizzle: In a 1- to 1½-quart/1 to 1.4 L saucepan, combine the granulated sugar, butter, and lemon juice. Set the pan over medium heat. Stir gently to dissolve the sugar. While the cake is still warm, use a pastry brush to gradually soak the cake with glaze—it will take a few minutes for the cake to absorb all the liquid. Let cool completely.

Prepare the icing: In a small bowl, whisk together the confectioners' sugar, half-and half or cream, vanilla, and salt and until smooth. Pour the icing over the cake. Let the icing set before slicing and serving.

COUNTER CAKE TIPS

The most easily identifiable of all counter cakes is the Bundt, with its iconic shape. When the Bundt pan was created in the 1950s by Nordic Ware in Minneapolis, it was modeled after traditional German molds for *Gugelhupf* (also known as *Bundkuchen*). The pan didn't quite take off at first, and the company considered discontinuing production several times (can you imagine?!). It wasn't until 1966, when the "Tunnel of Fudge Cake" placed second in the Pillsbury Bake-Off and exploded into pop culture, that the Bundt pan landed in nearly every kitchen in America. At that point, Nordic Ware started churning out up to thirty thousand pans a day to keep up with demand.

Today, Nordic Ware is still family-owned, and 95 percent of its expansive product line is still made right in St. Louis Park, Minnesota. The Bundt love lives on today, with the abundant look (a-Bundt-dant? Ugh, sorry) and ease of preparation being a symbol of Midwest hospitality. Nothing is quite as satisfying as baking a Bundt, tall and robust, that releases cleanly from the pan. Here's a few tips to ensure Bundt success (and for any thicker, denser counter cake, quick bread, or loaf cake, for that matter).

HAVE YOUR CAKE INGREDIENTS ALL AT ROOM TEMPERATURE. When making a cake of significant volume, such as a Bundt or thick loaf cake, it's very important that the batter be well mixed to get a nicely textured finished product. To speed things up, unwrap the butter and cut it into thin slices to help it to come to room temperature quickly, place your eggs in a bowl of balmy tap water, and take the chill off your milk or other liquids with the defrost setting of your microwave.

PREP A PROPER PAN. Bundt pans can be insanely intimidating to grease properly, with all their creases and crevices. My preferred method of greasing for most Bundts also happens to be the party line at Nordic Ware: Spray your pan all over with nonstick cooking spray, and then dust it with flour, tapping out the excess (add some cocoa powder to the flour for chocolate cakes, to avoid a ghostly floury layer). I take the extra step of inverting the pan onto paper toweling for a few moments to keep excess oil from pooling in the pan, before flouring it.

OVEN RACK PLACEMENT IS KEY. We often bake in the center of our oven, but thick cakes do better in the lower third of the oven. With more heat hitting the cake from the bottom of the oven, the center will bake thoroughly, without the top getting overdone during the long bake (usually an hour or more) that thicker counter cakes require.

AVOID SUPERDARK METAL PANS. The darker the pan, the thicker, firmer, and darker the crust of the cake. Some of the old-school Bundt pans have an almost black interior, and I avoid those. My favorite Bundt pans have a light-colored coating as their interior, silver- or gold-toned. I generally prefer light-colored metal pans for all baking, but especially for loaf cakes, to avoid burning the outer crust.

CONSIDER COOLING AS PART OF THE BAKE TIME. Remove the cake from the oven when a cake tester shows a few moist crumbs and isn't completely clean—it will continue to bake from residual heat. Also, with a larger, heavier cake, the structure needs time to set before it can be safely unmolded without tearing or collapsing, but you also don't want to wait so long that the cooled cake solders itself to the pan. Unless your recipe states otherwise, for Bundts, allow for 10 to 20 minutes of cooling time before inverting it out onto a wire rack to cool completely. For loaf cakes, go for 20 to 30 minutes before lifting it from the pan with its parchment liner and setting it on a rack.

CHOCOLATE CHIP MARBLE BUNDT CAKE

Serves 10 to 12

I HAVE A SOFT SPOT FOR THIS CAKE FROM LOGAN LEVANT OF THE FORMER BUTTER-cake Bakery in Los Angeles. Her bakery inspired me to make baking a part of my career more than a decade ago. This recipe also made me go out and buy my very first Nordic Ware Bundt pan. Years later, I have a rather aggressive wall of vintage Bundt pans in all shapes and colors decorating my office, so maybe I should start telling my husband the pan hoarding is kind of Logan's fault. At any rate, you really can't go wrong with this unbelievably moist counter cake, and its classic combination of vanilla and chocolate swirls.

A few tips for success here: Don't overswirl the batter; just a quick wave with a knife once or twice around the pan is all you need to create a beautiful marbled interior. As much as you'll want to devour this cake ASAP after baking, give it a couple of hours to really cool and rest out of the pan before serving—the flavor and texture are well worth the wait. Don't forget to flour the pan after spraying it with nonstick cooking spray; this cake likes to stick. But as a trade-off, this cake also stays extraordinarily moist for days on end, kept in a cake dome at room temperature.

2½ cups/500 g granulated sugar, divided

½ cup/64 g unsweetened cocoa powder*

½ cup/113 g hot water

¼ cup/84 g light corn syrup

2½ teaspoons pure vanilla extract, divided

1 cup/225 g unsalted butter, at room temperature, plus more for pan (optional)

Nonstick cooking spray for pan (optional)

2⅔ cups/340 g unbleached all-purpose flour, spooned and leveled, plus more for pan

2 teaspoons baking powder

½ teaspoon fine sea salt

4 large eggs, at room temperature

1 cup/225 g whole milk, at room temperature

1 cup/170 g semisweet chocolate chips

Either natural or Dutch-processed cocoa powder will work here.

In a 1- to 1½-quart/1 to 1.4 L saucepan, whisk together ½ cup/100 g of the sugar and the cocoa powder, hot water, and corn syrup. Over high heat, bring to a simmer, whisking occasionally until smooth. Remove the pan from the heat. Whisk in ½ teaspoon of the vanilla. Set the chocolate syrup aside.

Position a rack in the lower third of the oven and preheat it to 350°F/180°C. Butter or spray and lightly flour a 12- to 15-cup/2.8 to 3.6 L Bundt pan.

In a medium bowl, whisk together the flour, baking powder, and salt. In the bowl of an electric mixer fitted with the paddle attachment, combine the butter and remaining 2 cups/400 g of sugar. Beat on medium-high speed until fluffy and lightened in color, about 3 minutes. Beat in the eggs, 1 at a time. Scrape down the bottom and sides of the bowl. Beat in the remaining 2 teaspoons of vanilla.

On low speed, stir in the flour mixture and milk in 5 alternating additions. Gently fold in the chocolate chips by hand.

Scoop a third of the batter into a medium bowl. Whisk in the chocolate syrup. Pour another third of the vanilla batter into the prepared Bundt pan. Pour the chocolate batter over the first layer. Finish by pouring the last of the vanilla batter over the top. With a knife, lightly swirl the batters together with a figure-eight motion, once or twice around the pan.

Bake until a toothpick inserted into the center of the cake comes out mostly clean with a few moist crumbs, 60 to 70 minutes. Let cool the cake in the pan on a wire rack. Invert onto a serving platter. Store any leftovers in a cake dome at room temperature for 4 to 5 days.

AUNT PHYLLIS'S CRUSTY BUTTER POUND CAKE

Serves 15 to 20

GRAMMA WAS OF AN INTERESTING GENERATION, FOOD-WISE—BORN IN 1934, her early eating years were pre-convenience foods, and everything was made from scratch (my maternal great-grandmother had mad baking game, as the story goes). But by the time she was an adult and raising six (!) children of her own, packaged foods and box mixes had made their way into American kitchens, and she embraced that, too. Many a family birthday was celebrated with a box-mix yellow cake (but always with a homemade fudge frosting). One cake that she did make from scratch and talked about with a gleam in her eye was this pound cake, a recipe given to her by her sister-in-law—my great-aunt Phyllis of Memphis, Tennessee, my grandfather's only sister. Gramma described this cake to me as having a "sugar crust," and she's not wrong. While there's no sugar actually sprinkled over the batter before baking, it bakes into an irresistibly sweet, crunchy shell on the very top, the perfect foil to the velvety, tender interior.

The original recipe makes one large cake in a Bundt pan or tube pan, but you can also divide the batter and bake it in two standard loaf pans (or halve the recipe for one loaf). I recommend making the full recipe in two loaf pans because this cake freezes beautifully. So, bake one and freeze one—you won't regret it. Or even better, give it to a lucky neighbor.

1 cup/225 g unsalted butter, at room temperature, plus more for pan(s)

3 cups/360 g cake flour, spooned and leveled, plus more for pan(s)

1/2 teaspoon fine sea salt

1/4 teaspoon baking soda

3 cups/600 g granulated sugar

6 large eggs, at room temperature

1 cup/240 g full-fat sour cream

2 teaspoons pure vanilla extract

Preheat the oven to 325°F/170°C. Butter and flour a 12- to 15-cup/2.8 to 3.6 L Bundt pan or two 9 x 5-inch/23 x 12.7 cm loaf pans.

Sift the cake flour into a large bowl. Whisk in the salt and baking soda.

In the bowl of a mixer fitted with the paddle attachment, beat the butter on medium speed until creamy. Add the sugar and beat on medium-high speed until light and fluffy, about 5 minutes. Reduce the speed to medium-low, and beat in the eggs, 1 and a time. Scrape down the sides and bottom of the bowl and stir in the sour cream and vanilla on low speed. Add the flour mixture, 1/2 cup/64 g at a time, on low speed until the batter is smooth.

Pour the batter into the prepared pan(s) and bake until a toothpick inserted into the center comes out mostly clean with a few moist crumbs, about 90 minutes for the Bundt cake, and 60 to 70 minutes for 2 loaf pans. Let cool in the pan(s) for 20 minutes before unmolding and allowing to cool completely on a wire rack.

MOM'S CHERRY SHORTCAKE SQUARES

Makes 2 dozen squares

MY MOTHER IS MANY WONDERFUL THINGS. SHE IS A GREAT COOK, A TERRIFIC entertainer. A generally delightful woman. But she is not a prolific baker. The recipes she baked during my childhood were few in number, but made an impression. This simple sheet of cake squares was trotted out again and again in my childhood, and remains a favorite. It's another great example of making something fabulous out of just a few ingredients, and delighting a crowd without Herculean effort. It's just a pan full of happy. This big batch is easily halved by using a quarter sheet pan.

Nonstick cooking spray for pan

1 cup/225 g unsalted European-style butter, at room temperature

1½ cups/300 g granulated sugar

1 tablespoon freshly squeezed lemon juice

2 teaspoons pure vanilla extract

½ teaspoon fine sea salt

4 large eggs, at room temperature

2 cups/256 g unbleached all-purpose flour, spooned and leveled

1 (21-ounce/595 g) can high-quality cherry pie filling*

Confectioners' sugar for dusting

*The recipe I grew up with used the bright red canned variety with lots of glossy goo, and for nostalgia's sake, this is what I still use. I seek out brands that don't contain high-fructose corn syrup and say "more fruit" or something similar on the label—this typically indicates more cherries, less goo, and you'll have enough cherries to top each square.

Position a rack to the center of the oven and preheat it to 350°F/180°C. Spray a 10 x 15 x 1-inch/25 x 38 x 2.5 cm or 12 x 17-inch/30 x 43 cm rimmed baking sheet with cooking spray, line it with parchment paper, and lightly spray the parchment, too. (I like my squares a bit thinner, with crisp, golden edges, so I use a larger pan. The jelly-roll pan will give you a slightly loftier result and the fruit will be hidden a bit.)

In the bowl of an electric mixer, beat together the butter and sugar on medium-high speed until very light and fluffy, at least 5 minutes. (Don't skimp on the beating time—all the air in this cake comes from this stage!) Beat in the lemon juice, vanilla, and salt. Beat in the eggs, 1 at a time, giving each at least 30 seconds of beating to incorporate. Scrape down the bowl. Beat again for 1 minute. Reduce the mixer speed to low and stir in the flour. When there's a few streaks of flour left, finish stirring the batter by hand.

Scrape the batter onto the prepared sheet pan and smooth it into an even layer. Score the batter into 24 squares with a toothpick for easy, even placing of the cherries.

Stir the pie filling well. Place 3 cherries in the center of every square.

Bake until a toothpick inserted into the center of a square comes out clean, 25 to 30 minutes. Let cool completely in the pan on a wire rack. Just before serving, cut into 24 squares and dust with confectioners' sugar. Store any leftovers in an airtight container with layers of waxed paper or parchment for up to 3 days.

OZARK SKILLET CAKE

Serves 8

NAMED AFTER THE OZARKS REGION OF MISSOURI, OZARK PUDDING CAUGHT ON in popularity in the 1950s when Bess Truman revealed that she often made this dessert for her husband, President Harry S. Truman, and shared the recipe for the 1948 edition of *The Congressional Club Cookbook*. The original recipe is something like a *clafoutis*, an almost custardlike batter just barely holding together a mess of dried fruit, apple bits, and nuts aplenty, a celebration of native midwestern ingredients. I've tweaked this idea to make it a little more cakelike and sliceable, but still packed with all sorts of goodies, just the thing for a lazy fall weekend.

Unsalted butter for skillet

½ cup/60 g dried cranberries

2 large eggs

½ cup/113 g light brown sugar

½ cup/100 g granulated sugar

1 teaspoon pure vanilla extract

⅔ cup/85 g unbleached all-purpose flour, spooned and leveled

2 teaspoons baking powder

½ teaspoon ground cinnamon

¼ teaspoon fine sea salt

1 cup/120 g chopped pecans, toasted

1 medium-size pear or apple, peeled, cored, and chopped into ½-inch/1.25 cm chunks

Position a rack to the center of the oven and preheat it to 350°F/180°C. Butter a 10-inch/25 cm cast-iron skillet.

In a small, microwave-safe bowl, combine the cranberries and ¼ cup/57 g of water. Cover the bowl tightly with plastic wrap. Microwave on **HIGH** for 45 seconds. Keep the bowl covered and set aside while you prepare the batter.

In the bowl of an electric mixer fitted with the whisk attachment, combine the eggs, brown and granulated sugar, and vanilla. Beat on high speed until light in color and tripled in volume, about 5 minutes. Sift the flour, baking powder, cinnamon, and salt over the batter. Gently fold the dry ingredients into the batter.

Drain the cranberries and pat them dry with paper towels. Fold the cranberries and three quarters of the pecans into the batter. Pour the batter into the prepared skillet. Top with the pears or apples, then sprinkle with the remaining pecans. Bake until the cake is puffed and golden, about 35 minutes—a toothpick inserted into the center may come out quite moist, but not wet with batter, as the cake will continue to bake in the hot pan. Let cool until just warm and serve with lots of whipped cream or vanilla ice cream.

CHAPTER 6
BARS

THE TERM BARS, AS IN COOKIE BARS OR DESSERT BARS, IS PROBABLY one of the happiest, most Middle American words in existence. First of all, the flat *a* sound combined with an *r* can be endlessly drawn out and/or emphasized to really highlight all manner of midwestern accents. Plus, you can often get a double dip of that accent since the sight of a freshly cut 9 x 13 often makes folks say with delight, "Oh! Bars!" Perfect.

Related: Is there anything more glorious, more welcoming, more portable and shareable than a swath of treats in a 9 x 13? It follows that Mentality of Pie outlined in the introduction of Chapter 3—why give yourself arthritis shaping dozens of cookie dough balls when you can just shove the whole lot into one pan and call it done? Even better, the yield can be adjusted once the headcount is determined. Practical and delicious, just the way I like things, and a perfect candidate for bake sales, potlucks, and church basement buffets, cementing the importance of bars in the midwestern culinary landscape.

CHOCOLATE-ESPRESSO REVEL BARS

Makes 2 dozen bars

I'M ONE OF THOSE PEOPLE WHO HAVE A LOT OF TROUBLE WITH MISHEARING song lyrics. Like, a "hold me closer, Tony Danza"—level of trouble (all apologies to Sir Elton John). I also thought revel bars were actually called rebel bars for more years than I'd care to admit. In my defense, they are so dense with fudge, sandwiched between two layers of oatmeal cookie dough, they are absolutely something that could be considered rebellious, depending on the diet you're subscribing to on a given day.

My karaoke challenges aside, at the top of the list for many a midwestern bar cookie lover is the revel bar. As far as I can tell, the original concept of the revel bar might be credited to Iowa-based *Better Homes and Gardens* magazine as far back as 1968. That recipe uses a mixture of semisweet chocolate and sweetened condensed milk to create a trufflelike layer between the crust and topping, but as you can imagine, that combination becomes so sweet that it tends to overwhelm. In my version, I opt for a true truffle center with a bittersweet ganache, with a bump of espresso throughout.

Nonstick cooking spray for pan

FILLING AND ASSEMBLY:

½ cup/120 g heavy whipping cream

¼ cup/50 g granulated sugar

¾ teaspoon instant espresso powder

⅛ teaspoon fine sea salt

6 ounces/170 g bittersweet chocolate (60% cacao), coarsely chopped

DOUGH:

3 cups/300 g old-fashioned rolled oats

1¾ cups/225 g unbleached all-purpose flour, spooned and leveled

1½ teaspoons instant espresso powder

1 teaspoon baking soda

1 teaspoon fine sea salt

1 cup/225 g unsalted butter, at room temperature

1¾ cups/395 g firmly packed dark brown sugar

1 tablespoon pure vanilla extract

2 large eggs, at room temperature

½ cup/85 g semisweet chocolate chips

Position a rack to the center of the oven and preheat it to 350°F/180°C. Spray a 9 x 13-inch/23 x 33 cm light-colored metal baking pan with nonstick cooking spray and line it with parchment paper with a couple of inches of overhang on 2 opposite sides.

Prepare the filling: In a 1- to 1½-quart/1 to 1.4 L saucepan, combine the cream, granulated sugar, espresso powder, and salt. Set the pan over medium heat and bring the mixture to a bare simmer. Turn off the heat and add the bittersweet chocolate. Let sit for 1 minute, then whisk the mixture until smooth and glossy. Set aside to cool.

Prepare the dough: In a medium bowl, whisk together the oats, flour, espresso powder, baking soda, and salt.

In the bowl of an electric mixer fitted with the paddle attachment, beat the butter on medium speed until creamy, about 1 minute. Add the brown sugar and vanilla and beat until smooth and a bit lighter in color, about 1 minute more. Beat in the eggs, 1 at a time. Reduce the speed to low and gradually stir in the oat mixture until well blended. Transfer about a third of the dough to a clean bowl and set aside. To the dough remaining in the mixer bowl, stir in the chocolate chips.

Spread the chocolate chip–studded dough evenly across the bottom of the prepared pan. Pour the cooled chocolate ganache filling over the dough, drizzling it in thick ribbons—no need to smooth it evenly. Use your fingertips to pinch off generous tablespoons of the remaining cookie dough, and drop them randomly over the ganache filling.

Bake until the top is golden, the bars have begun to pull away from the sides of the pan, and there is the slightest wobble in the very center, 35 to 40 minutes. Let cool completely in the pan set on a wire rack until the ganache has set, about 2 hours. For easy cutting, refrigerate for 1 hour before cutting into bars. Store in an airtight container at room temperature for up to 3 days, or in the refrigerator for a week.

WEDNESDAY NIGHT BROWNIES

Makes 16 brownies

WHEN IT'S THE KIND OF HUMP DAY THAT MAKES YOU DO A DOUBLE TAKE AT THE calendar—because honestly, does this week have 11 days in it, or what?—it's important to have a reliable, one-bowl brownie in your repertoire. This is the kind of thing you can mix together right before sitting down to dinner, and have a warm, gooey brownie waiting for you in time for evening television. Preferably the kind of trashy television that makes you temporarily forget it's only Wednesday.

Nonstick cooking spray for pan

½ cup/113 g unsalted butter, cut into chunks

⅔ cup/150 g firmly packed dark brown sugar

⅔ cup/134 g granulated sugar

1 teaspoon pure vanilla extract

⅔ cup/64 g unsweetened Dutch-processed cocoa powder*

½ teaspoon baking powder

Generous ½ teaspoon fine sea salt

2 large eggs, fridge-cold

⅔ cup/85 g unbleached all-purpose flour, spooned and leveled

1 cup/170 g bittersweet (60% cacao), semisweet, or milk chocolate chips

*If you have black cocoa, this is an excellent place to do a half-and-half split.

Position a rack to the center of the oven and preheat it to 350°F/180°C. Spray an 8-inch/20 cm square light-colored metal baking pan with nonstick cooking spray and line it with parchment paper or aluminum foil.

In a large, microwave-safe bowl, combine the butter and the brown and granulated sugar. Microwave on **HIGH** until the butter is melted, about 1 minute. Whisk until smooth. Whisk in the vanilla, cocoa powder, baking powder, and salt. Whisk in the eggs, 1 at a time, just until blended—no need to incorporate too much air here. Switch to a spatula and fold in the flour. When just a few floury streaks remain, stir in the chocolate chips. Scrape the batter into the prepared pan and smooth the top.

Bake until the edges are set and just begin to pull away from the sides of the pan, about 25 minutes. Let cool in the pan for at least 20 minutes before slicing and serving.

TIP › *Chilling the pan before slicing the brownies will give you the cleanest cuts.*

NEXT-LEVEL CRISPY TREATS

Makes 10 to 15 bars

WHAT WOULD AN AMERICAN CHILDHOOD BE WITHOUT THE GLORY OF THE RICE Krispie treat? Honestly, have you ever met a person who doesn't love them? The Rice Krispie treat is the ultimate American hero. Sweet, crisp, chewy, melty, no polarizing flavors or spices. It's a beautiful, harmonizing thing, and a favorite of bake sales and low-maintenance bakers alike. (As an aside, the earliest record of a "baking sale" was held in May 1891, by the female members of a Methodist church in St. Paul, Minnesota, because of course it was.)

When I developed a recipe amplifying everything good about the original, I found the kind of addictive treat that makes people say "Take that pan away from me!" which is the very best compliment a baker can hear. Double butter, double mallows, a handful of white chocolate to add that *je ne sais quoi*. They're next-level.

Nonstick cooking spray for pan

1/2 cup/113 g unsalted butter

2 (10-ounce/560 g) bags miniature marshmallows, divided

3/4 teaspoon fine sea salt

4 ounces/113 g high-quality white chocolate, coarsely chopped

3/4 teaspoon pure vanilla extract

8 cups/256 g crispy rice cereal

For your crispy treat vessel, have ready any baking pan or dish with a capacity of 2 to 2½ quarts/1.9 to 2.4 L—a 9 x 13-inch/23 x 33 cm rectangular pan or casserole dish will do. Spray it lightly with nonstick cooking spray and dab away the excess.

In a 5-quart/475 L heavy-bottomed pot over medium-low heat, melt the butter. Add 15 ounces/425 g of the marshmallows (about 1½ bags) and the salt. Stir often, until the marshmallows have nearly melted. Add the white chocolate and stir until the mixture is smooth. Stir in the vanilla. Lower the heat to its lowest setting and add the cereal. Stir until well blended. Add the remaining 5 ounces/135 g of marshmallows and continue to fold gently until the added marshmallows just begin to melt at the edges, but are still very visible in the mixture.

Remove the pan from the heat and scrape the mixture into the prepared pan. Very gently pat the treat mixture into an even layer, being careful not to compact it. If it's very warm and sticky, a light spritzing of nonstick cooking spray on your palms will help you pat the mixture into place. Let sit at room temperature until cool, about 45 minutes, before cutting into generous portions. Store any leftovers in an airtight container at room temperature for up to 5 days.

SCOTCH-A-ROOS

Makes 3 dozen bars

THERE'S NO GETTING AROUND IT—SCOTCH-A-ROOS ARE THE VERY DEFINITION of midwestern excess. The best ones are reminiscent of a slab of sticky, gooey, crunchy candy bar filling, glossed over with a trufflelike chocolate and butterscotch topping. They're a classic that works for any celebration. Helps keep dentists in business, too.

One tip for perfectly-textured, chewy-crisp roos: Much like the Next-Level Crispy Treats on page 164, don't smash the crispy mixture into a tight, compact layer, which will harden them as they cool. Using a light hand ensures a soft, crave-worthy chew.

Nonstick cooking spray for pan

BARS:

1 cup/270 g creamy peanut butter, such as Skippy brand

1 cup/320 g light corn syrup

3/4 cup/170 g firmly packed light brown sugar

2 tablespoons/28 g unsalted butter

1/2 teaspoon pure vanilla extract

1/8 teaspoon fine sea salt

5 cups/185 g crispy rice cereal

TOPPING:

6 ounces/170 g bittersweet chocolate (60% to 70% cacao) chips or chopped bar chocolate

6 ounces/170 g butterscotch chips

Line a 9 x 13-inch/23 x 33 cm baking pan with aluminum foil with a couple of inches of overhang on 2 opposite sides and spray with nonstick cooking spray.

Prepare the bars: In a 4- to 5-quart/3.75 to 4.75 L heavy-bottomed pot, combine the peanut butter, corn syrup, brown sugar, butter, vanilla, and salt. Place the pot over medium-high heat and stir often until the sugar has dissolved and the mixture is smooth and just threatening to bubble. Remove the pan from the heat and stir in the cereal, blending thoroughly. Scrape the mixture into the prepared pan, and use a spatula to spread it gently into place, being careful not to compact the mixture.

Prepare the topping: In a microwave-safe bowl, combine the bittersweet chocolate and butterscotch chips. Microwave with 30-seconds bursts on **HIGH**, stirring well after each interval, until smooth. Pour over the crispy mixture and spread evenly. Refrigerate until the topping is set, about 30 minutes. Use the foil to lift out the slab and transfer to a cutting board. Cut into 36 bars. Store any leftovers in an airtight container for up to 5 days.

FROSTED SNICKERDOODLE BARS

Makes about 2 dozen bars

IS THERE ANYTHING MORE FANTASTICALLY HOMEY THAN THAT MOST MARVELOUS of soft-baked cookies, the snickerdoodle? The name is thought to have come from nineteenth-century New England, deriving from the word *Schneckennudeln*, a type of snail-shaped German cinnamon roll. Snickerdoodles are famously associated with the Pennsylvania Dutch and the Amish communities of Indiana, which explains how they made their way to the Midwest and have long been a homespun favorite here.

And, of course, if you can find a way to turn something, anything at all, into a recipe that can be crammed into a 9 x 13, it becomes extra midwestern. The swath of frosting on top gilds the lily here, but it's so worth it.

Nonstick cooking spray for pan

BARS:

2¾ cups/352 g unbleached all-purpose flour, spooned and leveled

2 teaspoons cream of tartar, sifted

1¼ teaspoons fine sea salt

1 teaspoon baking soda

1 teaspoon ground cinnamon*

1 cup/225 g unsalted butter, at room temperature

¾ cup/170 g light brown sugar

¾ cup/150 g granulated sugar

1½ teaspoons pure vanilla extract

2 large eggs, at room temperature

¼ cup/57 g whole milk

FROSTING:

¾ cup/170 g unsalted butter, at room temperature

1½ cups/180 g confectioners' sugar

1 teaspoon ground cinnamon, plus more for dusting (optional)

1 tablespoon plus 1 teaspoon whole milk

1 teaspoon pure vanilla extract

¼ teaspoon fine sea salt

*Vietnamese cinnamon (sometimes also labeled Saigon cinnamon) with its sweet-spicy punch reminiscent of Red Hots cinnamon candy, will bump the flavor of these bars from old-school to something really special.

Position a rack to the center of the oven and preheat it to 325°F/170°C. Line a 9 x 13-inch/23 x 33 cm light-colored metal baking pan with aluminum foil and spray it with nonstick cooking spray.

Prepare the bars: In a medium bowl, whisk together the flour, cream of tartar, salt, baking soda, and cinnamon.

In the bowl of an electric mixer fitted with the paddle attachment, beat the butter on medium speed until creamy. Add the brown and granulated sugar and vanilla and beat until light and fluffy, about 3 minutes.

Beat in the eggs, 1 at a time, giving each about 30 seconds of beating to fully incorporate. Beat in the milk. Reduce the mixer speed to low and gradually beat in the flour mixture. Finish stirring the batter by hand to make sure every is incorporated.

Spread the batter in the prepared pan and smooth the top. Bake for 25 to 30 minutes, or until the top looks puffy and beginning to turn golden. Rotate the pan 180 degrees, and while doing so, rap the pan on the oven rack until the bars deflate. Bake for 5 minutes more, or until the bars have pulled away from the sides of the pan and a toothpick inserted into the center comes out clean. The bars will still look quite soft. If they've puffed back up

during the last minutes of baking, rap the pan on the countertop once again. Let cool completely in the pan set on a wire rack.

Prepare the frosting: In the bowl of an electric mixer fitted with the paddle attachment, beat the butter on medium speed until creamy. Add the confectioners' sugar, cinnamon, milk, vanilla, and salt, and beat until smooth. Raise the mixer speed to high and beat until very light and fluffy, about 2 minutes. Spread the frosting over the cooled bars. Finish with a light dusting of cinnamon over the entire pan, if you wish. Store any covered in the refrigerator for up to 5 days.

BUCKEYE BARS

Makes 18 bars

THE BUCKEYE IS A CHERISHED CONFECTION IN THE MIDWEST, LITTLE BALLS OF peanut butter filling enrobed in chocolate, save for a small, circular window so that they resemble buckeye nuts, those woodsy little gems tumbling from trees native to Ohio, and the inspiration for the mascot of Ohio State University. As wild buckeyes are toxic in their raw form to every living being other than squirrels, you won't find them being eaten by humans. But that's just fine, because their confectionery counterpart is so good you won't even care about why they're called buckeyes in the first place.

The cute little candies are quite time consuming to make, so this bar version—cut into small fingers because a little goes a long way—delivers all the pleasure for very little effort. This can be easily doubled for a 9 x 13-inch/23 x 33 cm pan. It's essentially a whole pan of peanut butter cups, and way too quick and easy to make. Oh, man.

Nonstick cooking spray for pan

PEANUT BUTTER LAYER:

1½ cups/207 g very finely ground graham cracker crumbs*

1½ cups/180 g confectioners' sugar

10 tablespoons/140 g unsalted butter, melted and cooled

¾ cup/192 g creamy peanut butter, such as Skippy brand

2 ounces/57 g full-fat cream cheese, at room temperature

½ teaspoon pure vanilla extract

½ teaspoon fine sea salt

CHOCOLATE LAYER:

¾ cup/85 g semisweet or bitter-sweet chocolate chips

1 tablespoon creamy peanut butter

Flaky sea salt, such as Maldon for sprinkling (optional)

Equal to 1½ packets, or about 14 rectangles. Crush them in a food processor or large resealable plastic bag with a rolling pin. If using a food processor, just mix all the peanut butter layer ingredients together in it after crushing the grahams.

Spray an 8-inch/20 cm square baking pan with nonstick cooking spray and line it with parchment paper.

Prepare the peanut butter layer: In the bowl of an electric mixer fitted with the paddle attachment, combine the graham cracker crumbs, confectioners' sugar, melted butter, peanut butter, cream cheese, vanilla, and salt. Mix on medium-low speed just until well blended. Pat evenly into the prepared pan. Set in the refrigerator until lightly set and cool to the touch, about 20 minutes.

Prepare the chocolate layer: In a medium, microwave-safe bowl, combine the chocolate and peanut butter. Melt together in a microwave with 30-second bursts on **HIGH**, stirring well after each interval, until the mixture is smooth. Let cool slightly, then spread evenly over the peanut butter layer. Sprinkle with flaky sea salt, if you wish. Refrigerate until firm, at least 1 hour. Transfer the slab from the pan to a cutting board, and cut into fingers.

STATE STREET BROWNIES

Makes 25 brownies

THESE BROWNIES ARE NOT MEEK. TWO TYPES OF CHOCOLATE, LOADS OF BUT-TER and eggs and cream and more, all crammed into a relatively small 8 x 8-inch vessel, designed to be cut into tiny, rich, special little bites. But sometimes being over the top is just the thing. Like growing up as a suburban Chicago kid, anticipating Christmas with a thrilling train trip into the city, a freezing walk along State Street to press my nose up against the glittering holiday windows at Marshall Field's (RIP), binging on their famous truffle-esque Frango mints from the candy counter inside, and kiddie cocktails from the bar at the glamorous Palmer House hotel, just up the street. There's just nothing more deliciously extra than Chicago's State Street in December.

As it happens, the Palmer House is also the birthplace of the brownie, an American treat so iconic it's rare to consider its origins. But it was back in 1893 that Bertha Palmer, the socialite wife of the hotel's owner, requested that the pastry staff create a handheld boxed lunch dessert for the upper-class ladies attending Chicago's World's Fair. The Palmer House still serves that brownie, topped with an aggressive layer of walnut chunks and an apricot jam glaze, reminiscent of a German Sachertorte. I tinkered with the brownie's foundation, added some Frango mint-inspired flair, and created a celebration of two of Chicago's most beloved confections. Cut these into small squares—they're rich!

WHIPPED MINT MILK CHOCOLATE GANACHE:

9 ounces/256 g high-quality milk chocolate, chopped

1/3 cup/80 g heavy whipping cream

1/8 teaspoon fine sea salt

1 teaspoon pure peppermint extract*

BROWNIES:

Nonstick cooking spray for pan

7 ounces/200 g bittersweet chocolate (60% cacao), chopped

3/4 cup/170 g unsalted butter, cut into cubes

4 large eggs

3/4 cup plus 2 tablespoons/175 g granulated sugar

1 teaspoon pure vanilla extract

1 teaspoon pure peppermint extract

3/4 teaspoon fine sea salt

7 tablespoons/56 g unbleached all-purpose flour

GLAZE:

2 tablespoons/28 g unsalted butter

2 ounces/57 g bittersweet chocolate (60% to 72% cacao), chopped

1/4 teaspoon vegetable oil

Look for pure peppermint extract, not "mint" extract, which is usually a weaker blend of spearmint and peppermint that tastes vaguely of toothpaste and doesn't give these brownies the same oomph as pure peppermint.

Prepare the ganache: Place the chocolate in a medium, heatproof bowl. In a microwave-safe bowl, heat the cream with the salt, microwave on **HIGH** until hot to the touch but not boiling. Alternatively, heat the cream and salt in a 1- to 1½-quart/1 to 1.4 L saucepan over low heat. Pour the hot cream mixture over the chocolate. Let sit for 5 minutes. Whisk until smooth. Whisk in the peppermint extract. Set the bowl in the refrigerator and chill until the mixture is thickened and threatening to set firm, about 2 hours.

Prepare the brownie layer: Position a rack to the center of the oven and preheat it to 300°F/150°C. Spray an 8-inch/20 cm square metal baking pan with nonstick cooking spray and line it with parchment paper with a couple of inches of overhang on 2 opposite sides.

In a large, microwave-safe bowl, combine the chocolate and butter. Place the bowl in a microwave and melt with 45-second bursts on **HIGH**, stirring well after each interval. Alternatively, melt in a double boiler.

In a medium bowl, whisk together the eggs, sugar, vanilla, peppermint extract, and salt until slightly aerated, about 30 seconds. Scrape the egg mixture into the melted chocolate and whisk until satiny and thick. Add the flour. Switch to a spatula and gently fold just until no dry white streaks remain. Pour the batter into the prepared pan and smooth evenly. Bake until the edges are set and just begin to pull away from the sides of the pan, 30 to 35 minutes—the center will be quite soft. Let cool to room temperature in the pan set on a wire rack.

When the brownie layer has cooled and the ganache is completely cold, use a handheld electric mixer on high speed to whip the ganache to stiff peaks. Use a small offset spatula to spread the ganache over the brownie layer as smoothly as possible. Set the pan in the freezer to firm the ganache slightly, about 10 minutes.

Meanwhile, prepare the glaze: In a small, microwave-safe bowl, melt together the butter and chocolate in a microwave for about 45 seconds on **HIGH**, stirring until smooth. Alternatively, melt them together in a 1 to 1½-quart/1 to 1.4 L saucepan over low heat. Don't overheat the glaze, instead, give it just enough heat to encourage the chocolate to begin melting, and then let the residual heat from the butter and the bowl or pan do the rest of the work to smooth out the glaze as you stir. Whisk in the vegetable oil for extra shine.

To finish the brownies, when the ganache layer is just becoming firm to the touch, remove the pan from the freezer. Working quickly, drizzle the glaze over the ganache layer. Use a small offset spatula to evenly slick the entire surface with glaze. Refrigerate until the glaze and ganache are firm, at least 1 hour. To serve, run the back of a knife around the perimeter of the pan to loosen the slab, then use the parchment handles to transfer it to a cutting board. Warm a large, sharp knife with hot tap water, then dry it thoroughly. Immediately cut the slab into small squares, wiping the knife in between, and warming it again, if needed, to get clean cuts. Store any leftovers in an airtight container in the refrigerator for up to 1 week.

JAMMY WINTER FRUIT AND BROWNED BUTTER BARS

Makes about 2 dozen bars

WHEN IT'S THE DEAD OF WINTER AND THERE ARE NO FRESH, VIBRANT BERRIES or stone fruits to speak of (at least, not the type that hasn't been shipped thousands of miles and has the "meh" flavor and price tag to prove it), baking can seem kind of dreary. There are only so many brownies and chocolate chip cookies a person can take. It's then that apples and pears are the answer. Hearty with a long storage life, you're bound to find a couple rattling around the fridge just about any time of year.

These bars are a little like a Dutch apple pie in slab form, but made a little more interesting with the inclusion of pears, and with absolutely no pie crust making involved. In fact, if you're a lover of crumble-topped fruit pies, this is the recipe you need in your personal canon—both the crust and topping are made from the same streusel-like mixture, so you get double the dose of crumble here, with a jammy, winter fruit layer in between. PS: The jam filling is great on toast, all on its own, so if you have a glut of apples and pears, doubling the jam is not a bad idea at all.

JAM:

2 medium-size firm-ripe pears, such as Anjou, peeled, cored, and chopped into 1/2-inch/1.25 cm chunks (1½ to 2 cups/188 to 250 g chopped)

2 medium-size Honeycrisp apples, peeled, cored, and chopped into 1/2-inch/1.25 cm chunks (1½ to 2 cups/188 to 250 g chopped)

1/3 cup/75 g freshly squeezed orange juice

1/3 cup/67 granulated sugar

1/2 teaspoon pure vanilla extract

CRUST AND TOPPING:

Nonstick cooking spray for pan

2 cups/256 g cups all-purpose flour, spooned and leveled

1½ cups/150 g old-fashioned rolled oats

1 cup/225 g firmly packed light brown sugar

1 cup/120 g finely chopped walnuts

1 teaspoon ground cinnamon

3/4 teaspoon fine sea salt

3/4 teaspoon baking soda

1 cup/225 g unsalted butter, browned and cooled (see page 177)

1 large egg, at room temperature, beaten

1 teaspoon pure vanilla extract

2 tablespoons turbinado sugar for sprinkling

Prepare the jam: In a 2- to 2½-quart/1.9 to 2.4 L saucepan, combine the pear and apple chunks, orange juice, and sugar. Set the pan over high heat and bring the mixture to a boil.

Lower the heat to medium, cover, and cook until the fruit is tender, stirring occasionally, about 15 minutes. Use a potato masher or fork to mash the pears into small bits (but not completely smooth). Cook until the jam is thick and any excess liquid has all but disappeared, mashing often, 5 to 7 minutes more. Stir in the vanilla. Transfer the jam to a bowl and let cool to room temperature. You should have about 1½ cups/about 365 g of cooled jam.

Prepare the crust and topping: Spray a 9 x 13-inch/23 x 33 cm light-colored metal baking pan with nonstick cooking spray and line it with parchment paper.

In a large bowl, whisk together the flour, oats, brown sugar, walnuts, cinnamon, salt, and baking soda. Add the browned butter, egg, and vanilla and mix until a crumbly dough forms.

Firmly press half of the crumble mixture into the bottom of the prepared pan to form a crust. Chill the pan with the crust and the bowl with the remaining crumble mixture in the refrigerator until the jam has cooled.

Position a rack to the center of the oven and preheat the oven to 350°F/180°C.

Spread the jam over the crust, leaving a ½-inch/ 1.25 cm bare border around the edge of the pan. Sprinkle the remaining crust mixture over the jam, then press lightly with your palms all over the surface. Sprinkle with the turbinado sugar. Bake until slightly puffed and golden, about 35 minutes. Let cool completely in the pan set on a wire rack. Cut into bars and store in an airtight container for up to 3 days.

HOW TO BROWN BUTTER

If you're looking for the simplest way to bump up the flavor of pretty much any recipe calling for melted butter, browning it first is the ticket.

Place the butter in a 2- to 2½-quart/1.9 to 2.4 L saucepan over medium-high heat. Allow the butter to melt, then continue to cook the butter until it turns brown and smells nutty, about 7 minutes. Use your ears as well as your eyes—when the butter stops sizzling, that means the water has cooked out of the butter, while its butterfat and milk solids remain; the solids will be perfectly browned within seconds after the butter goes silent. Immediately pour the browned butter into a clean bowl (scraping out any brown bits along with it!) and let cool slightly before adding to your recipe (unless your recipe calls for hot melted butter, of course). Use as you would melted butter in any recipe, or freeze it solid and use it as you would sticks of regular butter.

CARAMEL CANVAS BLONDIES

Makes about 2 dozen bars

COMMUNITY COOKBOOKS ARE JAM-PACKED WITH RECIPES FOR UNADORNED BAR cookies like these, composed solely of pantry staples, with names like Butterscotch Bars or Toffee Bars, or any title indicating the power of the marriage of butter and brown sugar. In the Midwest, no-frills bars like these show up at bake sales, classroom parties, and box lunches, the ultimate in sweet-salty chew.

This recipe fulfills all my bar cookie dreams—blocky outer pieces with crisp edges and softer, denser middle ones to suit any mood, richer than most with sparks of salt throughout, a caramel-like foundation that can, of course, accommodate all matter of chocolate chips, nuts, candy bits, what have you (you'll want 2 to 3 cups of your chosen morsels, added after the dry ingredients). But truly, they need no add-ins to wow the crowd. I make them every chance I get.

Nonstick cooking spray for pan

3 cups/384 g unbleached all-purpose flour, spooned and leveled

2¼ teaspoons baking powder

1 teaspoon flaky sea salt, such as Maldon

½ teaspoon fine sea salt

2 cups plus 2 tablespoons/480 g firmly packed light brown sugar

3 large eggs, fridge-cold

1 large/20 g egg yolk, fridge-cold

1 tablespoon pure vanilla extract

1½ cups/339 g unsalted butter, browned and cooled

2 to 3 cups/about 300 to 450 g chocolate chips, nuts, or other mix-ins (optional)

Position a rack to the center of the oven and preheat it to 325°F/170°C. Spray a 9 x 13-inch/23 x 33 cm light-colored metal baking pan with nonstick cooking spray and line with parchment paper with a couple of inches of overhang on 2 opposite sides.

In a medium bowl, whisk together the flour, baking powder, and flaky and fine salt.

In a large bowl, using an energetic arm, whisk together the brown sugar, eggs, egg yolk, and vanilla until lighter in color and texture, about 1 minute.

Whisk in the cooled browned butter. Fold in the flour mixture just until no dry floury streaks remain. If you're adding mix-ins, stir them in now until just combined.

Scrape the batter into the prepared pan and smooth the top.

Bake until the blondies are fragrant and golden, with a slightly glossy surface and a raised, wrinkled perimeter beginning to pull away from the sides of the pan, about 40 minutes. Let cool completely in the pan set over a wire rack. Use the parchment paper to lift the blondie slab out of the pan and transfer to a cutting board. Cut into portions to suit the crowd you're serving. Store any leftovers in an airtight container at room temperature for up to 5 days.

MINDY SEGAL'S DREAM BARS

Makes about 30 bars

THE CHICAGO AREA IS FULL OF SOME OF AMERICA'S FINEST CHEFS, BOTH SWEET and savory. Mindy Segal is one of those chefs, a magician in the pastry world and one of my heroes. Her restaurant, Mindy's Hot Chocolate, is a must-visit, for dinner, dessert, or ideally both. What I love most about Mindy's style is that it's creative, bold, unapologetic, and always in tune with her midwestern roots.

Mindy's book *Cookie Love* should be on every home baker's shelf, and her riff on meringue-topped Dream Bars, a concept found in many a vintage cookbook, simply cannot be bested. I was thrilled when she agreed to let me share her recipe in these pages.

4 ounces/113 g bittersweet chocolate (60% cacao), melted

Nonstick cooking spray for pan

1 cup/225 g unsalted butter, at room temperature

1/2 cup/100 g granulated sugar

1 tablespoon water

1 teaspoon pure vanilla extract

2 large eggs, separated, at room temperature

2 cups/256 g unbleached all-purpose flour, spooned and leveled

1 teaspoon baking powder

1 teaspoon baking soda

3/4 teaspoon fine sea salt, plus a separate pinch for egg whites

1 cup/225 g firmly packed dark brown sugar

Line a large rimmed baking sheet with parchment paper. With an offset spatula, spread the melted chocolate into a rough, 9 x 13-inch/23 x 33 cm rectangle. Place the baking sheet in the freezer and freeze until completely firm, about 10 minutes.

Lightly coat a 9 x 13-inch/23 x 33 cm light-colored metal baking pan with nonstick cooking spray and line it with parchment paper with a couple of inches of overhang on 2 opposite sides.

In the bowl of an electric mixer fitted with the paddle attachment, beat together the butter and granulated sugar on medium speed until light in color, fluffy, and aerated, 3 to 4 minutes, scraping the bowl often. In a small bowl, add the water and vanilla to the egg yolks and whisk to blend. Keeping the mixer on medium speed, gradually add the egg yolk mixture and mix until smooth.

In a medium bowl, whisk together the flour, baking powder, baking soda, and salt. Reduce the mixer speed to low. Stir the flour mixture into the batter just until the dough comes together and still looks a bit shaggy. Remove the bowl from the mixer and finish stirring the dough by hand. Press the dough evenly into the prepared pan.

Remove the chocolate from the freezer and break it up into shards. Scatter the chocolate shards across the surface of the dough and then press into the dough (you'll want to press firmly so the shards are held fast into the dough, but work quickly so the heat of your hands doesn't melt the chocolate). Refrigerate until the dough is firm, about 30 minutes.

Position a rack to the center of the oven, and preheat it to 350°F/180°C.

In the bowl of an electric mixer fitted with the whisk attachment, whip the egg whites and a pinch of fine sea salt on medium speed until frothy, about 1 minute. Gradually add the brown sugar. Increase the speed to medium-high and whip to stiff, glossy peaks, about 3 minutes. Spread the meringue in an even layer over the chilled dough.

Bake until the meringue resembles a lightly toasted marshmallow, 23 to 25 minutes, rotating the pan 180 degrees about halfway through baking—do not overbake or the shortbread will be too crumbly to cut. Let cool completely in the pan. Once cool, refrigerate until thoroughly chilled.

Lift the bars out of the pan, using the parchment handles, and transfer to a cutting board. Cut into 30 small bars (a small bite goes a long way here). The bars can then be refrigerated in an airtight container for up to 5 days.

CHAPTER 7

SPECIAL OCCASION CAKES

→>> ◉◉◉ <<←

I'VE BROKEN THE CAKES IN THIS BOOK INTO TWO DISTINCT
categories: Casual and Fancier. The cakes in this chapter represent the latter, the
recipes you'll want to save for birthdays, baby showers, dinner parties, and the like.
If you want to become known for one knockout cake you can make for big-deal life
moments, or are looking to start new traditions by way of cake, I'm hoping you can
find your forever recipe here.

In a region full of practical, efficient bakers, a person doesn't need more than
one good recipe in each flavor category to have a solid celebration cake canon. That
said, the list of cakes in this section is concise, but covers all the bases in terms of
having just the right recipe to suit all manner of cake tastes, from fruit and spice to
rich and light, and of course, chocolate. (For those wackos who claim they "don't
like cake," there's always the pie chapter.)

Note these are recipes requiring forethought. That's not to say they are dif-
ficult recipes; rather, just that you'll enjoy the process more if you break some of
these recipes into steps, making cake layers one day, fillings or frostings the next,
that sort of thing. A few of these call for chilling time for maximum enjoyment, so
it takes a wee bit of planning, is all. But life's special occasions, sometimes seem-
ing so few and far between in our busy lives, call for a little extra TLC, wouldn't
you say?

CLEVELAND-STYLE CASSATA CAKE

Serves 10 to 12

ONE OF MY FAVORITE MIDWESTERN FOOD MEMORIES IS THE BIRTHDAY CAKE I requested for many years when visiting my father, known to me as "that strawberry and vanilla pudding cake"—a yellow sponge sheet in two layers, filled with fresh juicy berries and thick vanilla pastry cream, swathed in whipped cream frosting. As it turns out, that cake has a real name, and was actually just a more conveniently shaped version of the towering, round Cleveland-style cassata cake, a classic of the city's Little Italy neighborhood.

Cleveland cassata derives from the centuries-old *cassata siciliana*—essentially a cannoli in cake form, with a ricotta cheese filling, jewel-like candied fruit, and lavishly decorated. The LaPuma family, which emigrated from Sicily to Cleveland in the late 1800s, is credited with creating the first "Cleveland-style" cassata in the 1920s at their family bakery. Turns out the LaPuma kids didn't like the ricotta filling of the original (isn't that always the way?) and so came the remix, using locally-available ingredients. LaPuma Bakery still cranks out the same "modern" cassatas today, as do many other Cleveland-area bakeries, such as Corbo's and Presti's, and other old-school bakeries throughout the Midwest.

My version of a cassata is flavor-boosted with a nod to its roots: extra-virgin olive oil, a hit of lemon, and a subtle splash of balsamic vinegar to make the rubied berries even more vibrant.

BERRIES:

1 pound/453 g fresh strawberries, hulled and chopped into ½-inch/1.25 cm pieces

1 tablespoon/25 g granulated sugar

1 teaspoon balsamic vinegar

CAKE:

Nonstick cooking spray for pans

2 cups/120 g cake flour, sifted

1½ cups/300 g granulated sugar, divided

2½ teaspoons baking powder

½ teaspoon fine sea salt

¾ cup/170 g ice-cold water

½ cup/113 g extra-virgin olive oil

1 tablespoon finely grated lemon zest

1 teaspoon pure vanilla extract

7 large eggs, separated, at room temperature

1 teaspoon freshly squeezed lemon juice

ASSEMBLY:

2 cups Spoonable Vanilla Custard (page 309)

2 batches Make-Ahead Whipped Cream (page 308)

Prepare the berries: In a medium bowl, toss the strawberries with the sugar and balsamic vinegar. Let rest for at least 1 hour, or up to 1 day ahead in the refrigerator, tightly covered.

Prepare the cake: Position a rack to the center of the oven and preheat it to 325°F/170°C. Grease three 8-inch/20 cm round cake pans with nonstick cooking spray and line them with parchment paper.

In a large bowl, whisk together the cake flour, 1 cup/200 g of the sugar, and the baking powder and salt.

In a medium bowl, whisk together the cold water, oil, lemon zest, vanilla, and egg yolks until smooth.

Pour into the flour mixture and whisk vigorously until smooth, about 1 minute.

In the bowl of an electric mixer fitted with the whisk attachment, combine the egg whites and lemon juice. Whisk on medium-high speed until soft peaks form, about 2 minutes. Gradually add the remaining ½ cup/100 g sugar. Beat until the whites are firmer and opaque, but still soft in shape, about 1 minute more (overbeaten whites will cause the cake to collapse). Fold about a third of the whipped whites into the batter until smooth, then fold in the remaining whites. Divide the batter equally among the prepared pans.

Bake until golden, a toothpick inserted into the center of a layer comes out clean, *and* the top springs back when lightly pressed, 40 to 45 minutes (a toothpick will be clean a few minutes before the top springs back). Let cool completely in the pans on a wire rack—the cakes may shrink slightly as they cool.

Assemble the cake: Drain the strawberries well, catching the juice in a medium bowl.

When the cake layers have cooled, peel away the parchment paper. Place 1 layer on a cake stand and tuck strips of parchment under the cake to protect the cake stand from drips. Use a pastry brush to moisten the top of the layer with a few tablespoons of strawberry juice (you won't use all the drained juice). Top with half of the berries. Spoon half of the custard over the berries. Repeat the process with the second cake layer, berries, and custard. Top with the final cake layer. Frost the cake with the whipped cream, finishing with lots of swoops and swirls. Chill for at least 3 hours. This cake is best served the day it's assembled. Leftovers keep for up to 2 days, tightly covered and refrigerated.

TIP › *This party cake is a make-ahead wonder: The custard, fruit, and whipped cream frosting can be made a day ahead, and the cake layers 2 days ahead, kept tightly wrapped (separately) and refrigerated.*

AUNT VI'S CHEESECAKE

Serves 10

IN A DESCRIPTION THAT COULDN'T BE MORE MIDWESTERN IF I TRIED, AUNT VI wasn't my aunt. She wasn't even my great-aunt. She was Gramma's best friend Kathy Humphreys's aunt. The Humphreyses lived next door to my grandparents for a number of years and were the best of friends. The couples kicked up their heels together, vacationed together, raised children together, and I always felt a bit like an honorary grandchild to Jack and Kathy Humphreys.

So, the title of this recipe should actually be Kathy's Aunt Vi's Cheesecake. And apparently the lady could rock a cheesecake like none other. Between the unique crumb crust tasting of the very best buttered toast, to the luxurious topping of whipped cream, once I tried this recipe, I had completed my search for a cheesecake I can make for the rest of my life.

CRUST:

6 ounces/170 g zwieback toasts, or 1 (3½-ounce/100 g) package Holland Rusks (to make about 1½ cups/100 g crumbs)

2 tablespoons granulated sugar

¼ teaspoon fine sea salt

4 tablespoons/57 g unsalted butter, at room temperature

FILLING:

2 (8-ounce/225 g) packages full-fat cream cheese, at room temperature

1 cup/200 g granulated sugar

1 cup/240 g full-fat sour cream

2 large eggs, at room temperature

2 teaspoons pure vanilla extract

TOPPING:

½ cup/120 g heavy whipping cream, chilled

1 teaspoon granulated sugar

½ teaspoon pure vanilla extract

Position a rack to the center of the oven and preheat it to 350°F/180°C. Have ready a 9-inch/23 cm round springform pan.

Prepare the crust: In the bowl of a food processor, grind the zwiebacks to fine crumbs (you may need to do this in 2 batches). Add the sugar and salt. Process again for 30 seconds. Add the butter and blend until evenly moistened.

Tip the crust mixture into the pan. Pat the crumbs firmly and evenly across the bottom of the pan and halfway up the sides. Bake until firm and golden, about 8 minutes. Let cool completely. Wipe out the bowl of the food processor with a paper towel.

Prepare the filling: Add the cream cheese to the processor and blend until smooth and creamy. Add the sugar and blend for 30 seconds. Scrape down the bowl and add the sour cream. Blend until smooth. With the motor running, add the eggs, 1 at a time. Scrape down the bowl, add the vanilla, and process until the batter is well blended.

Pour the batter into the cooled crust. Bake for 20 minutes. Turn off the oven and leave the cheesecake in the oven for 1 hour. Transfer to a wire rack to cool completely, about 1½ hours.

Prepare the topping: In the bowl of an electric mixer, whip the cream, sugar, and vanilla together on medium speed until the cream holds firm peaks. Smooth the whipped cream over the cooled cheesecake. Chill in the refrigerator for at least 4 hours, or overnight. Store any leftovers tightly covered for up to 3 days.

CHEESECAKE, CHICAGO STYLE

As if the battle between Chicago deep dish pizza and New York–style pies wasn't heated enough, I'd like to play devil's advocate and discuss cheesecake. Yes, believe it or not, there are both New York cheesecakes, which are better known by name alone, and Chicago-style cheesecakes, which are superior. (By now, we know I'm a Chicagoan. This is my book, and I'm choosing to play that card right now. Hear me out.) The difference between the two styles is subtle but important.

New York–style cakes, such as those made famous by Junior's and Lindy's, often include the addition of heavy whipping cream resulting in a dense, thick, satiny filling not too far removed from the texture of cream cheese itself. Very little air gets incorporated into a New York cheesecake. It's the kind of thing where one small slice can be split between two people, and a couple of rich bites is all you need. It has a place, I will give it that.

But when I'm in a cheesecake mood, I want ultimate indulgence. I want to be able to eat many bites and I don't want to share. This is where Chicago-style cheesecake comes in. These cakes start with cream cheese, but use sour cream instead of heavy whipping cream, which ups the cultured dairy flavor and balances the richness. The batter is typically whipped a bit, and might even incorporate a few tablespoons of flour, which give the cheesecake a lighter, suedelike texture and a firm, bronzed top and sides.

I grew up with Eli's, the quintessential Chicago-style cheesecake. It has a shortbread crust and is bare on the sides, its signature look. Chicago restauranteur Eli Schulman first perfected his cheesecake recipe for his steakhouse restaurant in the early 1970s and quickly gained a following. In 1980, the cake debuted at the Taste of Chicago, and it has been a dessert celebrity ever since. It's important to note I've also been told more than once along this Midwest baking research trail that Schulman might have swiped the base of his cheesecake formula from Little Jack's, a legendary Chicago restaurant that ran from 1905 to 1962 on the city's west side, and was well known for its cheesecake. But I'm just the messenger here.

There's another famous Chicago-style cheesecake worth mentioning, and it all started in the 1940s with a woman from Detroit named Evelyn Overton. Inspired by a recipe clipped from a local newspaper, she started a small cheesecake baking business in her basement. For nearly twenty-five years, she supplied cheesecakes to local restaurants.

Once their kids were grown, she and her husband used all their savings to move to Los Angeles and open a business there, called the Cheesecake Factory Bakery. With that success, their son helped them to expand the concept as a restaurant, opening the Cheesecake Factory in Beverly Hills in 1975, and becoming a symbol of the glory that is the American chain restaurant. Today, the star of the show is still that solid Chicago-style cheesecake, with more than three dozen riffs on the original recipe.

CHOCOLATE BUMPY CAKE

Serves 15 to 20

SANDERS CONFECTIONERY IS A DETROIT INSTITUTION. SINCE 1875, SANDERS HAS cranked out legendary chocolates, candies, dessert sauces, ice cream treats and more, as retail products and in their brick and mortar locations. One of Sanders's most famous and beloved items is its Bumpy Cake, a combination of deeply chocolate cake and unique little rails of vanilla buttercream crossing the top, under a slick of glossy fudge icing. You can buy the cake in some grocery stores in the Midwest, but it's even better when you set aside the time to make it yourself. There are a few steps involved here, but there's no better birthday gift for your favorite Michigander.

CAKE:

Nonstick cooking spray for pan

2 cups/256 g unbleached all-purpose flour, spooned and leveled

2 cups/400 g granulated sugar

1/2 cup/48 g unsweetened cocoa powder*

1 1/2 teaspoons baking soda

3/4 teaspoon fine sea salt

1 cup/225 g well-shaken buttermilk, at room temperature

1/2 cup/113 g hot brewed coffee or hot water

1/2 cup/113 g vegetable or canola oil

2 large eggs

2 teaspoons pure vanilla extract

FILLING:

1 cup/200 g granulated sugar

1/4 cup/32 g cornstarch

1/8 teaspoon fine sea salt

1 cup/225 g whole milk

1 teaspoon pure vanilla extract

1/2 cup/113 g unsalted butter, at cool room temperature

ICING:

1 cup/225 g unsalted butter, divided

1 cup/200 g granulated sugar

1/2 cup/113 g well-shaken buttermilk

1/3 cup/113 g dark corn syrup

1/3 cup/32 g unsweetened cocoa powder

1/4 teaspoon fine sea salt

1 cup/120 g confectioners' sugar

1 teaspoon pure vanilla extract

*My first choice here is a half-and-half mix of regular Dutch-processed and black cocoa powders, for dynamite color and flavor. But if all you have is natural cocoa, that will work, too.

Prepare the cake: Position a rack to the center of the oven and preheat it to 350°F/180°C. Spray a 9 x 13-inch/23 x 33 cm light-colored metal baking pan with nonstick cooking spray.

In a large bowl, whisk together the flour, granulated sugar, cocoa powder, baking soda, and salt.

In a medium bowl, whisk together the buttermilk, coffee, oil, eggs, and vanilla. Pour the wet ingredients in the dry. Beat with an electric mixer until smooth. Pour the batter into the prepared pan. Bake until a toothpick inserted in the center of the cake comes out clean, 30 to 35 minutes. Set the pan on a wire rack to cool completely.

Meanwhile, prepare the filling: In a 2- to 2½-quart/1.9 to 2.4 L saucepan, whisk together the granulated sugar, cornstarch, and salt. Whisk in the milk. Bring to a boil over medium-high heat; boil for 1 minute. Remove from the heat and whisk in the vanilla. Transfer to the bowl of an electric mixer and let cool completely. Beating with the paddle attachment on medium speed, beat in 1 tablespoon of butter at a time. Increasing the speed to medium-high, beat until light and fluffy and resembling whipped cream, about 5 minutes.

When the cake has cooled completely, load the filling into a pastry bag fitted with a 1-inch/2.5 cm large round tip. Pipe nine 9-inch/23 cm lines crosswise over the cake, 1 inch/2.5 cm apart. Freeze until the filling is solid, at least 30 minutes.

When the filling is solid, keep the cake in the freezer while you prepare the icing: In a 2- to 2½-quart/1.9 to 2.4 L saucepan, combine ½ cup/113 g of the butter and the sugar, buttermilk, corn syrup, cocoa powder, and salt. Place the pan over medium-high heat and bring the mixture to a boil. Clip a candy thermometer to the side of the pan and cook until the mixture reaches 235°F/113°C—no higher. Whisk in the remaining butter, 1 tablespoon at a time. Stir in the confectioners' sugar and vanilla, whisking until the icing is smooth. Remove the cake from the freezer.

Immediately pour the icing in waterfall-like ribbons over the surface of the cake. If needed, gently rewarm any icing clinging to the pan, and pour it again. Freeze the cake until the icing is set, about 15 minutes, or refrigerate until ready to serve. Store any leftovers tightly covered in the refrigerator for up to a week.

RASPBERRY POKE CAKE

Serves 15 to 20

YOU KNOW ABOUT POKE CAKES, RIGHT? BOX-MIX CAKE, A GOOD SOAKING OF Day-Glo Jell-O, and clouds of Cool Whip is a 1970s beacon of processed, everything-instant cookery. And I'll be honest, I can't hate.

I grew up with a festive Christmas poke cake, wherein my mother baked a white box-mix cake into two round layers, drizzled one with red Jell-O (Strawberry? Cherry? Is there a difference? Let's say red-flavored), and one with green (lime, of course). After a generous frosting of Cool Whip, she would then craft "holly leaves" from cross-sections of sugared gummy spearmint leaves and a few cinnamon Red Hots candy. It was a vision and the pinnacle of everything I wanted in a childhood dessert. Kitsch on kitsch on kitsch. Glorious.

As word got out that I was making this book, I started to lose count of the number of midwestern folks, a few of them even legitimate, totally respected pastry chefs, who said something to the effect of, "Well, ya gotta have a poke cake in there, doncha?" And I realized I would indeed have to rethink the poke cake. This is my love letter to that old chestnut, but with all real ingredients instead.

CAKE:

Nonstick cooking spray for pan

3 cups/360 g cake flour, spooned and leveled

1 teaspoon baking soda

1 teaspoon baking powder

3/4 teaspoon fine sea salt

6 large egg whites, at room temperature

1 1/3 cups/298 g well-shaken buttermilk, at room temperature

2 teaspoons pure vanilla extract

1 cup/226 g unsalted butter, at room temperature

2 cups/400 g granulated sugar

FILLING:

2/3 cup plus 3 tablespoons/190 g cold water, divided

2 1/2 teaspoons unflavored gelatin

12 ounces/340 g fresh or frozen unsweetened raspberries

1/3 cup/67 g granulated sugar

2 teaspoons freshly squeezed lime juice

TOPPING:

8 ounces/225 g full-fat cream cheese, at room temperature

2 cups/480 g heavy whipping cream, chilled

1 cup/120 g confectioners' sugar

1 teaspoon pure vanilla paste or pure vanilla extract

Prepare the cake: Position a rack to the center of the oven and preheat the oven to 350°F/180°C. Spray a 9 x 13-inch/23 x 33 cm light-colored metal cake pan with nonstick cooking spray.

Sift the cake flour into a large bowl. Whisk in the baking soda, baking powder, and salt.

In a large measuring cup, whisk together the egg whites, buttermilk, and vanilla extract until smooth.

In the bowl of an electric mixer fitted with the paddle attachment, combine the butter and granulated sugar. Beat for 3 minutes on medium-high speed, or until very light and fluffy. Reduce the mixer speed to low. In 5 alternating batches, stir in the dry and wet ingredients, beginning and ending with the dry. Scrape down the bowl often to ensure everything is incorporated—a well-mixed cake will give you that tight box-mix crumb we're after.

Scrape the batter into the prepared pan and smooth the top. Bake until a toothpick inserted into the center comes out clean, 40 to 45 minutes. Let cool in the pan set on a wire rack for 10 to 15 minutes.

Meanwhile, begin preparing the filling: In a small cup, whisk together 3 tablespoons of the cold water and gelatin and set aside.

In a 2-quart/1.9 L saucepan, combine the raspberries, granulated sugar, lime juice, and remaining 2/3 cup/147 g of cold water. Place the pan over medium heat and bring the mixture to a boil, mashing the berries with a fork or potato masher. Once the berries have completely broken down, remove the pan from the heat. Whisk in the lump of gelatin until melted. Pour the purée through a

sieve into a spouted measuring cup, pressing on the solids with a spatula to get every bit of purée through—you should have just about 11/2 cups/200 ml of strained liquid.

Use the handle of a wooden spoon (about 1/2 inch/1.25 cm in diameter) to poke holes all over the cake, spacing them about 1 inch/2.5 cm apart. (You may need to wipe the handle a few times if any cake starts clinging to it.)

In a thin stream, slowly pour the hot raspberry filling all over the hot cake, filling each hole and drizzling a bit over the top as you go—it usually takes 2 rounds of pouring to get all the filling into the cake. Place the pan in the refrigerator to chill for about 2 hours.

Prepare the topping: In the bowl of an electric mixer fitted with the whisk attachment, beat the cream cheese on medium-high speed until very soft and creamy. Transfer to a small bowl.

Pour the cream into the mixer bowl (no need to clean it). Add the confectioners' sugar and vanilla extract or paste. Whip to soft peaks. Scrape in the softened cream cheese and continue to beat until stiff peaks form. Spread the topping over the cake. Serve immediately, or chill until ready to serve, up to 3 hours ahead. If chilling, allow the cake to soften at room temperature for 20 to 30 minutes before serving. Store leftovers in the refrigerator, covered, for up to 3 days.

BUTTER PECAN LAYER CAKE

Makes one 3-layer cake

ALTHOUGH PECANS TEND TO HAVE A SOUTHERN REPUTATION, THE PECAN TREE grows just as widely in the south-central Midwest as it does in the deeper South. In fact, the Latin name for the pecan tree is *Carya illinoinensis*. Who knew?

Nothing celebrates the pecan quite like butter pecan ice cream—the richness of that buttery, custard-yellow cream as the backdrop for crunchy, toasty pecans is an irresistible classic. This recipe bakes up that combination in cake form, with clouds of a creamy, dreamy, nutty frosting. Rich, yellow European-style butter in the cake and frosting brings the whole thing even closer to its ice cream inspiration. It typically comes in 8-ounce blocks, so I buy two, use them for the cake and frosting, and use a couple of tablespoons of standard butter for toasting the pecans.

Nonstick cooking spray for pans

PECANS:

2 tablespoons/28 g unsalted butter

2 cups/225 g raw pecan halves, finely chopped

CAKE:

2½ cups/320 g unbleached all-purpose flour, spooned and leveled

1 teaspoon baking soda

½ teaspoon fine sea salt

8 ounces/225 g unsalted European-style butter

2 cups/400 g granulated sugar

2 teaspoons pure vanilla extract

4 large eggs, at room temperature

1 cup/225 g well-shaken buttermilk, at room temperature

FROSTING:

8 ounces/225 g unsalted European-style butter

3½ cups/420 g confectioners' sugar

Scant ¼ teaspoon fine sea salt

2 teaspoons pure vanilla extract

2½ tablespoons half-and-half

4 ounces/113 g full-fat cream cheese, at room temperature, cut into small pieces

Position racks to the upper and lower thirds of the oven, and preheat the oven to 350°F/180°C. Spray three 8-inch/20 cm round cake pans with nonstick cooking spray and line the bottoms with parchment paper.

Prepare the pecans: In a large skillet over medium heat, melt the butter. Add the pecans. Stir constantly until browned and fragrant, 3 to 4 minutes. Transfer the pecans to a plate to cool.

Prepare the cake: In a medium bowl, whisk together the flour, baking soda, and salt.

In the bowl of an electric mixer fitted with the paddle attachment, beat the butter on medium-high speed until creamy, about 30 seconds. Add the granulated sugar and vanilla and beat for 3 more minutes, until very light and fluffy. Beat in the eggs, 1 at a time. Reduce the mixer speed to low, and in 5 alternating additions, add the flour mixture and the buttermilk, beginning and ending with the flour. Finish folding the batter by hand. Fold in half of the pecans. Divide the batter equally among the prepared pans and smooth the tops. Bake until a toothpick inserted into the center of each cake comes out clean, 25 to 30 minutes. Let the cakes cool completely in the pans set on wire racks.

Prepare the frosting: In the bowl of an electric mixer fitted with the paddle attachment, beat the butter on medium speed until creamy. Add the confectioners' sugar and salt and beat until blended. Add the vanilla and half-and-half and increase the mixer speed to high. Beat until very light in texture, almost like whipped cream, about 3 minutes. Stop the mixer and scrape down the bowl. Add the cream cheese bits and beat on medium speed until the frosting is well blended and smooth, about 1 minute. Stir in the remaining pecans by hand.

Assemble the cake: Invert 1 layer onto a serving plate and remove the parchment paper. Dollop 3/4 cup/175 ml of frosting onto the center of the cake and smooth evenly, all the way to the edges. Repeat with a second cake layer. Add the third cake layer, and press lightly to adhere. Generously frost the sides and top of the cake with the remaining frosting. Chill the cake for 30 minutes in the refrigerator to slightly firm the icing before slicing and serving.

AUNT MARGE'S BIRTHDAY CAKE

Serves 15 to 20

WHEN I SCOURED FAMILY RECIPE FILES AND POLLED SECOND AND THIRD COUSINS for their family favorites, Aunt Marge's buttermilk-based yellow cake came up again and again. She was my grandmother's oldest sister, a mother of six, and an obvious bearer of classic all-American tastes, always pairing this yellow cake with a fudgy milk chocolate frosting.

If you like your yellow cake fluffy yet sturdy, like a cake from a box mix, then this is the recipe for you. For best results, measure the cake flour carefully: if you're measuring by volume, spoon it lightly into the cup and level it with a knife, making for a feather-light cup of flour.

Nonstick cooking spray for pan

3 cups/360 g cake flour, spooned and leveled

1 teaspoon baking powder

1 teaspoon baking soda

1 teaspoon cream of tartar

1/2 teaspoon fine sea salt

1 cup/225 g unsalted butter, at room temperature

2 cups/400 g granulated sugar

2 teaspoons pure vanilla extract

4 large eggs, separated

1 cup/225 g well-shaken buttermilk, at room temperature

1 recipe Silky, Creamy Chocolate Frosting (page 306)

Position a rack to the center of the oven and preheat it to 350°F/180°C. Spray a 9 x 13-inch/23 x 33 cm light-colored metal baking pan with nonstick cooking spray.

Sift the cake flour into a large bowl. Whisk in the baking powder, baking soda, cream of tartar, and salt.

In the bowl of an electric mixer fitted with the paddle attachment, beat the butter on medium-high speed until creamy, about 30 seconds. Add the sugar and vanilla and beat until very light and fluffy, about 3 minutes. Add the egg yolks, 1 at a time, giving each about 10 seconds to blend into the batter before adding the next. Reduce the mixer speed to low. In 5 alternating batches, add the flour mixture and the buttermilk, beginning and ending with the flour mixture. Finish folding the batter by hand until smooth.

In a medium bowl, using clean beaters, beat the egg whites until they are stiff, but not dry. Fold about a third of the egg whites into the batter to slacken it a bit. Fold in the remaining egg whites carefully. Scrape the batter into the prepared pan and smooth the top. Bake until deeply golden and a toothpick inserted into the center comes out clean, 50 to 55 minutes, rotating the pan 180

degrees halfway through baking and tenting with foil if it's browning too quickly.

Let the cake cool completely in the pan set on a wire rack. When cool, slather with Silky, Creamy Chocolate Frosting.

CARROT CAKE FOR A CROWD

Serves 15 to 20

MAKING THIS SIMPLE, SOFTLY SPICED CAKE HAS BEEN A BALM FOR ME MORE TIMES than I can count. It was the first thing I baked after the births of both children, the recipe I reached for right after Gramma's passing. And before things get way too heavy around here, let me say I've also made this cake for celebrations, dinner guests, and just for fun. Its method is so fantastically efficient and easy, it always makes me feel as though I've got a handle on life, if just for the moment.

Carrot "cake" recipes abound, dating back to the carrot puddings that appeared in many world cuisines as far back as the 17th century. But it seems the first recipes resembling current-day carrot cake—using wheat flour and leavened with baking powder—showed up in a cookbook from the Twentieth Century Club in Wichita, Kansas, in 1929. *The Chicago Daily News Cookbook* of 1930 included a carrot cake recipe, too, but it still wasn't really catching on outside of the region. That is, until cream cheese frosting crept onto American palates in the 1960s. And as any cream cheese frosting lover can attest, you can basically slather that business on anything that's not nailed down and you'll be deliriously happy. So, the moment carrot cake was paired with cream cheese frosting and the word got out, carrot cake took off, and now, well, here we are, unable to imagine one without the other.

CAKE:

Nonstick cooking spray for pan

2¾ cups/352 g unbleached all-purpose flour, spooned and leveled

1¼ teaspoons baking powder

1 teaspoon baking soda

1¼ teaspoons ground cinnamon

½ teaspoon freshly grated nutmeg

⅛ teaspoon cloves

½ teaspoon fine sea salt

1 pound/453 g carrots, peeled and trimmed

1½ cups/300 g granulated sugar

½ cup/113 g packed light brown sugar

4 large eggs

1 teaspoon pure vanilla extract

1½ cups/339 g vegetable oil

FROSTING:

12 ounces/340 g high-quality white chocolate, such as Lindt, finely chopped*

12 ounces/340 g full-fat cream cheese, at room temperature*

1 teaspoon pure vanilla extract

If you are baking the cake in 8- or 9-inch/20 or 23 cm square pans and layering them, increase both the white chocolate and cream cheese to 16 ounces/453 g each.

Prepare the cake: Position a rack to the center of the oven and preheat it to 350°F/180°C. Spray a 9 x 13-inch/23 x 33 cm baking pan with cooking spray and line the bottom with parchment paper. Alternatively, you can bake the cake in two 8- or 9-inch/20 or 23 cm square pans, sprayed and papered.

In a large bowl, whisk together the flour, baking powder, baking soda, cinnamon, nutmeg, cloves, and salt.

Fit a food processor with the shredding disk and shred all the carrots. Dump the carrots into the bowl containing the flour mixture. Stir until evenly mixed.

Place the processor bowl used to shred the carrots back on its base and fit with the steel S blade. Add the granulated sugar, brown sugar, eggs, and vanilla and process thoroughly. With the processor running, pour in the oil in a steady stream.

Pour the sugar mixture into the carrot mixture and stir well with a rubber spatula until the batter is free of floury lumps. Scrape the batter into the prepared pan and smooth evenly. Bake until a toothpick inserted into the center comes out clean, 35 to 40 minutes. Set the pan on a wire rack and let the cake cool completely.

Meanwhile, Prepare the frosting. Melt the white chocolate in a double boiler, or in a microwave-safe bowl using 30-seconds bursts on MEDIUM in a microwave, stirring well after each interval until smooth. Let cool.

Place the cream cheese and vanilla in either a food processor fitted with the steel S blade or in the bowl of an electric mixer fitted with the paddle attachment. Beat the cream cheese on medium-high speed until soft and creamy, about 1 minute. Add the melted white chocolate and beat just until the frosting is blended and smooth.

Slather the cake with the icing. Tightly cover and refrigerate any leftovers for up to 5 days.

SCOTT'S CHOCOLATE CAKE

Serves 10

THE "SCOTT" OF THIS CAKE IS MY DARLING HUSBAND. WHEN HIS FIRST BIRTHDAY AS a married man rolled around, it was mid-September and it was *hot* in our little un-air-conditioned apartment in Los Angeles. But scorching temperatures be damned, I was determined to demonstrate my domestic abilities as a newly minted wife and bake him a birthday cake from scratch. Thanks to blind moxie and a complete lack of experience in making layer cakes, I didn't consider the effect of heat on tender cake rounds and soft buttercream. The stacked cake layers split into fourths soon after the frosting was applied—I tried in vain to pin the cake together with toothpicks and solder the whole droopy creature in the freezer, to no avail. The birthday cake was really more of a birthday pile that year, with candles haphazardly stuck in it. We laughed and I cried a little. But it was still insanely delicious. And that is a testament to how extraordinary this cake really is.

Over the years I've tweaked the recipe for texture and taste, and become much better at building layer cakes. Even though it's so fabulous it deserves to be paraded out for every dinner party, picnic, bake sale, and other random people's birthdays, I save this chocolate behemoth for just once a year, in honor of my favorite husband.

CAKE:

Nonstick cooking spray for pans

2¼ cups/270 g cake flour, spooned and leveled

1½ teaspoons baking soda

1 teaspoon fine sea salt

1 cup/226 g unsalted butter, at room temperature

1½ cups/300 g granulated sugar

1 teaspoon pure vanilla extract

4 ounces/113 g bittersweet chocolate (70% to 72% cacao), melted and cooled

3 large eggs

⅓ cup/75 g vegetable or canola oil

1 cup/225 g cold water

FROSTING:

3 cups/360 g confectioners' sugar, sifted

1½ cups/339 g unsalted butter, at room temperature

2 tablespoons whole milk or cooled brewed coffee

1½ teaspoons pure vanilla extract

Generous ½ teaspoon fine sea salt

6 ounces/170 g bittersweet chocolate (70% to 72% cacao), melted and cooled

2 ounces/57 g semisweet chocolate, finely chopped, plus more for sprinkling (optional)

Position an oven rack to the center of the oven and preheat it to 350°F/180°C. Coat two 8-inch/20 cm round cake pans with nonstick cooking spray, line the bottoms of the pans with circles of parchment paper, and then spray again for extra nonstick insurance.

Sift together the cake flour, baking soda, and salt into a large bowl.

In the bowl of an electric mixer fitted with the paddle attachment, on medium-high speed beat together the butter, granulated sugar, and vanilla until light and fluffy, about 3 minutes. Add the melted chocolate and beat for 1 minute to blend. In a small bowl, whisk together the eggs and oil until emulsified. On medium speed, beat the egg mixture into the chocolate mixture. Continue to beat to a light, mousselike texture, about 2 minutes.

Gradually mix in the flour mixture in 3 batches, alternating with the cold water and mixing for 30 seconds after each addition. When all of the flour mixture and water has been added, scrape the bowl once more and then mix for 1 minute more on medium speed, or until the batter is smooth and mousselike once again. It should look like clouds of chocolate.

Pour the batter evenly into the prepared pans until about two-thirds full, and smooth the surfaces with a spatula. Bake until the cakes spring back when touched and a cake tester comes out clean, about 35 minutes. Let the cakes cool in the pans on a rack for at least 40 minutes. Turn out the cooled layers onto a parchment-lined baking sheet, wrap with plastic wrap, and chill for 1 hour, or up to 1 day ahead—this is a very tender cake and the chilling time makes it easier to frost.

Meanwhile, prepare the buttercream: In the bowl of an electric mixer with the paddle attachment, combine the confectioners' sugar, butter, milk or coffee, vanilla, and salt. Beat on medium-high speed until light and airy, at least 3 minutes. Add the cooled bittersweet chocolate. Beat until well blended, 1 minute more. Fold in the chopped semisweet chocolate by hand.

Turn 1 of the cooled cake layers upside-down onto a cake stand and peel away the parchment. Spread about a third of the frosting on this layer. Place the second layer on top and remove the parchment. Apply a thin, almost invisible-in-spots layer of frosting on the outside of the cake as a crumb coat to glue any errant crumbs in place. Chill for 20 minutes to set. Frost top and sides of the cake with the remaining frosting. Sprinkle with additional chocolate chunks, if desired.

Aunt Vi's Cheesecake

Crust - mix ½ C melted butter
2 T sugar

---

1 stick butter
1½ cups graham cracker crumbs
1 cup chopped walnuts
1 small pkg (6 oz) Nestle's choc chips
1 - 3½ oz. can coconut
1 can Eagle condensed milk

Melt butter in 13×9
add others in
Bake 25 min or
until browned
350°

Magic Cookie

WORLD'S BEST SUGAR COOKIES

1 cup butter or margarine
1 cup powdered sugar
1 cup granulated sugar
1 cup vegetable oil
2 eggs, beaten
2 teaspoons vanilla
5 cups flour
1 teaspoon baking soda
1 teaspoon cream of tartar
¼ teaspoon salt

Cream together the butter and sugars. Beat well. Add oil, eggs and vanilla. Combine flour with remaining ingredients and beat into batter. Mix well.

Roll into balls the size of a large walnut, or the size
with

Fudge

1 can cond. milk
1 - 12 oz. bag of chips
micro for 1 min
Stir to mix
add 1 T
½ to ¾

---

1 Baked pie shell.

Lemon Cream Pie

Tower angel cake
easy but memorable

This dessert will have your family believing you spent the afternoon making it. However, it's a shortcut idea that makes use of a store-bought angel food cake. It's cut into four layers, spread with a delicious filling, then chilled until dinner time.

TOWER ANGEL CAKE

1 package (8 ounces) cream cheese, softened
¼ cup sugar
¼ cup whipping cream, whipped

½ cup diced maraschino cherries
1 can (8¼ ounces) crushed pineapple, drained
½ cup chopped pecans
1 large angel food cake

Whip cream cheese until soft and fluffy. Mix in sugar, stir in whipped cream, maraschino cherries, pineapple and pecans. Cut angel food cake into four layers. Spread filling between layers and on top of cake. Chill. Yield: 12-16 slices.

Cream together ½ lb butter
1½ C sugar
add one at a time 4 o.

Mrs. Braun's Oatmeal Cookies

1 cup shortening ⎤
1 cup dark brn sugar ⎬ combine
1 cup granulated sugar ⎦

2 eggs ⎤
1 tsp. vanilla ⎬ add

1½ cups flour ⎤
1 tsp. salt ⎬ sift together
1 tsp. baking soda ⎦ and add to above

3 cups oatmeal - stir in
Golden raisins & chopped walnuts

CHAPTER 8
SUMMER SWEETS

APRIL AND EARLY MAY ARE A SLOW CLIMB IN THE MIDWEST, A meteorological tug-of-war not completely unlike tearing a Band-Aid off hair by hair. When you have three different jackets out and two pairs of boots, plus maybe a pair of sandals because of that one weird Thursday where it was 75°F and then snowed overnight, it can be a little demoralizing.

But if you can hang on, in comes the glory of midwestern June. The air sings, the color of the sky is like the fictional flavor of blue raspberry. The trees transform from skeletal, splintered frameworks into heroic, vibrant green salads on trunks. There is a mere suggestion of humidity, glorious for human skin and hair, but not mid-August peanut butter air.

All at once, June hits me in the face and the heart. One deep inhale while driving with the windows down right around Memorial Day, and my brains flips back through summer memories like a rigid stack of Polaroids, *snap snap snap snap*.

June here feels like a cleansing, a freedom, busting out of a race track gate. It exhales cut grass, wet Popsicle sticks, a little bit of Freon, and coppery water from a lawn sprinkler. June runs like a long gravel road with tall grass on either side, unfurling into two and a half beautiful, school-free months. Whether I think back ten or thirty-five midwestern summers ago, the sensation is the same. In January, it's a feeling best described as the distant familiar.

The sweets I suddenly crave in early summer fall right in line with those memories—frozen custard, fruit salads (some of them quite kitschy), creamy no-bake desserts, gleaming and quivering gelatins. While I suppose any of these can be enjoyed year-round, it's a perfect fit June through August.

In California, June didn't come in this way—the air is different, the scenery literally evergreen. The distant familiar of an Illinois summer is hard to access when you've gone so long without it. But the seasonal turnover here is powerful, and I'm so glad that it—and the recipes that come along with it—are part of the rhythm of our life again. In fact, it's nearly June right now, as I write this. It's so good to be home, you guys.

CHOCOLATE ÉCLAIR DESSERT

Serves 12 to 15

LAKE GENEVA, WISCONSIN, IS BARELY AN HOUR NORTH OF CHICAGO, BUT IT FEELS a world away. It's one of those funny little lake towns that plays up the nautical decor and its history of being a summer retreat for the Midwest's wealthiest captains of industry in the first half of the 1900s. For a good chunk of my childhood, my paternal grandparents had a house there that we'd visit with my dad, an airy ranch with a built-in swimming pool, which felt totally *Dynasty* at the time. In summer, we'd swim from eight a.m. until dinner, except for the hour of torture when we were forced to eat lunch and *then* were barred from the water at the risk of contracting life-threatening "cramps" after eating. Now that I'm a parent, I know the cramps were a myth, but provided a break for weary adults who just wanted to sit with a freaking beer for a while and not throw pennies into the water for us to dive down and retrieve, or toss us into the deep end, or allow us to ride weightlessly on their backs. It's cool, Dad, I respect it now.

The only thing that made the hour of pool restriction bearable was when my grandmother brought out éclairs from the bakery in town. They were fridge-cold mini éclairs, chubby pastry fingers about 4 inches long, slicked with chocolate icing and topped with a pastel buttercream rose. Stuffed with chilled vanilla custard, they were pure heaven when eaten poolside in the shade. They were also so good it was worth the extra 10 minutes of cramp prevention tacked on if we ate a second. I wonder what the cramp wait time would be for this dessert, which is basically a whole pan of éclairs. I'm thinking two hours poolside, easy.

PASTRY:

Nonstick cooking spray for pan

½ cup/113 g whole milk

½ cup/113 g lukewarm water

½ cup/113 g unsalted butter, cut into small pieces

Scant ½ teaspoon fine sea salt

1 cup/128 g unbleached all-purpose flour, spooned and leveled

4 large eggs, at room temperature

ASSEMBLY:

1 batch Spoonable Vanilla Custard (page 309)

1 batch Make-Ahead Whipped Cream (page 308)

⅓ cup/100 g chocolate hazelnut spread

Prepare the pastry: Position a rack to the center of the oven and preheat it to 400°F/200°C. Spray a 9 x 13-inch/23 x 33 cm baking dish with nonstick cooking spray.

In a 2-quart/1.9 L heavy-bottomed saucepan, combine the milk, lukewarm water, butter, and salt. Bring the mixture to a boil

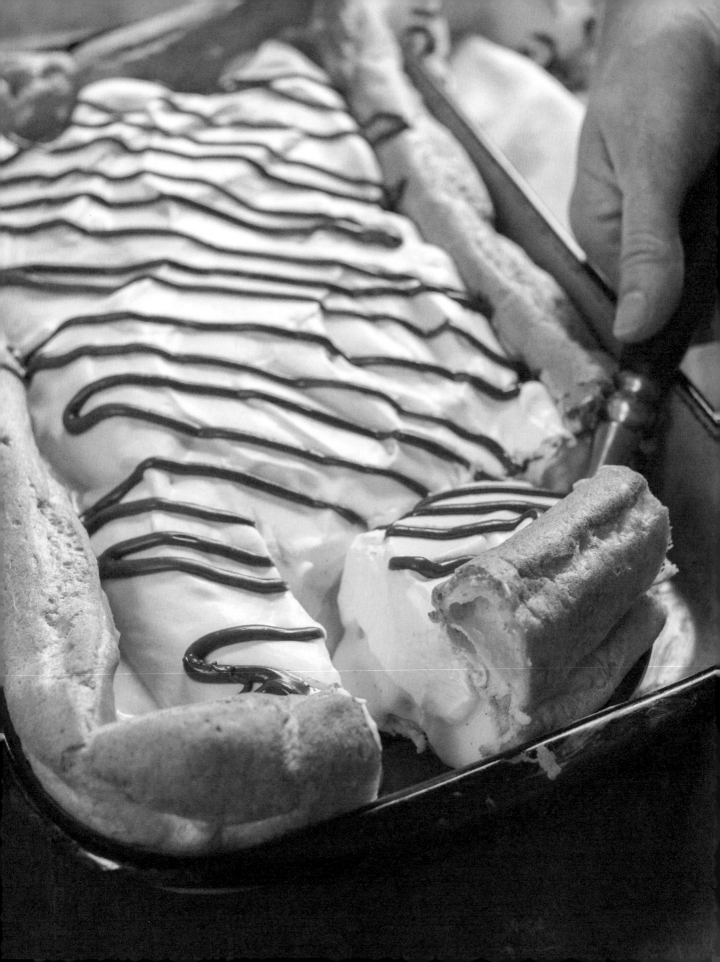

over medium-high heat. Add the flour all at once, lower the heat to medium-low, and immediately begin stirring. Stir vigorously until the dough forms a loose ball and a light crust forms on the bottom of the pan. Stir for 1 minute more to dry the dough.

Turn out the dough into the bowl of an electric mixer fitted with the paddle attachment. On medium speed, beat in the eggs, 1 at a time. Beat until the dough is thick and smooth. Test the doneness by pinching a bit of dough between your thumb and forefinger, then pulling them slowly apart—if you can stretch the dough to a string about 1 inch/2.5 cm long, it's done.

Spread the dough into an even layer in the prepared pan, using a combination of a spatula and dampened fingertips. Bake until puffed and golden, about 25 minutes. Let cool completely in the pan set on a wire rack.

Whisk the chilled custard until smooth. Fold half of the whipped cream into it until well blended. Spread over the cooled crust. Top with the remaining whipped cream. In a small, microwave-safe bowl, warm the chocolate hazelnut spread in a microwave on **HIGH** until fluid, about 30 seconds, then drizzle it over the whipped cream. Refrigerate for at least 2 hours before serving, or up to 1 day ahead (cover loosely with plastic wrap if chilling for more than 3 hours).

TIP › *For a banana pudding effect, and if you're able to serve this dessert soon after its final chill so the fruit doesn't get too brown, it's so, so good to layer in 2 medium-size sliced bananas, tossed with 1 tablespoon of freshly squeezed lemon juice. Lay the slices over the custard before adding the whipped cream topping.*

RED BERRIES AND CREAM GELATIN MOLD

Serves 12

WE MAY NOT HAVE FAMILY CRESTS IN AMERICA, BUT WE DO HAVE WEIRD FAMILY recipes. You know the ones, the slightly odd side dishes at family potlucks that never make sense to an outsider. And they may not get completely devoured, but if they were ever missing, people would notice. (Another defining quality of the wackiest family recipes—they tend to just *appear* on the table at every gathering, as though out of thin air and not made by an actual person. Mystical!) In the Midwest, more often than not, that recipe will be some kind of gelatin-based situation, whether it be a "salad" (see page 214), or molded dessert.

The combination of red Jell-O and whipped cream, probably in the form of a "nondairy whipped topping" and stuffed into the divot left behind by an oiled Bundt pan, is pure Heartland buffet glory. As it turns out, when you start with red Jell-O as your inspiration, it's easy to find fresh berries and real fruit juice that produce that color in nature, with even better flavor. And when you add a layer of lush, creamy buttermilk panna cotta, you really can reinvent the wheel. Maybe this from-scratch stab at my family's gelatinous favorite will inspire you to try and remix yours. Unless yours is made with green Jell-O. Good luck with that.

RED BERRY LAYER:

Nonstick cooking spray for pan

4 cups/900 g cranberry juice cocktail, divided

5½ teaspoons unflavored gelatin

⅔ cup/132 g granulated sugar

1 cup/170 g hulled and quartered fresh strawberries

1 cup/170 g fresh red raspberries

PANNA COTTA LAYER:

⅓ cup/75 g cold water

1 tablespoon unflavored gelatin

2 cups/480 g heavy whipping cream

6 tablespoons/75 g granulated sugar

⅛ teaspoon fine sea salt

1 cup/225 g well-shaken buttermilk

½ teaspoon pure vanilla extract or pure vanilla bean paste

Prepare the red berry layer: Generously spray a 10- to 12-cup/2.4 to 2.8 L Bundt pan or gelatin mold with nonstick cooking spray. Invert the pan onto paper towels to allow any excess to drip away.

In a small, bowl, whisk together 1 cup/225 g of the cranberry juice cocktail and the gelatin. Set aside to soften for 10 minutes.

Meanwhile, in a 2- to 2½-quart/1.9 to 2.4 L saucepan, combine the remaining 3 cups/675 g of cranberry juice cocktail and the sugar. Place the pan over medium-high heat and bring to a simmer, stirring to dissolve the sugar, about 1 minute. Remove the pan from the heat and whisk in the gelatin. Place the pan in the refrigerator and allow the gelatin to cool and thicken slightly, about 1 hour. During this time, you can gently stir it a time or two to check on it, but do not whisk, or you'll form bubbles in the gelatin. After an hour or so, it should be thickened but still flow in a stream, not unlike hair-styling gel.

Pour the gelatin into the prepared mold. Test the gelatin's thickness by dropping a raspberry into it—it should sink just below the surface without settling in to the bottom of the pan. Drop the rest of the berries over the gelatin—you may need to press some berries lightly to get them to sink into the gelatin and be suspended in it. Place the pan in the refrigerator and chill until the red berry layer is set but slightly sticky on the surface when touched with a fingertip, about 2 hours. (If it sets too firm, the second layer will not adhere.)

While the first layer is setting, prepare the panna cotta: In a small bowl, whisk together the water and gelatin. Set aside to soften.

In a 2- to 2½-quart/1.9 to 2.4 L saucepan, combine the cream, sugar, and salt. Stir over medium heat until the sugar has dissolved—do not allow the mixture to come to a simmer. Remove the pan from the heat and whisk in the gelatin. Whisk in the buttermilk and vanilla extract or paste. Set aside to cool at room temperature—do not refrigerate.

When the red berry layer has partially set, pour the cooled panna cotta mixture over it. Place the pan back in the refrigerator and chill until completely set, a minimum of 12 hours. Gelatin reaches its full setting ability with 24 hours of chilling time.

To unmold the dessert, lightly spray a serving plate with nonstick cooking spray and dab away the excess with a paper towel. Use the pads of your fingertips to gently pull the gelatin away from the sides and center tube of the mold to "break the seal." Fill a sink or large bowl with hot tap water. Dip the mold in the hot water for 5 to 10 seconds. Remove and dry off the mold with a towel. Place your serving plate over the mold and invert it. Shimmy the mold back and forth until you hear the gelatin release. Carefully remove the mold. Slice and serve. The gelatin keeps in the refrigerator uncovered for up to 3 days.

ON DESSERT SALADS

When it comes to the "dessert salad" culture of the Midwest, where do we even begin? Maybe it's best just to call out the elephant in the room—these recipes are most certainly wacky, and really, resemble anything but actual salad. To be fair, they might have one or two saladlike ingredients—say, fresh apple chunks, pineapple tidbits, or mandarin orange segments—but usually that's canceled out by the addition of packaged Day-Glo gelatin, instant pudding, or tubs of whipped topping, among other eyebrow-cocking add-ins, like vegetables that would indeed be found in an actual salad. (A recipe from a vintage Lutheran church cookbook called "Yellow Jell-O" involves lemon gelatin, cabbage, pineapple, and diced cucumbers. The headnote says simply *"Germans love this!"* Do they, though?)

For sweet dessert salads, the whimsical names alone encourage as many questions as the ingredients: Glorified Rice, Watergate Salad, Snickers Salad (yes, the candy bar), Cookie Salad. Ambrosia is another popular selection, but is claimed as much by the South as the Midwest. In short, an exemplary dessert salad is the kind of thing that makes you hate yourself for how much you love it.

It's interesting to try and figure out exactly how and why this dessert salad phenomenon came about, and why it's so prevalent in the Midwest. The prominence of churchgoers, particularly Catholics and Lutherans, definitely has a hand in it—potluck-based community meals postservice are still very much a thing in the central states, and dessert salads are a cheap and easy way to feed a crowd. It could also have something to do with the strength of Scandinavian and Nordic roots here and their tastes; there are several traditional foods of those cultures that are gelatinous, creamy, and, um, goopy, for lack a better word (think: lutefisk, for example, or any number of thick, almost-bouncy fermented dairy products like *skyr* or *viili,* which have been blended with fruit and sugar and served as dessert for hundreds of years). As a specific example, glorified rice might have been inspired by the delicious Scandi rice puddings that go by several names in those countries (see page 291).

But regardless of their origins, dessert salads have a place on our picnic tables and in our hearts, and almost everyone from the region has a favorite (however reluctant they are to admit it), most likely a family recipe from a singular aunt who's known for bringing it to any get-together requiring an edible contribution. For me, nothing is better on the Fourth of July than a certain dessert salad that my Auntie Amy has been making since the days of Tupperware parties (on page 215). It has such a fantastically bizarre combination of ingredients (pineapple juice, flour . . . vinegar?!), you'll never even believe me when I tell you that somehow, it actually does taste like a taffy apple. The great mysteries of the Midwest, I tell you.

AUNTIE AMY'S
TAFFY APPLE SALAD

Serves 8

NOW, AS DESSERT SALADS GO, THE ORIGINAL VERSION OF THIS RECIPE IS FAIRLY low on pre-packaged ingredients, save for that iconic whipped topping in the red, white, and blue tub. And sometimes I make it that way, just for the exact taste memory of it. But I've found that with a few tweaks, most dessert salads calling for nondairy whipped topping can also be made by using a mixture of cream cheese and real heavy whipped cream with a little gelatin, and the results are great. The quiet tang of the cream also tends to balance out sweetness in a fantastically modern way.

As you make the custard step of this recipe, it will all seem (and smell!) very bizarre and basically, I'm just asking you to blindly trust me. For the apples here, I love Honeycrisp when they're in season, or Jonathans. Pick a variety with a pretty skin, since the apples remain unpeeled in this recipe, lending to that "taffy apple" quality.

CUSTARD:

½ cup/113 g pineapple juice, divided

1 teaspoon unflavored gelatin

½ cup/100 g granulated sugar

1 tablespoon unbleached all-purpose flour

1 large egg

1 tablespoon cider vinegar

ASSEMBLY:

3 ounces/85 g full-fat cream cheese, at room temperature

1 cup/240 g heavy whipping cream

⅓ cup/40 g confectioners' sugar

½ teaspoon pure vanilla extract

4 medium-size Honeycrisp or Jonathan apples, cored, cut into ¾-inch/2 cm chunks (about 4 cups/450 g chopped)

1 cup/120 g salted cocktail-style peanuts, coarsely chopped, divided

Prepare the custard: In a small cup, whisk together 2 tablespoons of the pineapple juice and the gelatin. Set aside to soften. In a 1- to 1½-quart/1 to 1.4 ml saucepan, whisk together the sugar and flour until lump-free. Whisk in the remaining pineapple juice, egg, and vinegar. Set the pan over medium heat and cook, whisking constantly, until large bubbles begin to form. Continue to whisk and cook for 1 minute more. Remove the pan from the heat and whisk in the gelatin until melted. Pour the custard through a sieve into a small, clean bowl. Cover the surface with plastic wrap and refrigerate until completely chilled, about 2 hours.

In a large bowl, using a handheld mixer, beat the cream cheese until very soft and creamy. Add the custard, which will be set firm. Beat until the mixture is smooth. In a separate, medium bowl, combine the whipped cream, confectioners' sugar, and vanilla. Beat until stiff peaks form. Add the whipped cream to the cream cheese mixture and fold to blend well. Add the apples and three quarters of the nuts. Fold gently to blend. Cover and chill for at least 2 hours. Just before serving, scatter the top with the remaining nuts. This salad is best served the day it's made, but leftovers will hold, covered and refrigerated, for up to 2 days.

PEACHES AND CREAM
SCHAUM TORTE
Serves 8 to 10

ALTHOUGH IT RESEMBLES THE POPULAR AUSTRALIAN PAVLOVA, THE MERINGUE-crowned schaum torte actually predates it. Translated as "foam cake," it was brought to America by German immigrants who settled in the Midwest between 1839 and 1850, with the first published recipes coming out of Wisconsin in 1870. Setting it further apart, unlike the free-form pavlova, schaum torte is a bit more refined, baked in round cake pans and is often stacked in layers to serve a crowd with major wow factor.

Fans of Wisconsin supper clubs (I myself am a superfan) will recognize individual schaum tortes with crisp, marshmallow-bellied meringue disks piled high with ice cream, seasonal fruit, and clouds of whipped cream. Life doesn't get much better than a wood-paneled dining room, a leatherette-bumpered bar, pub cheese and Ritz crackers, kiddie cocktails, and icy old-fashioneds for the grown-ups with Wisconsin's finest Korbel brandy. And with ice-cream drinks and schaum torte on the dessert menu, you've just gone straight to heaven.

MERINGUE:

Nonstick cooking spray for pans

6 large egg whites, at room temperature

1/2 teaspoon fine sea salt

2 teaspoons white or cider vinegar

1 teaspoon pure vanilla extract

1/2 teaspoon pure almond extract

2 cups/400 g granulated sugar

FILLING AND ASSEMBLY:

1 cup/240 g heavy whipping cream, chilled

2 teaspoons granulated sugar

1/2 teaspoon pure vanilla extract

1 quart/453 g premium vanilla ice cream, or 1 batch Homemade Frozen Custard (page 219)

3 medium-size peaches, pitted and sliced into 1/2-inch/1.25 cm-thick slices (to equal 2 1/2 cups/425 g), or 1 (1-pound/450 g) bag unsweetened frozen peach slices, thawed

Prepare the meringues: Position a rack to the center of the oven and preheat it to 275°F/135°C. Lightly spray two 8-inch/20 cm round cake pans with nonstick cooking spray. Line the bottoms of the pans with rounds of parchment paper.

Pour the egg whites and salt into the bowl of an electric mixer fitted with the whisk attachment. Beat the whites until frothy on medium-high speed, about 1 minute. Add the vinegar, vanilla, and almond extract. Continue to beat until the egg whites hold soft peaks. Add the sugar very slowly, 1 tablespoon at a time. When all the sugar has been added, increase the mixer speed to high and beat for 1 minute more, or until the meringue is very thick, stiff, and glossy.

Divide the meringue equally between the cake pans, and use the back of a spoon to smooth it evenly. Bake until lightly golden and hollow when tapped, about 1 hour. Turn off the oven. Prop the oven door open with a wooden spoon and allow the layers to cool completely in the oven, about 1 hour. (The layers can be made 1 day ahead—wrap the cooled pans tightly with plastic wrap.)

Assemble the torte: In a medium bowl, using a handheld mixer, whip the cream with the sugar and vanilla to stiff peaks. Run a very thin, flexible knife around the edges of each pan to loosen the meringues. Turn out 1 layer upside-down onto a serving platter and carefully remove the parchment paper. Spoon the ice cream over the meringue in small scoops and top with half of the peach slices. Turn the second layer out of its pan, remove the parchment, and stack on top, right-side up. Dollop the whipped cream on top, and add the remaining peach slices. Cut and serve immediately, with a large serrated knife.

HOMEMADE FROZEN CUSTARD

Makes 1 generous quart/liter custard

THERE'S SOMETHING SO WONDERFULLY NOSTALGIC ABOUT FROZEN CUSTARD, it's so simple and yet so flavorful, a balm on a hot summer day. The seasonal openings and closings of small town custard stands give rhythm to the passage of time in a way so few things do anymore. I mean, a summer night, wearing shorts and sandals, throwing all the kids in the car, and heading out for a cone after dinner on a Tuesday, just because? Sitting at wobbly table while the sun sets, next to kids in Little League jerseys with waffle cones, chocolate-dipped and sprinkled, and tired mothers using a scoop as Xanax. Grandmothers ordering a neat little single cup; dads with their milk shakes, because that's such a dad thing to do. That's the good stuff, right there.

But if you ever have the urge to make your own, I'm going to leave this winner right here. With a subtle kiss of brown sugar and a swirl of sour cream, there's just enough crave-worthy edge here to make you wonder if you should get into the frozen custard business.

6 large egg yolks

1½ cups/338 g whole milk

1 cup/240 g heavy whipping cream

⅓ cup/75 g light brown sugar

⅓ cup/67 g granulated sugar

3 tablespoons/63 g corn syrup

⅛ teaspoon fine sea salt

¼ cup/60 g full-fat sour cream

2 teaspoons pure vanilla bean paste or pure vanilla extract

In a large bowl, whisk the egg yolks until well beaten.

In a 2- to 2½-quart/1.9 to 2.4 L saucepan, combine the milk, cream, brown and granulated sugar, corn syrup, and salt. Bring to a bare simmer over medium-high heat, being careful not to let the mixture boil.

Remove the pan from the heat and slowly drizzle the hot milk mixture into the egg yolks, whisking vigorously until all the liquid has been added. Pour the egg mixture back into the saucepan and place it back on the stove over medium heat. Clip a candy thermometer to the pan. Stirring constantly, cook the custard until slightly thickened and registers a temperature of at least 160°F/71°C. Pour the custard through a sieve into a large bowl. Whisk in the sour cream and vanilla bean paste. Cover the bowl and chill thoroughly in the refrigerator, at least 4 hours or overnight.

Freeze the custard in an ice-cream machine according to the manufacturer's instructions. Transfer the soft-set frozen custard to a 1-quart/1 L container with a tight-fitting lid and freeze until firm.

MIDWEST + FROZEN CUSTARD = TRUE LOVE

History reveals that frozen custard first made an appearance on New York's Coney Island in 1919. But like oh-so-many great American inventions, it didn't take off on a larger scale until the 1933 World's Fair in Chicago, and boy, did the Midwest take that baton and run with it. Soon after, frozen custard took hold in the next-largest midwestern city nearby, Milwaukee, also known as "Cream City." (As it turns out, the nickname actually refers to the cream-colored bricks, made from native clay, that so many of the city's buildings are constructed with. But it also fits beautifully with Milwaukee's relationship with frozen custard, so let's go with it.)

With access to top-notch Wisconsin dairy and a massive ice-harvesting industry, Milwaukee was ripe for getting into the ice cream manufacturing game after the World's Fair. Additionally, with so much farmland, eggs were also plentiful, and since the difference between ice cream and custard is the lack of air pumped in, and the addition of lots of egg yolks to create a denser, smoother (and, I'll say it—more delicious) product, Milwaukee had the ability to produce frozen custard easily and inexpensively. With a strong urban center to catch onto the trend and help spread the word, Milwaukee was the perfect place to grow the frozen custard culture remaining in the Midwest today. Although now would be a good place to mention that St. Louis people wouldn't let me finish this treatise on frozen custard without mentioning Ted Drewes and its famous Concretes, a custard creation so thick that they're presented to customers upside-down.

Milwaukee's most famous frozen custard sellers include Kopp's, Gilles, Kitt's, and Leon's, and of course there's the Culver's chain, which has become a big name all over the region and beyond. People love to pit them against one another and fight over who churns out the best. But I'm partial to the roadside mom-and-pop stands that are only open seasonally. If you can resist tiny shops with names like Custard's Last Stand or Not Licked Yet, you might not be a real person. It all adds to the glory of a sublime, golden, drippy cone.

WATERMELON SHERBET

Makes about 1½ quarts/1.4 L sherbet

WHETHER YOU CALL IT "SHER-BETTE." AS ITS SPELLED AND HOW IT PROBABLY should be pronounced, or "Shur-Burt" as though you're Ernie on _Sesame Street_ responding to your roommate, this is a lighter, fairly retro, and fabulously refreshing alternative to ice cream. This watermelon riff is especially good to know about when you've been gifted an enormous watermelon for one reason or another. Like, say, you've hosted a summer barbecue and someone decided to bring one for the kids, but the adults all drank a little too much and forgot to crack it open? You know what I mean.

At any rate, Midwest summers are synonymous with watermelon. Watermelons are a prized crop of the Great Plains of the Midwest, namely South Dakota and its Black Diamond variety, round as a beach ball with a striking matte, blackish-green skin the color of seaweed, with a snow white inner rind. Its flesh is so sweet and vibrant it nearly glows. If hot pink had a flavor, this would be it.

4 cups/680 g chopped seed-less watermelon (1-inch/2.5 cm chunks)

¾ cup/150 g granulated sugar

2 tablespoons freshly squeezed lemon juice

2 tablespoons freshly squeezed lime juice

⅛ teaspoon fine sea salt

¼ cup/57 g cold water

2½ teaspoons unflavored gelatin

1 cup/225 g half-and-half

In a large bowl, combine the watermelon, sugar, lemon juice, lime juice, and salt. Cover the bowl and chill for 30 minutes in the refrigerator, or until the sugar has dissolved.

Meanwhile, in a small, microwave-safe bowl, whisk together the cold water and gelatin. Set aside to soften for 5 minutes. Place the bowl in the microwave and heat for 15 seconds on **HIGH** to melt the gelatin. Alternatively, scrape the gelatin into a 1- to 1½-quart/1 to 1.4 L sauce-pan and melt it gently over low heat.

Transfer the watermelon mixture to a blender. Blend for 1 minute. Add the melted gelatin and blend in for 30 seconds. Blend in the half-and-half. Pour the mixture back into the large bowl and cover. Chill in the refrigerator for at least 3 hours, or overnight.

Pour into an ice-cream maker and freeze according to the manufacturer's instructions. Transfer to an airtight container, cover tightly, and freeze until firm. Soften slightly before scooping and serving.

NO-CHURN HEAVENLY HASH ICE CREAM

Makes about 2 quarts/1.9 L ice cream

WE RARELY HAD ICE CREAM IN THE HOUSE GROWING UP. IF WE DID, IT WAS USUALLY a half-gallon of Dean's Neapolitan left over from a birthday party, usually finished within the following 24 hours and ending with my mother yelling, "Who ate all the ice cream?!"

However, there were a few moments when ice cream could be found in the freezer just for ice cream's sake. And I use the word *found*, because it was always hidden, probably from me, behind a bunch of freezer-burned whatnot. Found ice cream was usually Heavenly Hash, a wonderful combination of flavors and textures that had its heyday and has since all but disappeared, which is a damn shame. So, I'm bringing it back, with a fun, no-machinery-required technique, because the combination of chocolate and marshmallow and crunchy bits of almond and chocolate chips is perfection, and the answer to all of life's stresses. In short, this is the kind of ice cream you can make with your kids, but also deserve to hide from your kids.

2 cups/480 g cold heavy whipping cream

1 (14-ounce/392 g) can sweetened condensed milk

⅓ cup/32 g unsweetened Dutch-processed cocoa powder, sifted

½ teaspoon pure vanilla extract

¼ teaspoon fine sea salt

2 cups/100 g mini marshmallows, toasted

½ cup/60 g chopped raw almonds, toasted and cooled

3 ounces/84 g bittersweet chocolate, finely chopped

Place a 9 x 5-inch/23 x 12.7 cm metal loaf pan in the freezer.

In the bowl of an electric mixer fitted with the whisk attachment, whip the cream to firm peaks.

In a medium bowl, whisk together the sweetened condensed milk, cocoa powder, vanilla, and salt. Fold a third of the whipped cream into this mixture to lighten it, then fold in the remaining cream until well blended. Fold in the toasted marshmallows, almonds, and chopped chocolate. Spoon into the chilled loaf pan. Chill, uncovered, in the freezer until firm, at least 4 hours.

BLACK RASPBERRY CHIP ICE CREAM

Makes 1 generous quart/1.2 L ice cream

THIS RECIPE IS INSPIRED BY TWO OF OHIO'S FINEST—GRAETER'S ICONIC ICE CREAM flavor, and ice cream queen Jeni Britton Bauer, who has taken over the world with her company Jeni's Ice Creams and her mad scientist approach to the craft of making ice cream. Jeni's clever technique of adding a chunk of cream cheese to ice cream bases emulsifies the mixture without eggs, adds richness, and tempers sweetness. I especially love to use her trick for ice creams with a lot of fruit purée in them, like this one, because it keeps the texture scoopable and velvety, never icy.

Black raspberries—or blackcaps, as they're affectionately known—are among some of the most delicious, fragile, and fleeting fruits on earth. If I had to describe them, I suppose the most obvious way would be a cross between a blackberry and a raspberry, but they're more mysterious, more primitive in flavor, with juice so intensely colored that it's a little alarming.

They grow wild in spots in the Midwest—I let out an Oprah-esque "black raaaaaspbeeeeriiiieeesss!" when I discovered some long-neglected brambles in my own backyard—and only appear for about three weeks in July. When ours finally come in, I immediately start a freezer stash, picking just a couple of handfuls a day before the birds can get to them. I'll often supplement the haul with a trip to a U-pick berry farm in the same time frame. The hoarding is worth it when you get to make this ice cream.

4 cups/450 g fresh or frozen black raspberries, thawed if frozen

1½ cups/360 g heavy whipping cream

1½ cups/337 g whole milk

1 cup/200 g granulated sugar

3 tablespoons/63 g light corn syrup

⅛ teaspoon fine sea salt

3 ounces/85 g full-fat cream cheese

2 tablespoons cornstarch

1 to 2 teaspoons freshly squeezed lemon juice

4 ounces/113 g bittersweet chocolate (60% cacao), melted

In a food processor or blender, purée the berries. Pour and firmly press through a sieve into a measuring cup—you should have about 1⅓ cups/300 g of purée.

In a 3- to 4-quart/2.8 to 3.75 L saucepan, combine the cream, milk, sugar, corn syrup, and salt. Bring to a bare simmer over medium heat, stirring until the sugar in dissolved. Remove from the heat.

Place the cream cheese and the cornstarch in 2 separate bowls. Ladle ¼ cup/57 g of the hot milk mixture into each bowl. Whisk both mixtures until smooth.

Pour the cornstarch mixture into the saucepan and return it to medium heat. Bring to a low boil until slightly thickened, and cook for 2 minutes, whisking often. Remove the pan from the heat and whisk in the cream cheese mixture. Pour in the black raspberry purée and whisk to blend. Add lemon juice to taste, just enough to really make it sing. Transfer the mixture to a large bowl.

Cover the bowl and chill thoroughly in the refrigerator, at least 4 hours or overnight. Freeze in an ice-cream machine according to the manufacturer's instructions.

While the ice cream is churning, line baking sheet with parchment paper. Spread the melted chocolate into a rough 7 x 9-inch/18 x 23 cm rectangle. Freeze until set, about 10 minutes. Chop the chocolate into small bits. When the ice cream has finished churning, fold in the chocolate bits. Transfer the ice cream to a container with a tight-fitting lid and freeze until firm.

ANGEL FLUFF

Serves 10

FOR REASONS STILL UNKNOWN, WHEN I FIRST FOUND THIS MYSTERIOUS, SPARSELY written recipe—a Missouri State Fair winner, no less—I was determined to unpack this Angel Fluff. With no fruit, it doesn't quite qualify as a "dessert salad." It's too sweet to go alongside other savory dishes on a Chinet potluck plate. It's hard to picture it being served as a stand-alone dessert. It's too sturdy to be a pudding. What is even happening here?

I talked to myself with a furrowed brow during the entire preparation of the vaguest of formulas. I made a batter reminiscent of a sponge cake, but baked it into a crisp cookie? I quartered marshmallows with kitchen scissors? I bound it all together with unsweetened whipped cream? I was completely prepared for this marshmallowy bowl of crazy to go right into the trash.

Well. That absolutely did not happen. Because after a rest in the fridge, the whole thing transformed. The exposed edges of the marshmallows gave up just enough gelatin to embolden the cream.

The crispy cookie bits softened and swelled, lending a custardy, genoise flavor to the whole thing. It ended up being something like a creamy angel food cake. I was captivated. I could not stop swiping spoonfuls straight from the refrigerator over the course of two days. When I did, I could see others in my household were covertly doing the same. There was an uptick of spoons in the sink. So, apparently, "eat randomly, secretly, straight from the fridge" is the category for this recipe. Reserve your judgment, don't ask too many questions, and just get on in here. You won't regret it.

2 large eggs

3/4 cup/150 g granulated sugar

1/4 teaspoon fine sea salt

2 teaspoons pure vanilla extract, divided

1/4 cup/32 g unbleached all-purpose flour, spooned and leveled

1 teaspoon baking powder

1 (10-ounce/280 g) bag large marshmallows

2 cups/480 g heavy whipping cream, chilled

Position a rack to the center of the oven and preheat it to 325°F/170°C. Line a 12 x 17-inch/30 x 43 cm rimmed baking pan with parchment paper (the paper is a must, to get the baked cookie out of the pan).

In the bowl of an electric mixer fitted with the whisk attachment, combine the eggs, sugar, and salt. Beat on high speed until light and tripled in volume, about 5 minutes. Beat in 1 teaspoon of the vanilla. Fold in the flour and baking powder. Scrape the batter onto the prepared baking sheet and smooth it into a thin layer, nearly filling the pan. Bake until golden and crisp, about 15 minutes. Let cool in the pan set on a wire rack. Wash the bowl and whisk and fit them back onto the mixer.

Meanwhile, use kitchen scissors to snip the marshmallows into quarters (tedious but worth it—the exposed edges of the marshmallows help the fluff bind together better than mini marshmallows would). Pour the cold cream into the bowl of the mixer. Add the remaining vanilla. Whip the cream to stiff peaks.

Crumble the cookie into small bits into the whipped cream. Add the marshmallows. Fold to blend. Cover the bowl tightly with plastic wrap and chill in the refrigerator for at least 2 hours before serving. Keep any leftovers covered in the fridge for up to 3 days.

ROASTED STRAWBERRY LONGCAKE WITH YOGURT WHIPPED CREAM

Serves 10 to 12

WHY ASSEMBLE A BUNCH OF INDIVIDUAL STRAWBERRY SHORTCAKES LIKE A SUCKER, when you can make a whole pan at once? This recipe is basically a strawberry cobbler, but rather than putting raw shortcake dough on top of raw fruit, I prefer to let the strawberries roast and caramelize a bit on their own first, and then put the shortcakes on top of the bubbling fruit, where they immediately begin to bake from the bottom as well as the top, staying fluffy and moist in the center. With this method, you can adapt this recipe for the grill on moderate heat, using a big cast-iron skillet.

Whipping cream with a dollop of full-fat Greek yogurt gives lightness and a bit of tang to cut through the fatty cream. It's great on fruit desserts and pies, too. My preference for baking with yogurt is always to use the whole-milk variety, which I consider heaven in a plastic cup.

BERRIES:

2½ pounds/1.1 kg g fresh strawberries

½ cup/113 g light brown sugar

2 tablespoons cornstarch

⅛ teaspoon fine sea salt

1 tablespoon freshly squeezed lemon juice

BISCUITS:

6 tablespoons/75 g granulated sugar

1 teaspoon finely grated lemon zest

1¾ cups/224 g unbleached all-purpose flour, spooned and leveled, plus more for dusting

2 tablespoons yellow cornmeal

1½ teaspoons baking powder

½ teaspoon baking soda

½ teaspoon fine sea salt

6 tablespoons/84 g cold unsalted butter, diced

¾ cup/180 g cold whole-milk Greek yogurt

¾ teaspoon pure vanilla extract

Coarse sugar, such as sanding sugar, turbinado, or demerara, for sprinkling

YOGURT WHIPPED CREAM:

1 cup/240 g cold heavy whipping cream

½ cup/120 g cold whole-milk Greek yogurt

2½ tablespoons granulate-sugar, or to taste

½ teaspoon pure vanilla extract

Position rack to the center of the oven and preheat it to 475°F/246°C.

Prepare the berries: Wash, dry, and hull the strawberries. For smaller berries, halve them, and if they're large, quarter them, so that the pieces are roughly the same size.

In a 9 x 13-inch/23 x 33 cm baking dish, use your hands to mix together the brown sugar, cornstarch, and salt. Add the berries and lemon juice and toss with your hands until there are no white powdery patches. Roast in the oven for 15 minutes, stirring the berries and scraping the pan halfway through the baking time, until the juices are bubbling and beginning to caramelize on the sides of the pan.

Prepare the biscuits: In a medium bowl, combine the granulated sugar and lemon zest. Use your fingertips to rub the mixture together until moist and fragrant. Add the flour, cornmeal, baking powder, baking soda, and salt and stir to blend. Drop in the butter pieces and use your fingertips to rub the butter into the dry ingredients until it resembles fine, even crumbs. Add the yogurt and vanilla. Use a flexible spatula to gently fold the mixture until a soft dough forms—don't overmix. Turn out the dough onto a lightly floured work surface. Divide the dough into 10 equal portions.

After the berries have been roasting for 15 minutes, remove the pan from the oven. Lower the oven temperature to 425°F/220°C. Drop the biscuits on top of the fruit. Sprinkle the tops of the biscuits with the coarse sugar. Return the pan to the oven and bake until the biscuits are golden and firm, about 20 minutes. Let cool for at least 20 minutes.

Prepare the yogurt whipped cream: Pour the cream into a large bowl. Using a handheld mixer, beat the cream on high speed just until it begins to thicken. Add the yogurt, granulated sugar, and vanilla. Beat on high speed until stiff peaks form. Dollop generously over each serving.

CHAPTER 9
SAVORIES

MOST OFTEN, BAKING MEANS SWEETS—CAKES, COOKIES, PIES, PASTRIES—all the goodies we've visited thus far in these pages. But one of my very favorite categories of baking has very little to do with tapping into the sweet tooth, and entertaining savory cravings instead.

When cooler weather hits and saucy, one-pot meals are in regular rotation, savory side bakes are a savior, allowing you to skip yet another boring store-bought loaf of "artisan" bread that's at least a day old. When you want to really make friends and influence people, nothing will do that better than making your own dang sandwich bread. When you're invited to a holiday party and find out—horrors!—it's a potluck, mere hours before you have to drag yourself out the door, bringing something freshly baked and savory instead of sweet is always welcome when the dessert buffet is bound to stretch ten times further than the dinner table (much like the chapters of this book).

And when you've had the kind of day where all you want for dinner is something bready and at least half a bottle of wine, it's a grand excuse to warm up the house with a hot oven and spicy, salty, cheesy, herby scents.

NEBRASKAN RUNZAS

Makes 12 sandwiches

RUNZAS (A.K.A. *BIEROCKS* OR *KRAUTBURGERS*, AMONG OTHER NAMES) ARE A POCKET sandwich, a puffy, yeasted dough baked around a savory meat filling. They likely originated in Russia in the 1800s, and came to the Midwest with the Volga Germans, a population of German people who lived along the Volga River in southeastern Russia in the 18th century and settled in Nebraska, Kansas, and the Dakotas in the early 20th century.

In Nebraska, you'll find runzas with a longer, rectangular shape; whereas in Kansas, they tend to be shaped more like circular buns. Either way, they're traditionally filled with a simple combination of onions, ground beef, and cabbage, and that's perfectly delicious. But one day while shopping for the cabbage, my eyes fell on a packet of "superfood" slaw mixture of green and red cabbage, shredded broccoli stems, kale, carrots, Brussels sprouts, and more. Trying to ignore the shouts of midwesterners past with this admittedly hippie twist on the classic, I decided upon tasting that I loved the pop of texture and color this new combination of vegetables gave the sandwiches, as well as the reduced prep time, and now it's what I use all the time.

DOUGH:

2¼ teaspoons instant yeast

3 tablespoons/42 g warm water (110° to 115°F/43° to 46°C)

5 cups/640 g unbleached bread flour, spooned and leveled, plus more for dusting

6 tablespoons/75 g granulated sugar

1 teaspoon fine sea salt

1½ cups/337 g warm whole milk (110° to 115°F/43° to 46°C)

½ cup/1 stick/113 g unsalted butter, melted

2 large eggs, at room temperature

Oil for bowl

FILLING:

2 tablespoons/28 g vegetable oil

1 medium-size onion, finely diced (about 2 cups/320 g)

2 garlic cloves, minced

1 pound/450 g ground beef (85% lean)

1 tablespoon Worcestershire sauce

4 cups/400 g shredded cabbage or cruciferous combination of your choice (see headnote)

Fine sea salt and freshly ground black pepper

1½ cups/170 g coarsely grated extra-sharp Cheddar cheese

2 tablespoons/28 g unsalted butter, melted, for serving

Position racks to the upper and lower thirds of the oven, and preheat it to 350°F/180°C. Line 2 baking sheets with parchment paper.

Prepare the dough: In a small cup, whisk together the yeast and warm water.

In the bowl of an electric mixer fitted with the dough hook, combine the flour, sugar, and salt.

In a medium bowl, whisk together the warm milk, melted butter, eggs, and dissolved yeast mixture. Whisk until smooth. Pour into the flour mixture and stir with a wooden spoon to form a shaggy dough. Set the mixer to medium speed and knead until the dough is smooth and elastic, 5 to 6 minutes. Place the dough in an oiled bowl, cover tightly, and let rise in a warm place for 30 minutes. Punch the dough down, cover, and let rise for another 30 minutes.

Meanwhile, prepare the filling: In a large skillet over medium-high heat, heat the oil. Add the onion and garlic and sauté until soft and just beginning to turn golden, about 5 minutes. Add the ground beef and cook until browned, 5 minutes more. Add the Worcestershire sauce and cabbage and cook until tender, about 8 minutes. Season to taste with salt and pepper. Remove the pan from the heat and allow the filling to cool. Once cooled, stir in the cheese.

Assemble the sandwiches: Turn out the dough onto a lightly floured work surface, and divide into 12 equal portions. Roll each portion into a ball, then use a rolling pin to form the dough balls into rough 6-inch/15 cm circles (if the dough fights you as you're trying to roll it out, let it rest for 5 minutes and start again). Place a generous 1/3 cup/about 100 g of filling in the center of each circle. Fold half of the dough over the filling, and pinch the edges to seal, rolling them up slightly all around the edge. Place the runzas, seam-side down, on the prepared baking sheets.

Bake until golden, 20 to 25 minutes. Let cool on the sheets for 10 minutes. Brush lightly with the melted butter just before serving. Any leftovers reheat well the next day.

GARLICKY, BUTTER-SWIRLED PULL-APART ROLLS

Makes 14 rolls

THINK OF THESE WARM, GOLDEN SPIRALS AS SAVORY CINNAMON ROLLS. OR A garlic bread you can unfurl. You can either make these all in one go, allowing the dough to have just an hour during its first rise, or, if you're a planner—good for you!—go for a longer cold rise in the refrigerator up to 12 hours ahead. It's worth it for the flavor boost.

DOUGH:

4 tablespoons/84 g unsalted butter

3/4 cup/170 g well-shaken buttermilk, at room temperature

2 tablespoons warm water (110° to 115°F/43° to 46°C)

1¼ teaspoons instant yeast

2 teaspoons granulated sugar

1 large egg, at room temperature

2¾ cups/352 g unbleached bread flour, spooned and leveled, plus more if needed and for dusting

1¼ teaspoons fine sea salt

Nonstick cooking spray or oil for bowl and pan

FILLING:

2 tablespoons olive oil

8 large garlic cloves, finely minced (to equal a generous 1/3 cup/50 g)

Fine sea salt

4 tablespoons/57 g butter, at room temperature

1/2 teaspoon dried basil

1/2 teaspoon dried oregano

Freshly ground black pepper

1/2 cup/50 g grated Parmesan cheese, plus more for sprinkling

1 teaspoon freshly squeezed lemon juice

1 large egg, separated

1 tablespoon water

Prepare the dough: In a large, microwave-safe measuring cup, melt the butter in a microwave on **HIGH**, about 1 minute—it should be hot, but not bubbling. Whisk in the buttermilk. You should now have a liquid that's just warm to the touch.

In the bowl of an electric mixer, whisk together the warm water and yeast. Let dissolve for a few minutes. Whisk in the buttermilk mixture, sugar, and egg. Add the flour and salt and mix with a wooden spoon until a shaggy dough forms. Attach the bowl to the mixer along with the dough hook. Knead on medium speed until the dough is smooth and freely clears the sides of the bowl, 6 to 7 minutes. If the dough is still clinging to the sides of the bowl after the first 2 minutes of kneading, add additional flour,

2 tablespoons at a time, until the dough clings just to the center 2 inches/5 cm of the bottom of the bowl while kneading.

Turn out the dough onto a lightly floured work surface and knead a few times by hand until smooth and springy. Shape the dough into a ball. Spray the mixer bowl with nonstick cooking spray or oil it lightly and place the dough back into it. Cover the bowl with plastic wrap. Allow the dough to rise in the refrigerator for 6 to 12 hours for maximum flavor, or if you're short on time, let rise in a warm place until it has doubled, about 1 hour.

If you've gone for a cold rise, remove the dough from the refrigerator and let it warm up at room temperature for about 30 minutes.

Prepare the filling: In a 1- to 1½-quart/1 to 1.4 ml saucepan, heat the olive oil over medium-low heat. Add the garlic and a few pinches of salt. Stirring often, gently cook the garlic until nearly translucent, about 5 minutes—don't allow it to brown. Remove the pan from the heat and allow the mixture to cool to room temperature.

In a small bowl, beat the butter by hand until soft and creamy. Blend in the cooked garlic and oil, ¾ teaspoon of the salt, basil, oregano, a few grinds of the pepper, the Parmesan, and the lemon juice and egg yolk.

In a small cup, beat the egg white with the water and a pinch of salt until liquefied. Grease a 10-inch/25 cm cast-iron skillet, or similar-sized heavy baking pan with nonstick cooking spray or oil.

Lightly flour a work surface and turn out the dough onto it. Press the dough into a rough rectangle, with a long side closest to you. Use a rolling pin to roll the dough out into a 10 x 14-inch/25 x 35.5 cm rectangle. Spread the filling on the dough, leaving a ½-inch/1.25 cm bare border on all sides. Roll the dough away from you into a tight log. Brush the filling-free border with the egg white mixture. Finish the roll and pinch tightly to seal. Cut the log into 14 equal rolls. Place the rolls in the prepared skillet. Cover with plastic wrap and allow the rolls to rise until puffy, about 1 hour.

Position a rack to the center of the oven and preheat it to 350°F/180°C. Brush the tops of the rolls with the egg white mixture and sprinkle with grated Parmesan.

Bake until puffed and golden, about 30 minutes (the internal temperature should register at least 190°F/88°C on an instant-read thermometer). Let cool for about 10 minutes before serving from the skillet.

SWEDISH LIMPA

Makes one 15-inch/38 cm loaf

SHORT FOR *VORTLIMPA*—WITH *VORT* REFERRING TO THE FERMENTED BREWERS' WORT left over from beer making, and *limpa* meaning "loaf"—this Swedish bread is a classic with many variations. In its most old-school form, the bread is a funky, spiced, dark rye made with that afore-mentioned wort, or more often for home bakers, a good stout. It's intense.

Scandinavian bakeries across the Midwest tend to carry lighter, more crowd-pleasing versions of limpa that swap out the beer for water, buttermilk, or even orange juice, and contain light or medium rye flour combined with white flour, giving the bread a soft and spongy interior and a thin crust. Al Johnson's Swedish Restaurant in Sister Bay, Wisconsin, a quirky place where unamused goats live and munch away on the grass-lined roof, serves stacks of light limpa with sweet butter alongside its paper-thin Swedish pancakes topped with plenty of lingonberries. This is the kind of limpa I love, and what I'm sharing with you here. It makes excellent toast and is a terrific foundation for those irresistible open-faced Scandi sandwiches called *smørrebrød*.

Limpa looks like a simple, humble loaf, but hold it up to your nose and take a bite, and a veritable carnival of flavors and fragrances come parading out. There's a slight sweetness, and always some combination of potent seeds to add extra zing—usually fennel, anise, and caraway, and perhaps some cardamom, too. Please note that I'd rather hit up an Ikea on Black Friday than eat something with caraway, so I leave it out of my personal formula.

6 tablespoons/84 g warm water (110° to 115°F/43° to 46°C), divided

¼ cup/57 g firmly packed light brown sugar

2 tablespoons/28 g unsalted butter

1 tablespoon finely grated orange zest

2 teaspoons fine sea salt

1 teaspoon instant yeast

¼ teaspoon granulated sugar

1 cup/225 g well-shaken butter-milk, at room temperature

2½ cups/320 g unbleached all-purpose flour, spooned and leveled, plus more for dusting

1 cup/105 g medium rye flour, spooned and leveled

¼ teaspoon baking soda

½ teaspoon fennel seeds

½ teaspoon anise seeds

Nonstick cooking spray or oil for bowl

1 tablespoon unsalted butter, melted, for brushing

In a 1- to 1½-quart/1 to 1.4 L saucepan, combine ¼ cup/57 g of the warm water with the brown sugar, butter, orange zest, and salt. Warm gently over medium heat until the butter is melted and the sugar has dissolved. Set aside to cool until warm to the touch.

In a small cup, whisk together the remaining 2 tablespoons of warm water, the yeast, and the granulated sugar. Let sit for 5 minutes.

In the bowl of an electric mixer fitted with the paddle attachment, combine both wet mixtures. Whisk in the buttermilk. Add the all-purpose flour, rye flour, baking soda, and seeds. Mix on low speed until the dough comes together in a shaggy ball. Exchange the paddle attachment for the dough hook, then knead the dough on medium-low speed until smooth and elastic, 5 to 7 minutes.

Turn out the dough onto a lightly floured work surface and knead by hand for a few minutes. Spray the mixer bowl with nonstick cooking spray or oil it lightly and place the dough in the bowl. Cover tightly and allow to rise in a warm spot until doubled in bulk, about 1 hour.

Line a 12 x 17-inch/30 x 43 cm baking sheet with parchment paper. Transfer the dough from the bowl to the work surface and shape into an oval about 12 inches/30 cm in length. Cover with plastic wrap and let rise again for 1 hour. Meanwhile, position a rack to the center of the oven and preheat it to 375°F/190°C.

Brush the top of the loaf with the melted butter. Bake until golden and hollow-sounding when tapped, about 40 minutes (the internal temperature should register at least 190°F/88°C on an instant-read thermometer). Let cool on a wire rack before slicing.

BREWERS' CHEDDAR BREAD

Serves 10

THIS EASY QUICK BREAD IS PACKED WITH ZIPPY FLAVORS CELEBRATING THE incredible beer brewing and cheese-making traditions of the Midwest. You can use any combination of beer and hard cheeses you have on hand. But to make a bread that belies its humble appearance and really helps usher in cooler weather and comfort food season, I love using an Oktoberfest lager, crisp and spicy, paired with the sharpest Wisconsin Cheddar I can find.

Nonstick cooking spray for pan

1½ cups/170 g coarsely grated extra-sharp Cheddar cheese

¼ cup/32 g finely grated Parmesan cheese

3 cups/384 g unbleached all-purpose flour, spooned and leveled

1 tablespoon baking powder

1 tablespoon granulated sugar

¾ teaspoon fine sea salt

¼ teaspoon freshly ground black pepper

1 large shallot, peeled and finely minced

1 garlic clove, finely minced

2 tablespoons/28 g unsalted butter, melted, divided

1 tablespoon Dijon mustard

1½ cups/340 g cold beer

Position a rack to the lower third of the oven and preheat it to 350°F/180°C. Spray a 9 x 5-inch/23 x 12.7 cm loaf pan with nonstick cooking spray and line it with parchment paper.

In a small bowl, toss together the cheeses. Remove ¼ cup/30 g and set aside for the topping.

In a large bowl, whisk together the flour, baking powder, sugar, salt, and pepper. Add the remaining 1½ cups/172 g of the cheese mixture and the shallot and garlic and stir to combine. Make a well in the center of the dry ingredients, and pour in 1 tablespoon of the melted butter and the mustard. Use a fork to stir together the butter and mustard until smooth. Add the beer, and use a wooden spoon to mix the batter gently just until it comes together and there are no dry pockets—don't overmix.

Scrape the batter into the prepared pan and smooth the top. Drizzle the remaining 1 tablespoon of butter over the top of the batter. Scatter over the reserved ¼ cup/30 g of cheese. Bake until a toothpick inserted into the center comes out clean, 50 to 60 minutes. Let cool in the pan set on a wire rack for 20 minutes, then remove the loaf from the pan to cool further. Store any leftovers, tightly wrapped, at room temperature for up to 2 days.

TIP › *Serve the bread warm from the oven the first day, and toast slices of any leftovers the next.*

SUNFLOWER STATE BREAD

Makes one 9 x 5-inch/23 x 12.7 cm loaf

WHILE KANSAS MIGHT BE KNOWN AS THE SUNFLOWER STATE—AND INDEED, STUNNING sunflower farms, such as Grinter Farms in Lawrence, draw thousands of tourists every year—sunflowers are actually more abundant in the Dakotas, with South Dakota being the nation's biggest producer. If you've ever seen a stunning goldenrod carpet of midwestern sunflowers, their big, goofy faces turned up at the sun like children sucked into their favorite cartoon, you won't soon forget it.

Sunflowers first grew wild in Arizona and Texas, prized by Native Americans who used the entire plant for everything from foodstuffs to textile dyeing, body painting, and medicine. Spanish explorers brought the sunflower to Europe in the 1500s, and over the next 300 years, it grew in popularity in Europe and then in Russia, where the flowers became a national obsession, mostly for their oil.

The cultivated seeds eventually made their way back to North America in 1930, when Canada started the first government-sponsored sunflower-breeding program. These farms then extended down into parts of Minnesota and the Dakotas, and eventually Kansas, too. So, like any good food story, it took multiple cultures to discover a plant, make it awesome, and then return it to whence it first came so as to flourish. And if you've made it this far, I'll bet you're hungry. How about some carbs to celebrate the sunflower? When you're in the mood for a nubbly, wholesome loaf, this is the kind of bread you're looking for.

1¹/₃ cups/166 g bread flour, spooned and leveled

1 cup/225 g warm whole milk (110° to 115°F/43° to 46°C)

2¹/₄ teaspoons instant yeast

1¹/₂ teaspoons granulated sugar

1 cup/128 g whole wheat flour, spooned and leveled

¹/₂ cup/50 g old-fashioned rolled oats

¹/₂ cup/60 g unsalted, shelled raw sunflower seeds

2 tablespoons/28 g unsalted butter, melted

2 tablespoons/42 g honey

1 teaspoon fine sea salt

Nonstick cooking spray or oil for bowl

In the bowl of an electric mixer fitted with the paddle attachment, beat together the bread flour, milk, yeast, and sugar on low speed for 3 minutes. Cover tightly and let rest in a warm place until doubled, about 30 minutes. Add the whole wheat flour, oats, sunflower seeds, melted butter, honey, and salt. Fit the bowl back on the mixer along with the dough hook attachment. Knead on medium speed for 5 to 6 minutes. Transfer to a smooth work surface and knead by hand several times—the dough should feel springy and elastic, and need very little flour—if any—to keep it from clinging to the work surface. Spritz the mixer bowl lightly with nonstick cooking spray or oil it lightly and place the dough back into it. Cover tightly again and let rise until doubled, 30 minutes.

Turn out the dough onto the work surface once again and knead several times before shaping it into a loaf to fit a 9 x 5-inch/23 x 12.7 cm pan. Cover with plastic wrap and rest for a final 30-minute rise.

Position a rack to the lower third of the oven and preheat it to 375°F/190°C. Bake until deeply golden and hollow-sounding when tapped, about 35 minutes (the internal temperature should register at least 190°F/88°C on an instant-read thermometer). Let cool in the pan set on a wire rack for 10 minutes. Turn out the bread to cool completely before slicing.

ENGLISH MUFFIN BREAD

Makes one 9 x 5-inch/23 x 12.7 cm loaf

I FIRMLY BELIEVE THAT ALMOST ANY BREAD CAN BE IMPROVED UPON BY TOAST-ING it and slicking it with salted butter. This bread, basically a giant English muffin with enough nooks and crannies to make Mr. Thomas blush, is intended to be baked specifically for the purpose of toasting it the next day. And happily, as yeasted bread recipes go, it doesn't get much more low-ef-fort than this. In my travels across the region, I most often saw this bread baked in an old-fashioned German *Rehrucken* (crimp loaf pan), which I love the look of; it's often found as a hinged, cylindrical pan with pretty ridges all around its circumference, and flat ends so that every last slice is identical in shape and size. I managed to snag one of these pans at a thrift store, but a regular loaf pan works just as well.

Nonstick cooking spray for pan

3 tablespoons/30 g yellow cornmeal, divided

2¼ teaspoons instant yeast

⅓ cup/75 g warm water (110° to 115°F/43° to 46°C)

1 tablespoon granulated sugar, divided

3 cups/384 g unbleached all-purpose flour, spooned and leveled

1½ teaspoons fine sea salt

¼ teaspoon baking soda

1 cup/225 g well-shaken buttermilk, at room temperature*

2 tablespoons plus 1 teaspoon/32 g vegetable oil

1 tablespoon unsalted butter, melted

*It's very important that the buttermilk not be fridge-cold, so that the dough can rise well.

Lightly spray a 9 x 5-inch/23 x 12.7 cm metal loaf pan with nonstick cooking spray, wiping away any excess that pools in the edges of the pan. Dust the pan all over with about 2 tablespoons of the cornmeal, tapping out the excess.

In a small bowl, whisk together the yeast, warm water, and 1 teaspoon of the sugar. Let rest for a couple of minutes.

In the bowl of an electric mixer fitted with the paddle attachment, whisk together the flour, the remaining 2 teaspoons of sugar, salt, and baking soda. On low speed, stir in the buttermilk, oil, and finally the yeast mixture. Increase the speed to high and mix for 1 minute, stopping halfway through to scrape down the bowl. The dough will be soft and sticky. Scrape the dough out into the prepared pan. Oil your hands lightly and pat the dough gently and evenly into the pan. Sprinkle the top with the remaining tablespoon of cornmeal. Cover with plastic wrap and let rise until doubled and the dough comes about 1 inch from the top of the pan, about 1 hour.

During the rise, position a rack to the center of the oven and preheat it to 400°F/200°C. Bake the bread until golden and risen, with a hollow sound when tapped in the center, 22 to 25 minutes (the internal temperature should register at least 190°F/88°C on an instant-read thermometer). Turn out the bread onto a wire rack. Brush lightly all over with the melted butter. Let cool completely before slicing.

A BLUEPRINT FOR SAVORY BREAD PUDDING

Serves 8

When the British came to the Midwest in the late 1700s, they also brought the kind of comfort food the region is now known for, such as the Cornish pasties on page 256, the glorious tradition of a roast dinner—meat, potatoes, vegetables, and gravy all together—and one of my favorite building block recipes of all time, bread pudding. Bread pudding is one of those marvelous kitchen concepts that's often overlooked, but is excellent to keep top-of-mind, because it's less about having a real "recipe" than it is about having a wonderful blank canvas at which to throw just about anything you're craving, or trying to get rid of. It can be sweet and dessertlike, with sugars and chocolate and fruits, but my favorite way to have bread pudding is to make it savory. Add a bright little side salad and a glass of wine, and I need nothing else in this life.

With a 1-pound/455 g loaf of bread (a little past its prime is actually ideal), six large eggs, and 3 cups/675 g of liquid dairy with at least some percentage of fat (milk, half-and-half, cream, a combination of all three, why not?), you are well on your way to a main dish or unctuous side that's at once creamy, crispy, soft, comforting, and seriously thrifty.

FIRST, GET YOURSELF A GOOD BAKING VESSEL. Bread pudding likes a nice deep, insulated baking dish rather than a metal pan. You want something in the neighborhood of 2½ to 3 quarts/2.4 to 2.8 L, square, round, oval, whatever. Spray the vessel with non-stick cooking spray or butter it generously. Set your oven rack to the center and preheat your oven to 375°F/190°C.

After you've got your building blocks in place, **THINK ABOUT YOUR ADD-INS**, usually based on what you've already got knocking around. Will your bread pudding be carnivorous? Bacon, ham, leftover poultry, ground beef, sausage—all great candidates. Just make sure they're cooked first.

IF YOU'RE INCORPORATING VEGETABLES, it's nice to cook them just a little first as well, with a quick softening in olive oil or butter or both, and a little salt and pepper. Onion, garlic, scallions, mushrooms, peppers of all sorts—these are some of my favorite savory add-ins. I also love a broccoli and/or cauliflower and cheese version for a nice vegetarian option, and in that case, I give the florets a few minutes in a steamer basket, just to tenderize them. Allow your cooked mixtures to cool to room temperature.

SAVORY BREAD PUDDING IS AN EXCELLENT VEHICLE FOR CHEESE. You want about 1½ cups/180 g of shredded, grated, or diced cheeses in total. Throw in multiple types to clean out that fridge drawer, or be more intentional with sharp Cheddar, Gruyère, Parmesan, fontina . . . the possibilities are endless. Reserve a little for sprinkling on top.

FOR SEASONINGS, START WITH SALT AND FRESHLY GROUND PEPPER, AND ADD FLAIR TO YOUR LIKING. Since you're whisking a batter with raw eggs, it's tough to "season to taste," but I tend to season a batch of this size with about ½ teaspoon of salt and a few grinds of black or white pepper. I love lots of fresh herbs in bread pudding, especially fresh thyme, sage, or parsley, but lesser amounts of stronger, dried herbs can work out just fine.

THEN COMES THE MARRIAGE OF ALL THE ELEMENTS. In the biggest bowl you've got, whisk together the eggs, milk, and about ½ teaspoon salt until completely smooth (the salt will help denature the proteins in the eggs and liquefy them). Tear or cut the bread into 1-inch/2.5 cm chunks—leave the crusts on or not, depending on how hard the crust is. If it's a soft loaf all over, use the whole thing. I like to use about half of the crust from a crusty artisan-type loaf, so there's plenty of texture and more bread to soak up the custard. No crust, and you'll have a much creamier, puddinglike result. Totally up to you. Let the bread soak for 5 to 10 minutes.

Fold in your cooked meats, vegetables, cheeses, and/or herbs and spices, including a few grinds of black pepper (remember that you added salt at the beginning with the milk and eggs).

TURN OUT THE BREAD PUDDING MIXTURE INTO THE PREPARED BAKING DISH. Sprinkle the top with a little extra cheese. Bake, uncovered, until puffed and golden and a knife inserted into the center comes out clean—anywhere from 45 to 60 minutes, depending on the size and depth of your baking dish. Let cool on a wire rack for 15 minutes before serving.

CHEESY, HERBY CASSEROLE BREAD

Serves 8

LEONA SCHNUELLE OF CRAB ORCHARD, NEBRASKA, ABSOLUTELY SLAYED AT THE 1960 Pillsbury Bake-Off with her Dilly Casserole Bread, winning the whole dang competition, and it soon became a sensation with home cooks all across the country. It's the simplest of yeast breads that can still be found in many a vintage recipe box, making its "no-knead" technique cool before no-knead bread was even a thing among modern food lovers.

As it happens, the original recipe is easy to pump up with bolder, fresher flavors. The original version calls for dried minced onion and dill seeds, which have a camphor-esque quality that isn't my favorite flavor. Instead, I prefer to load up my dough with lots of scallions, fresh dill, and a tiny spoonful of dried dill, which gives you more of a layered dill flavor. Rounding it all out with a lift of lemon zest, a handful of Parmesan, and crunchy sea salt truly makes buttering optional with this recipe remix.

2¼ teaspoons instant yeast

¼ cup/57 g warm water (110° to 115°F/43° to 46°C)

1 cup/240 g 4 percent milk-fat cottage cheese

2 tablespoons granulated sugar

1 tablespoon extra-virgin olive oil

1 large egg

1 teaspoon fine sea salt

¼ teaspoon baking soda

⅓ cup/32 g minced scallions

⅓ cup/16 g finely chopped fresh dill leaves

3 tablespoons/15 g finely grated Parmesan cheese

1 teaspoon dried dill

Grated zest of ½ medium-size lemon

2½ cups/320 g unbleached all-purpose flour, spooned and leveled

Nonstick cooking spray for casserole dish

Flaky sea salt, such as Maldon, for sprinkling (optional)

In the bowl of an electric mixer, whisk together the yeast and warm water. Let rest for 5 minutes, then add all the ingredients, except the flour, cooking spray, and flaky sea salt, and whisk to blend well. Add the flour to the bowl, and fit the bowl on the mixer with the paddle attachment. Mix on low speed until a stiff but sticky dough forms, about 1 minute. Scrape the bowl down well and form it into a loose ball in the bottom of the bowl. Cover the bowl with plastic wrap. Let rise in the refrigerator for 8 hours or overnight, or in a warm place for 1 hour, until doubled.

Coat a 2-quart/1.9 L round ceramic casserole dish with nonstick cooking spray. Remove the dough from the bowl and shape it into a tight round: Using both hands, pull sides of dough underneath the ball of dough, rotating it as you pull and tuck the bottom of the ball underneath. Keep repeating the motion until the dough forms a tight, smooth round on top with no visible creases. Flip the ball over in 1 hand, and use all the fingers of the other hand to firmly draw in and pinch together all the ragged edges in 1 spot in the center, resembling a drawstring purse. Flip the dough ball over and place it in the prepared casserole dish. Let rise in a warm place until doubled—if your first rise was in the refrigerator, this will take about 1½ hours; if it was a warm first rise, 45 minutes.

Position a rack to the center of the oven and preheat it to 350°F/180°C. Sprinkle the top of the dough with flaky sea salt, if you like. Bake until the bread is deeply golden and sounds hollow when tapped in the center, 45 to 50 minutes (the internal temperature should register at 200°F/93°C on an instant-read thermometer). Let cool in the dish for 5 minutes before turning out onto a wire rack to cool further. Slice and serve while the bread is still slightly warm.

TIP › *When it comes to proofing the bread for the first rise, you have two options. You can mix the dough in the morning or even the night before baking, and allow it to have a cold rise in the refrigerator for at least 8 hours, which gives the bread impressive flavor. Or, if you're short on time, you can get by just fine with a warm rise of 1 hour before shaping and resting a second time.*

BROWN IRISH SODA BREAD

Makes one 8-inch/20 cm round

BESTED IN POPULATION ONLY BY THE GERMANS, THE IRISH WERE—AND CONTINUE to be—one of the most important immigrant groups that helped shape the Midwest. Irish soda bread is the perfect example of a poor country doing a lot with very little, and in a very efficient way. Soda bread is actually a quick bread, no yeast and very little handling required. In relation to the long history of Ireland, soda bread is actually a fairly recent development, since baking soda wasn't introduced there until the 1840s. The cross sliced into the top of a round loaf of soda bread is said to have been introduced to ward off the devil and protect the household.

I have a big love of Irish soda bread, partly because we had it every St. Patrick's Day, when Gramma would cook a batch of corned beef and really play up the whole Irish branch of our family tree, if only for a day. The soda bread we had was store-bought and an example of what's found most often in midwestern bakeries—the sweeter, white-flour variety, with a soft, custard-colored interior and currants or raisins added. And without the dried fruit, this is thought to be the most traditional kind of soda bread, since Irish flour is made of soft wheat and yields light, cakey baked goods. But soda bread can take on many forms and flavors, and even bend to the savory side, built on the simple formula of some type of flour, baking soda, salt, and an acidic dairy ingredient, such as buttermilk or yogurt.

2 cups/256 g all-purpose flour, spooned and leveled, plus more for dusting

2 cups/240 g 100 percent whole-wheat flour, spooned and leveled

1½ teaspoons baking soda

2 teaspoons finely chopped fresh rosemary

1 teaspoon fine sea salt

½ teaspoon freshly ground black pepper

4 tablespoons/57 g cold unsalted butter, cut into ½-inch/1.25 cm pieces

2 cups/450 g cold, well-shaken buttermilk, plus more for brushing

1 tablespoon honey

1 teaspoon flaky sea salt, such as Maldon, for sprinkling (optional)

Position a rack to the center of the oven and preheat it to 425°F/220°C. Line a 12 x 17-inch/30 x 43 cm baking sheet with parchment paper and dust it with flour.

In a large bowl, whisk together the all-purpose and whole wheat flour, baking soda, rosemary, salt, and pepper. Add the butter pieces to the flour mixture. Using your fingertips, rub the butter into the flour mixture until it resembles a coarse meal.

In a large measuring cup, whisk together the buttermilk and honey. Make a well in the center of the flour mixture and pour in the buttermilk mixture. First use a large flexible spatula, and then your hands, to mix the dough into a sticky mass—don't overmix.

Turn out the dough onto the prepared baking sheet and shape it into a 6-inch/15 cm ball. Use a large, floured sharp knife to slice a deep X across the top of the bread, about halfway through the ball. Lightly brush the loaf with buttermilk. Sprinkle with flaky sea salt, if you wish.

Bake at 425°F/220°C for 15 minutes. Lower the oven temperature to 350°F/180°C and bake for 30 to 35 minutes more, or until the bread is deeply golden and sounds hollow when tapped. Remove the bread from the pan and let cool on a wire rack.

PULLMAN LOAF

Makes one 13 x 4-inch/33 x 10 cm loaf

IN OUR WHOLE-GRAIN, RUSTIC, ARTISAN BREAD-OBSESSED WORLD, I FEEL THAT white sandwich bread gets the shaft far too often. I mean, yes, the squishy, plasticky type you can form into Ping-Pong ball facsimiles isn't exactly great eating when there are better-tasting, higher-quality breads just about everywhere these days. But do not overlook the simple pleasure of a straight-forward, milk-based, tight-crumbed white bread, especially if it comes along with a great story.

Also known as *pain de mie*, this bread has European roots going back to the 1800s, where bakers made it in specially made lidded pans that would trap steam and turn out a loaf with minimal crust. The resulting loaves turned out perfectly square and soft. In the Midwest, this style of bread is known as Pullman loaf, and got its name during the railroad boom of the mid- to late 1800s. The Pullman Car Company was an Illinois-based leader in the industry, turning traveling by rail into an experi-ence, complete with comfortable sleeping and dining cars. The square-shaped pain de mie was a superb fit for the compact kitchens on the trains; without a domed top, twice as many loaves could stack into the smallest of storage spaces.

¼ cup/57 g warm water (110°to 115°F/43° to 46°C)

1 teaspoon granulated sugar

2¼ teaspoons instant yeast

4¼ cups/544 g unbleached all-purpose flour, spooned and leveled, plus more for dusting

1½ teaspoons fine sea salt

1¼ cups/280 g warm whole milk (110° to 115°F/43° to 46°C)

3 tablespoons/42 g unsalted butter, melted

Nonstick cooking spray or oil for bowl and pan

In a bowl of an electric mixer, whisk together the warm water, sugar, and yeast. Let rest for 5 minutes.

Add the flour and salt to the mixer bowl. Pour in the milk and melted butter. Stir with a wooden spoon until a shaggy dough forms. Fit the mixer with a dough hook and knead the dough on medium speed until soft, smooth, and elastic, when the dough is clinging to the hook but moving cleanly off the sides of the bowl, 5 to 6 minutes.

Briefly remove the dough from the bowl, spray it with nonstick cooking spray or oil it lightly, and replace the dough in it. Cover with plastic wrap and allow it to rest until doubled in size, 30 to 45 minutes.

Lightly grease a 13 x 4-inch/33 x 10 cm Pullman pan and its lid with or nonstick cooking spray or oil.

Generously flour a work surface. Scrape the dough onto the work surface and gently press out the air, shaping the dough into a roughly 10 x 7-inch/25 x 18 cm rectangle as you do so. With the short end closest to you, fold the longer left side into the center of the rectangle, pressing the seam tightly. Repeat with the longer right side. Repeat this folding into the center with the 2 short sides. Rotate the dough 90 degrees so 1 longer side is now closest to you. Fold and press the longer sides into the center once more. Flip the dough over—you should now have a nice smooth loaf. Gently and evenly roll the dough back and forth to form a 13-inch/33 cm log. Place the dough in the prepared loaf pan.

Cover with plastic wrap and let the dough rise until in warm spot until it's 1 inch/2.5 cm from the lip of the pan, no higher, about 45 minutes. Overproofing will lead to a collapsed loaf.

Position a rack to the center of the oven, and preheat it to 400°F/200°C. Slide the cover onto the pan. Bake for 25 minutes. Remove the cover and bake for 20 minutes more, or until the loaf sounds hollow when tapped (the internal temperature should register at least 190°F/88°C on an instant-read thermometer).

Turn out the bread onto a wire rack and let cool completely before slicing. Store in an airtight container for up to 3 days.

NOTE > *To sample this taste of the past, with its golden crust and tender, soft-spongy interior that cries out to make your next picnic sandwich the very best it can be, you'll need a Pullman pan. The pans are not terribly expensive, plentiful online and in kitchen stores. The purchase is worth it for this wonderfully simple, flavorful bread. Alternatively, you can shape the dough into a 9-inch loaf and use 9 x 5-inch/23 x 12.7 cm metal loaf pan. Let the dough rise a final time until it's 1 inch (2.5 cm) over the lip of the pan. Bake, uncovered, for 35 to 40 minutes, tenting the loaf with aluminum foil halfway through the baking time.*

SMOKY CHEDDAR-CRUSTED CORNISH PASTIES

Makes 6 pasties

IN THE UPPER PENINSULA OF MICHIGAN, PASTIES ARE ESSENTIAL. AND WHEN YOU'RE taking in the stunning landscape, so beautiful you'll feel as if you're in trapped in a Monet, the hand-held savory pies just feel right. Cornish pasties have British roots, first arriving in the Midwest in the late 1700s. But it was the mining boom in the Upper Midwest that made the grab-and-go, satiating pies a mainstay, providing hearty, portable sustenance during a day of hard labor.

In my highly scientific polling of Michiganders, there are a few must-haves when it comes to a proper Cornish pasty. There must be beef, which can be ground or, as here, sirloin chopped finely. You might get away with some pork for its flavor, but don't talk about it too much. Onion is a must, as is rutabaga and potato. There are two camps, one that believes in serving the pasty with gravy, the other with ketchup. Pretty much every Yooper would give me the side-eye for making mine with this Cheddar-and-smoked-paprika crust, but that's a delicious risk I'm willing to take.

CRUST:

Ingredients for 1 double batch My Favorite Pie Crust (page 74)

6 ounces/170 g extra-sharp Cheddar cheese, coarsely grated

1 teaspoon smoked Spanish paprika

FILLING:

1/2 pound/225 g sirloin, cut into 1/2-inch cubes

1/2 pound/225 g ground pork

1/2 cup/75 g diced rutabaga (1/4-inch/6 mm pieces)

1/2 cup/75 g diced potato (1/4-inch/6 mm pieces)

1/3 cup/50 g diced carrot (1/4-inch/6 mm pieces)

1/3 cup/25 g finely sliced scallions, white and light green parts

1 heaping teaspoon tomato paste*

1 large garlic clove

3/4 teaspoon fine sea salt

1/4 teaspoon freshly ground black pepper

1/8 teaspoon cayenne pepper

ASSEMBLY:

1 large egg

1 tablespoon water

Pinch of fine sea salt

All-purpose flour for dusting

*Buy the kind in the tube so small amounts like these aren't annoying.

Prepare the crust: Add the cheese and paprika to the unprocessed dry ingredients for the pie crust in the bowl of a food processor and process until the mixture resembles a coarse meal. Make the rest of the pie crust recipe as directed on pages 74–75. Gently knead the dough several times to bring it together into a claylike ball, working it a little longer than you normally would, to develop a touch of gluten that will help hold the pasties together. Divide the dough into 6 equal portions. Shape each into a disk, and wrap each tightly in plastic wrap. Chill the dough for at least 2 hours.

Prepare the filling: Combine all the filling ingredients in a medium bowl.

Assemble the pasties: Position a rack to the center of the oven and preheat it to 400°F/200°C.

In a small cup, beat together the egg, water, and salt.

On a lightly floured surface, roll each piece of dough into an 8-inch/20 cm circle. Divide the filling equally among the circles, placing the filling on half (1 semicircle) of each piece. Brush the perimeter of the circle with egg wash. Fold the other side over the filling, and crimp the edges together with a fork. Place the pasties on an unlined, rimmed baking sheet. Slice a few vents in the top of each pasty. Brush lightly all over with egg wash. Bake for 15 minutes. Lower the oven temperature to 350°F/180°C and continue to bake until golden all over and browned and crisp on the bottoms, 35 to 40 minutes more. Let the pasties cool briefly on a wire rack before serving.

BIG, SOFT PRETZELS

Makes six 5-inch/12.5 cm pretzels

I WAS VERY MUCH A PART OF THE MALL GENERATION IN MY JUNIOR HIGH AND HIGH school years. During the former, I saved my pennies for Lisa Frank notebooks, fruity-fragranced erasers, and stickers galore at the Hello Kitty store. In the latter years, I was an Abercrombie and Fitch obsessor, and hoarded Henleys and bulky sweaters, while dreaming of a boyfriend who smelled of their heady cologne and played lacrosse. In both eras, I never left the mall without buying a big, soft pretzel with pebbles of chalk white salt. I also found time for pretzel-eating in school cafeterias, and it often served as my lunch, with a chilled can of Cherry Coke on the side. In the all-things-fat-free craze of the 1990s, I really thought I was the pinnacle of health with that one.

These days, I don't eat nearly as many soft pretzels as I should, and I'm betting you don't, either. When Oktoberfest rolls around in the Midwest, the pretzel making at many bakeries goes into over-drive, rivaling that of any mall kiosk, a frenzy of twisting, boiling, and baking. But it turns out that they're so fun to make at home, even a small batch is worth the effort. If you really want to have a taste of the Midwest, you'll serve these with some beer cheese soup for dipping.

DOUGH:

1 cup plus 2 tablespoons/254 g warm water (110° to 115°F/43° to 46°C)

2¼ teaspoons instant yeast

1 teaspoon granulated sugar

3 tablespoons/42 g unsalted European-style butter, melted

3½ cups/448 g bread flour, spooned and leveled, plus more for dusting

1 teaspoon fine sea salt

Nonstick cooking spray or oil for bowl

BOILING SOLUTION:

2 quarts water

¼ cup/72 g baking soda

2 tablespoons granulated sugar

FINISHING:

1 large egg

1 tablespoon water

Pinch of fine sea salt

Coarse salt for sprinkling

1 tablespoon unsalted European-style butter, melted

Prepare the dough: In the bowl of an electric mixer, whisk together the warm water, instant yeast, sugar, and melted butter. Let the mixture rest for 5 minutes. Add the flour and salt. Use a wooden spoon to stir the mixture into a shaggy dough.

Fit the bowl onto the mixer with the dough hook. Knead the dough until smooth and elastic and clearing the sides of the bowl, 6 to 7 minutes. Lightly flour a work surface, scrape the dough out of the bowl, and

knead the dough several times by hand. Form the dough into a ball. Spray the mixer bowl with nonstick cooking spray or oil it lightly and place the dough in it. Cover the bowl tightly with plastic wrap and allow the dough to rise until doubled in size, about 45 minutes.

Position a rack to the center of the oven and preheat it to 450°F/230°C. Line a 12 x 17-inch/30 x 43 cm baking sheet with parchment paper.

Using masking tape, mark off a 24-inch/61 cm length along a work surface. Lightly flour the surface and turn onto the dough out it. Divide the dough into 6 equal portions. Roll and stretch each piece of dough into a thin rope, about 24 inches/ 61 cm in length. The dough may be quite resistant to stretching in the beginning, so it's easiest to first shape all the pieces into chunkier tube shapes, and then rotate through the pieces a few times, gradually lengthening each piece into a rope and allowing each portion to relax a bit before stretching it out further. Twist each rope into a pretzel: start by creating a U shape. Grasp 1 end in each hand. Twist together twice, exchanging the ends between hands. Lay the ends at the inside bottom curve of the pretzel, pressing them down firmly. Lay them on the prepared baking sheet.

Prepare the boiling solution: In a 3- to 4-quart/2.8 to 3.75 L saucepan, combine the water, baking soda, and sugar. Bring the mixture to a boil over high heat, then lower the heat to a simmer. Working with 1 pretzel at a time, gently lower each pretzel into the boiling solution, cooking 20 seconds per side. Remove each pretzel from the liquid with a slotted spatula (a fish spatula works well), and allow it to drain for a moment before placing it back on the baking sheet. Once all the pretzels have been boiled, in a small cup, beat together the egg, water, and salt until liquefied. Brush the pretzels lightly with the egg wash, then sprinkle with coarse salt.

Bake until deeply golden, shiny, and firm on the outsides, 12 to 15 minutes. Let cool briefly, then brush lightly with the melted butter. Serve warm.

ITALIAN BREAD

Makes 1 large loaf

GROWING UP, IT WAS MY MATERNAL GRANDFATHER, JERRY FOROPOULOS, WHO did much of the cooking for our big, loud extended family. It was he of strong hugs, Memphis roots, and thanks to his Greek and Sicilian genes, bearer of that insane last name—who ran the stove like a DJ, multiple pots and pans going at once, like his famous red gravy (never "sauce") clattering with pork neck bones. It was umami-packed before umami was a thing, with a flavor no one in our family has ever been able to replicate.

Grampa passed away suddenly at the beginning of my eighth grade year, the first real, important, heartbreaking death I experienced. These days, pots of his red gravy appear in my dreams whenever I've spent a little too much time working and not enough time with family. I always wake up a little hungry, knowing it was him, sending me that message in a way I understand.

During those family dinners in my formative years, the main dish was mostaccioli with that red gravy, and let's just forget the salad, okay? Alongside would be a scratched wooden bread board with thick slices of Italian bread and knife-shattered golden crumbs, manna from heaven with a combination of thin, crisp crust and a stellar, airy, almost cottony interior. There's simply no better utensil for squeegeeing your pasta plate, elbow to elbow around the table.

3/4 cup plus 2 tablespoons/ 197 g warm water (110° to 115°F/43° to 46°C)

2 tablespoons olive oil, divided

2¼ teaspoons instant yeast

1½ teaspoons granulated sugar

2½ cups/320 g unbleached all-purpose flour, spooned and leveled, plus more for dusting

1 teaspoon fine sea salt, plus a pinch for egg wash

3 tablespoons/24 g yellow cornmeal

1 large egg white

1 tablespoon water

In the bowl of an electric mixer, whisk together the warm water, 1 tablespoon of the olive oil, and the yeast and sugar. Let rest for 5 minutes. Add the flour and salt. Stir with a wooden spoon until a shaggy dough forms. Fit the dough hook onto the mixer. Knead on medium speed for 5 to 6 minutes, or until the dough is smooth and elastic. Cover the bowl with plastic wrap and allow the dough to rest for about 30 minutes.

Lightly flour a work surface. Turn out the dough and pat it into a rough 10 x 15-inch/25 x 38 cm rectangle. Tightly roll up the dough lengthwise, as you would for cinnamon rolls (see page 30 for more details). Pinch the seam tightly, as well as the 2 ends, and tuck the ends under to form a smooth, slightly oblong loaf.

Line a 12 x 17-inch/30 x 43 cm baking sheet with parchment paper and scatter it with the cornmeal. Lay the loaf, seam-side down, on the pan. Brush the top and sides with the remaining tablespoon of olive oil. Cover with plastic wrap and refrigerate for at least 3 hours, or up to 24 hours ahead.

Position a rack to the center of the oven and preheat it to 425°F/220°C. Pull the loaf from the refrigerator and rest at room temperature for 15 minutes. Using a thin, sharp knife, cut 3 or 4 diagonal slashes in the top of the loaf. Bake for 10 minutes. Reduce the heat to 400°F/200°C. Bake for 15 more minutes. In a small cup, beat the egg white with the water and a pinch of sea salt. Remove the pan from the oven. Brush the loaf with the egg wash. Return the pan to the oven and bake until golden and crisp on the outside, about 5 minutes more (the internal temperature should register at least 190°F/88°C on an instant-read thermometer). Let cool for at least 15 minutes before serving.

BLUE CHEESE AND SCALLION CORNBREAD

Serves 8

WHEN TEMPERATURES PLUMMET AND WE ENTER SOUP-, STEW-, AND CHILI-MAKING weather, cornbread becomes a bit of a necessity. Much as with the bran muffins on page 63, I grew up loving Jiffy brand cornbread mix from the box, and I wouldn't turn my nose up at it today. But when you make it from scratch, you can get the ratio of cornmeal to flour and sugar just right, and cram lots of blue cheese and scallions into it. And yes, southern cornbread disciples, I said flour and sugar—this recipe is unapologetically Yankee-style. Without the cheese and scallions, this is a great foundation recipe to have in your back pocket whenever a meal calls out for side of cornbread.

Nonstick cooking spray for pan

1 cup/165 g medium-grind, degerminated yellow cornmeal

1 cup/128 g unbleached all-purpose flour, spooned and leveled

1/4 cup/50 g granulated sugar

1 tablespoon plus 1 teaspoon baking powder

1/4 teaspoon baking soda

1 teaspoon fine sea salt

4 ounces/113 g blue cheese, crumbled, divided*

1/3 cup/25 g finely sliced scallions (2 to 3 large scallions, white and light green parts)

1 cup/240 g full-fat sour cream or whole-milk Greek yogurt

3 large eggs, at room temperature

3 tablespoons/42 g unsalted butter, melted and cooled

3 tablespoons/42g vegetable oil

My first cheese choice here is Maytag blue—Iowa's pride and joy, salty and funky and piquant. If I can't find it, I look for a firm, crumbly, unpasteurized cow's milk blue that's got a spicy kick to it, such as Gorgonzola Piccante, a.k.a. Mountain Gorgonzola.

Position an oven rack to the center of the oven and preheat it to 400°F/200°C. Spray an 8-inch/20 cm square metal baking pan with nonstick cooking spray.

In a large bowl, whisk together the cornmeal, flour, sugar, baking powder, baking soda, and salt. Mix in three quarters of the cheese and all of the scallions

with your fingertips, to keep them from clumping together.

In a medium bowl, whisk together the sour cream, eggs, melted butter, and oil until smooth. Pour the wet ingredients into dry and fold gently until there are no more dry pockets in the batter—don't overmix. Pour the batter into the prepared pan and smooth the top. Sprinkle with the remaining cheese crumbles. Let the batter rest in the pan for 15 minutes.

Bake until golden and a toothpick inserted into the center comes out with moist crumbs, about 25 minutes. Let the bread cool slightly in the pan before turning it out, slicing, and serving. It's best served the day it's made.

CHAPTER 10
WINTER HOLIDAYS

BORN IN THE LAST YEARS OF THE 1970S, MY CHRISTMAS MEMORIES begin with the vintage cool of Sinatra and Bing Crosby on vinyl, Crown Royal in the grown-ups' glasses, and lots of scratch-baked treats. With just a few years' time, the memories evolve into a 1980s rainbow explosion of plastic toys and prepackaged Christmas sweets, as the number of family members, namely children (my first cousins), began to increase.

But it's the earliest Christmases that cemented my opinions of what the holidays ought to be, and what I go back to in my mental files each December. In that living room in my grandparents' 1950s ranch house in Rolling Meadows, Illinois, the lights are low, some walls dark wood-paneled, others covered in chaotic, vermilion paisley wallpaper. The Christmas tree bowed under the weight of multicolored lights, ornaments crafted by little hands from salt dough and pipe cleaners, and those silvery shreds of tinsel no one seems to use anymore. (Was it found to be cancerous, much like everything else? Or did people just get tired of the beaters of their vacuums getting suffocated between December and January?)

Additional decor included a glossy green, hand-painted ceramic tree, lit up from within and covered in confetti-like colored lights, a DIY project that was all the rage in the '70s (I recently rescued one from a flea market to put this memory back in my own house). A bright red velvet bow was stuck on each of six framed 8 x 10 school photos that hung on the wall adjacent to the tree, one for my mother, frozen permanently as a high school senior, and the rest for her older brother and four younger siblings. In the kitchen, there was the terry cloth hand towel with a crocheted handle, my favorite bit of Christmas kitsch emblazoned with "Merry Merry" on one side and "Happy Happy" on the other. One could enjoy its festivity and usefulness well into January by simply reversing the way it hung from the sink cabinet.

The Christmas treats I remember the most, of course, are the cookies. Archway Cherry Nougats (RIP) were the thing I whined for the most at the store. But there were plenty of scratch goodies, too—shiny gold Hostess fruitcake tins, the fruitcake long since eaten, filled with Christmas cookies. Toll House chocolate chip cookies no larger than two or three bites, and crisp, minty meringues tinted pale green and studded with tiny bits of chocolate, which we called "forgotten cookies." The star of the show for me, though, were my Gramma's sugar cookies, sandy, crunchy, deep with buttery flavor, and always scattered with coarse rainbow sanding sugar, which may not have been textbook Christmassy in its colors, but it was perfect to me. It was in a corner of the front room, crouched low with greedy handfuls of cookies, that I listened to the strains of Andy Williams coming from the hi-fi, wondering what gifts I might score.

Thinking back to those years, it seems the outside air was colder, and the insides warmer. Christmas break was guaranteed to be snowy, and our little bodies would be alternately damp with snow and damp with sweat, our feet stuffed into plastic sandwich bags inside our boots as waterproof insurance, wool itching on our wrists and foreheads as we pulled our sleds up to the top of the hill once more. It was a simpler, greedier, more delicious time.

WHITE FRUITCAKE

Makes one 10-inch/25 cm cake

GLEAMING WITH ROYAL BLUE, RED, AND GOLD, ONE OF MY FAVORITE BITS OF Christmas frippery are the old tins from Hostess holiday fruitcakes past, with their signature cameo in the center of each lid. Maybe you've seen these now-vintage tins in your grandmother's house, holding sewing supplies or any number of odds and ends. But for me, seeing them as a kid meant holiday baking was about to begin, with the tins at the ready to store all of the delicious results. I'm convinced Christmas cookies taste better after being stored in one.

The Hostess brand, still known for Twinkies, Wonder Bread, and the like, also built a reputation for its Christmas fruitcakes way back in the day, as far back as the 1920s. When the Continental Baking Company bought Indianapolis-based Taggart Baking Company in 1925, it got the Hostess brand in the deal. Continental operated an enormous commercial bakery in Chicago, which employed one of my great-grandmothers for a time, and continued the fruitcake tradition for decades, usually sold in those aforementioned tins.

The fruitcake that came in them was the furthest thing from the heavy, boozy brown bricks that have become a Christmas punchline. Hostess's holiday fruitcake was a "white fruitcake," more like a buttery pound cake packed with nuts and candied fruit, and infinitely tastier. This recipe is my ode to that cake, and those oh-so-beautiful tins.

Nonstick cooking spray for pan

1½ cups/180 g golden raisins

3 tablespoons/42 g bourbon or dark rum

6 ounces/170 g candied cherries, halved

4 ounces/113 g candied orange peel, chopped into ¼-inch/6 mm bits

4 ounces/113 g candied pineapple, chopped into ¼-inch/6 mm bits

2 cups plus 1 tablespoon/264 g unbleached all-purpose flour, spooned and leveled, divided

1¼ teaspoons baking powder

1 teaspoon fine sea salt

½ teaspoon freshly grated nutmeg

6 large eggs, separated

1 cup/200 g granulated sugar, divided

1 cup/225 g unsalted butter, at room temperature

1½ teaspoons pure vanilla extract

¾ teaspoon pure almond extract

⅔ cup/160 g heavy whipping cream, at room temperature

4 ounces/113 g pecan halves, toasted and broken into ½-inch/1.25 cm pieces

Position an oven rack to the lower third of the oven and preheat it to 325°F/170°C. Spray a 10-inch/25 cm tube pan with nonstick cooking spray.

In a small, microwave-safe bowl, combine the raisins and bourbon. Cover the bowl with plastic wrap. Microwave on **HIGH** for 1 minute. Set aside to soak for at least 10 minutes.

In a medium bowl, toss all the candied fruit bits with 1 tablespoon of the flour to separate the pieces.

In another medium bowl, whisk together the remaining flour and the baking powder, salt, and nutmeg.

In the bowl of an electric mixer fitted with the whisk attachment, beat the egg whites to soft peaks on medium-high speed. Slowly add ½ cup/100 g of the sugar, and beat until the meringue reaches stiff peaks. Transfer to a clean bowl and set aside.

Fit the bowl back on the mixer (no need to clean it) and change to the paddle attachment. Beat together the butter, remaining ½ cup/100 g of sugar, and the vanilla and almond extract on medium-high speed until very light and fluffy, about 5 minutes. Add the egg yolks, 1 at a time. Slowly pour in the cream. Reduce the mixer speed to low, and stir in about half of the flour mixture. Stir about a third of the meringue into the batter to lighten it up. Then, gently fold in the remaining meringue. Stir in the soaked raisins and any remaining liquid, candied fruit, and nuts. Fold in the remaining flour mixture. Spoon the batter into the prepared pan and smooth evenly.

Bake until a toothpick inserted into the center comes out with just a few moist crumbs, about 1 hour—don't overbake. Cover tightly with aluminum foil, and let cool completely. This cake keeps for up to a week, wrapped tightly in plastic wrap and stored in an airtight container.

APRICOT AND ORANGE BLOSSOM KOLACKY

Makes about 4 dozen kolacky

ONE OF THE FIRST THINGS PEOPLE MENTION WHEN YOU TALK ABOUT CHRISTMAS baking Midwest-style is *kolacky*. Like its Jewish cousin rugelach, kolacky starts with an easy cream cheese dough and is filled with various fillings, usually fruity ones, but they are simpler to form, and they look so pretty tucked into cookie tins.

My kolacky recipe takes advantage of the ease and lightness of a cream cheese dough, and combines it with a scratch-made apricot filling woken up with a tiny bit of orange blossom water—infinitely more flavorful than a canned filling.

DOUGH:

4 ounces/113 g full-fat cream cheese, at room temperature

4 ounces/113 g unsalted butter, at room temperature

3 tablespoons/38 g granulated sugar

1½ teaspoons finely grated orange zest

1 teaspoon pure vanilla extract

½ teaspoon pure almond extract

½ teaspoon fine sea salt

1 cup/128 g unbleached all-purpose flour, spooned and leveled, plus more for dusting

Confectioners' sugar for dusting

FILLING:

1 cup Apricot and Orange Blossom Lekvar (page 302)

Prepare the dough: In the bowl of an electric mixer fitted with the paddle attachment, beat together the cream cheese, butter, and granulated sugar on medium-high speed until light and fluffy, about 3 minutes. Add the orange zest, vanilla, almond extract, and salt, and beat for 1 minute more. Reduce the speed to low and gradually stir in the flour. To avoid overmixing, when a few streaks of flour remain finish mixing the dough by hand. Line a work surface with plastic wrap and turn out the dough onto it. Gently pat the dough into a rectangle and wrap tightly. Chill at least 2 hours, or overnight.

Position an oven rack to the center of the oven and preheat it to 350°F/180°C. Line 2 baking sheets with parchment paper.

To shape the cookies, lightly dust a work surface with flour. Roll out the dough to a rough 13 x 17-inch/33 x 43 cm rectangle, about 1/16-inch/2 mm thick (you need a thin dough to get crisp cookies that don't unfurl while baking). Re-flour the surface as needed to prevent sticking. Use a pizza cutter to trim ½ inch/1.25 cm from all 4 sides to make a clean, straight-edged 12 x 16-inch/30 x 40 cm rectangle. From there, cut the dough into 4 dozen 2-inch/5 cm squares. Place 1 scant teaspoon of filling in the center of each square,

spreading the filling across the square in a diagonal strip. Focusing on the 2 bare corners of the square, fold 1 over the filling, then fold the opposite corner on top, pinching gently to seal.

Place the cookies about 1½ inches/3.8 cm apart on the prepared baking sheets, 2 dozen to a sheet. (Place 1 sheet of cookies in the refrigerator while you bake the first.) Bake until lightly golden at the bottom and edges, about 20 minutes in total, rotating the sheet 180 degrees halfway through the baking time. Let the cookies cool briefly on the baking sheet before transferring them to wire racks to cool completely. Dust generously with confectioners' sugar. Store in an airtight container at room temperature for up to 5 days.

KOLACKY VS. KOLACHE

(A.K.A. "HOW DOES YOUR GRANDMA SAY IT?")

The differences between *kolacky* and *kolache* (page 38) are blurry at best, but important nonetheless. Across the globe, there are over one hundred pronunciations and spelling variations referring to an Eastern European baked good consisting a simple dough and a filling, usually a fruity one, most traditionally prunes or poppy seeds.

Generally speaking, in the Midwest the cookies you see on page 270 are known as kolacky, derivative of the Polish word *kolaczki*, and pronounced "koh-lah-key," "koh-latch-key," and more, mostly depending on whose grandmother is saying it.

Kolache ("koh-lah-chee," or "koh-lashe," among others) are the yeasted, bunlike Czech pastries on page 38. Both are old-world recipes, and came to the Midwest with immigrants who often wanted to re-create a taste of home. Czech immigrant and Chicago resident John Sokol helped make that effort a little easier by inventing a line of cake and pastry fillings made from imported European ingredients. Solo brand filling is still on grocery shelves today, with a decades-old kolacky recipe still printed on its labels, which can be found torn from the cans and tucked into countless midwestern recipe boxes. But Solo fillings were only one part of making kolacky a Christmas cookie staple.

The oldest versions of the cookie are made with a butter-based pastry, similar to a shortcrust. But the overwhelmingly popular, modern way to make kolacky is with a cream cheese dough, which wasn't invented until the 1930s. As a way to promote its cream cheese, Kraft developed the first cream cheese cookie dough, a lightly sweet, flaky, nonleavened dough that caught on like wildfire, particularly with Jewish Americans who were already magicians when it came to cooking and baking with cream cheese. Rugelach, a kolacky cousin and a decidedly American invention, came into existence soon after, and it wasn't long before other pastry-based cookies, like the kolacky you see here, started switching over to cream cheese dough, too.

CHEATER'S FUDGE

Makes 25 squares

NEARLY EVERY SLEEPY LAKESIDE TOWN WITH A PEAK SUMMER TOURIST SEASON has a cheery little shop with canoe-size trays of fudge, selling the portions by weight. Even if you've already had ice cream after a Friday fish fry that covered the entire table, there's still some kind of irresistible magic wrapped in those white waxed paper bags.

The undisputed midwestern champ of fudge is Michigan's Mackinac Island, where windowed shops allow customers to watch the magic of fudge-making. Old-fashioned fudge is a labor of love, and an ode to the science of candy making—the mixture is boiled to 235°F/113°C, cooled to exactly 110°F/43°C, and then manipulated on a marble slab to slowly cool it for a smooth, creamy finished result. It's tricky to do at home, but this vintage shortcut method brought to my attention by my friend Jessie Sheehan is a dangerously delicious way to cure fudge cravings on the fly. Since fudge is as synonymous with summer vacation indulgence as it is holiday treat making and gifting, this is an especially handy one to have in your files. It just as good plain as it is with any number of add-ins, such as toasted nuts, chopped caramel candies, or mini marshmallows.

Nonstick cooking spray for pan

1 pound/453 g bittersweet chocolate (60% cacao), chopped*

2 tablespoons unsalted butter

1 (14-ounce/397 g) can sweetened condensed milk

1/2 teaspoon fine sea salt

1/2 teaspoon pure vanilla extract

1/2 teaspoon flaky sea salt, such as Maldon

1 cup/140 g coarsely chopped walnuts or pecans, toasted and lightly salted**

*High-quality chocolate chips will work in a pinch!

**Immediately after toasting, sprinkle the nuts lightly with fine sea salt.

Line an 8-inch/20 cm square baking pan or similarly sized dish with aluminum foil. Spray the foil with nonstick cooking spray and dab away the excess with a paper towel.

In a large, heatproof bowl, combine the chocolate and butter. Set the bowl over a pan of simmering water over medium-low heat, making sure the water doesn't touch the bowl. Stir until completely melted. Remove the bowl from the heat. Add the sweetened condensed milk, fine sea salt, and vanilla and stir to blend. Stir in the flaky salt and nuts. Spread in the prepared pan and smooth the top.

Refrigerate until set, about 1 hour. Remove the fudge slab from the pan and cut into small squares. Store in an airtight container at room temperature for up to 2 weeks, or in the fridge for 1 month.

GRAMMA'S HEIRLOOM SUGAR COOKIES

Makes about 6 dozen cookies

TAKEN FROM A YELLOWED STRIP OF NEWSPRINT TUCKED INTO A RECIPE BOX FULL of Gramma's Greatest Hits, this is the crispest of sugar cookies, sandy-textured but tender with a gorgeous pale golden color begging for a smattering of sparkling colored sugars and sprinkles, no icing required. It's the first cookie I make every holiday season; when sheets of these start emerging from the oven, Christmas is finally on the way.

Like being a fan of a little-known indie rock band, I grew up thinking this most beloved recipe was special to my family, and in turn that we were geniuses because no one else knew about it, with its unique additions of vegetable oil, confectioners' sugar, and cream of tartar. Imagine my bewilderment when I found this exact recipe in a vintage Illinois state cookbook, titled Mary Todd Lincoln's Sugar Cookies. Yeah, I guess she probably got to this recipe first, then.

DOUGH:

5 cups/640 g unbleached all-purpose flour, spooned and leveled

1 teaspoon baking soda

1 teaspoon cream of tartar

1 teaspoon fine sea salt

1 cup/200 g vegetable oil

2 large eggs, at room temperature

2 teaspoons pure vanilla extract

1 cup/225 g unsalted butter, at room temperature

1 cup/200 g granulated sugar

1 cup/120 g confectioners' sugar

FINISHING THE COOKIES:

½ cup/100 g granulated sugar

Colored coarse sanding sugar or sprinkles for decorating

Position oven racks to the upper and lower thirds of the oven and preheat it to 350°F/180°C. Line 2 baking sheets with parchment paper.

In a large bowl, whisk together the flour, baking soda, cream of tartar, and salt.

In a medium bowl, whisk together the oil, eggs, and vanilla until smooth.

In the bowl of an electric mixer fitted with the paddle attachment, beat together the butter, 1 cup/200 g of the granulated sugar, and the confectioners' sugar on medium speed until fluffy and pale in color, scraping the sides and bottom of the bowl often. Reduce the mixer speed and gradually pour in the egg mixture, beating until the resulting mixture is smooth and somewhat uniform in texture, like a thin cake batter. Reduce the mixer speed to low and gradually add the flour mixture. Mix on low speed until all the dry ingredients are incorporated. The dough will be very soft.

Using a 1-tablespoon scoop, portion out the dough onto the prepared baking sheets, evenly spaced, 12 to a sheet.

To finish the cookies, pour the granulated sugar onto a plate. With your fingertips, ever so slightly dampen the bottom of a drinking glass with water. Dip the glass into the sugar to coat the bottom, and flatten each cookie to about a ¼-inch/6 mm thickness, coating the glass with more sugar in between each cookie. Sprinkle the flattened cookies with the decorative sugar or sprinkles.

Bake for about 13 minutes, rotating the sheets from top to bottom and front to back about halfway through, or until pale golden and just beginning to turn golden brown at the edges. Let cool on the baking sheets for 2 minutes, then transfer to a wire rack and cool completely. Store the cookies in an airtight container at room temperature for up to 1 week.

TIP › *Both the dough and the finished cookies stash away in the freezer like a dream, giving you another reason to make them the first baking project on your list—they wait in delicious patience while you get the other elements of your cookie tins together.*

SIMPLE ROLLED, ICED SUGAR COOKIES

Makes 2 to 3 dozen cookies, depending on size

WHEN YOU HAVE SMALL CHILDREN AT CHRISTMASTIME, COOKIE BAKING IS INEVITABLE. It's as though they come out of the womb expecting to bake cookies come December 1. And they can't just be any cookies. They have to be decorated, iced cookies, rolled and shaped with cutters dug from the nether regions of one's pantry. They are complicated cookies that cause as much mess as delight, between the flour and the icing and the sprinkles, applied with absolutely no technique whatsoever. The whole process equates to mere minutes of chaotic fun. And yet, we let them do it every year, because childhood memories. It's best just to let it happen, and having a good, foolproof recipe like this one means the resulting cookies will taste great, even if they all end up looking like the business end of a piñata.

COOKIES:

2¼ cups/288 g unbleached all-purpose flour, spooned and leveled, plus more for dusting

½ teaspoon baking powder

¼ teaspoon fine sea salt

½ cup/113 g unsalted butter, at room temperature

1 cup/200 g granulated sugar

1 teaspoon pure vanilla extract

¼ teaspoon pure almond extract

2 large eggs, at room temperature

ICING:

1⅓ cups/160 g confectioners' sugar

1 tablespoon meringue powder, or 1 large egg white

¼ teaspoon pure vanilla extract (optional)

2 tablespoons plus 1 teaspoon water

Various food colorings, sanding sugars, jimmies, etc., for decorating

Prepare the cookies: In a large bowl, whisk together the flour, baking powder, and salt. Set aside.

In the bowl of an electric mixer fitted with the paddle attachment, beat together the butter and granulated sugar on medium speed until light and fluffy, about 2 minutes. Beat in the vanilla and almond extract. Beat in the eggs, 1 at a time. With the mixer on low speed, beat in the flour mixture until the dough is soft and smooth. Gather the dough into a ball and pat it into a disk. Wrap in plastic wrap and refrigerate until firm, about 1 hour, or up to 3 days in the refrigerator and 6 months in the freezer.

Position a rack to the center of the oven and preheat it to 375°F/190°C. Line 2 baking sheets with parchment paper.

Lightly flour a work surface. Working with half of the dough at a time, roll it out to about ¼-inch/6 mm thick. Cut into your desired shapes with cookie cutters and place on the prepared baking sheets. Bake 1 sheet at a time, rotating the sheet halfway through baking time, until the cookies just begin to turn golden on the edges, 10 to 12 minutes. Let the cookies cool on the sheets for 2 minutes before transferring them to a wire rack to cool completely.

Prepare the icing: In a medium bowl, combine the confectioners' sugar, meringue powder or egg white, vanilla (if using), and 2 tablespoons of water. With a handheld mixer, beat on medium speed until stiff peaks form. Stir in 1 more teaspoon of water—the icing should be thick enough to be controlled, but still thin enough to spread cleanly across the surface of a cookie without leaving a track when spread. If necessary, add a bit more water to thin the icing.

Ice the cooled cookies and decorate as desired. Allow the icing to dry completely before storing in an airtight container for up to 1 week.

PEANUT BETTER BLOSSOMS

Makes 3 dozen cookies

WHAT WOULD AN AMERICAN CHRISTMAS COOKIE TIN BE WITHOUT THE UBIQUITOUS peanut butter blossom? It doesn't get much more midwestern than that. But at the risk of having to hand in my Illinois resident ID, I'm going to be completely honest: I've never really liked peanut butter blossoms. All too often, the cookie is bland, and the chocolate kiss tends to come off the cookie in one big hunk, completely eliminating the joyful experience of both peanut butter and chocolate in every bite. My version of this homespun classic uses natural crunchy peanut butter for a crave-worthy salty-sweetness, huge peanut flavor and texture. And as adorable as those chocolate kisses are, I think you'll agree they're bested in both flavor and appearance by a quick, glossy, trufflelike chocolate ganache.

The key to making these cookies soft and chewy is to not beat too much air into the dough before the flour is added, so be conservative with both your mixing speed and time, and bake them just until the edges are set and the centers are still very soft.

COOKIES:

1½ cups/192 g unbleached all-purpose flour, spooned and leveled

½ teaspoon baking soda

½ teaspoon fine sea salt

½ cup/113 g unsalted butter, at room temperature

½ cup/113 g firmly packed dark brown sugar

½ cup/100 g granulated sugar

1 teaspoon pure vanilla extract

¾ cup/192 g well-stirred natural, salted crunchy peanut butter

1 large egg, at room temperature

GANACHE FILLING:

3 ounces/75 g semisweet chocolate

3 tablespoons/42 g unsalted butter

Prepare the cookies: Position racks to the upper and lower thirds of the oven, and preheat it 350°F/180°C. Line 2 baking sheets with parchment paper.

In a medium bowl, whisk together the flour, baking soda, and salt.

In the bowl of an electric mixer fitted with the paddle attachment, beat together the butter, brown and granulated sugar, and vanilla on medium-low speed just until smooth and creamy, about 2 minutes. Add the peanut butter and mix until smooth. Beat in the egg. Reduce the speed to low, and gradually stir in the flour mixture until the dough comes together.

Place level tablespoons of dough about 1½ inches/4 cm apart on the prepared baking sheets, 20 per sheet (they don't spread much). Using a small measuring spoon with a deep well, or a melon baller, make a 1-inch/2.5 cm-diameter divot in the center of each cookie. Bake the cookies just until they are firm and turning golden brown at the edges but still very soft in their centers, about 12 minutes, rotating the sheets from front to back and top to bottom about halfway through the baking time. As soon as the cookies come out of the oven, reinforce the indentations with whatever tool you used before. Let the cookies cool for 5 minutes on the pans, then transfer to a wire rack to cool completely.

Prepare the ganache: Place the chocolate and butter in a microwave-safe bowl. Microwave on **HIGH** in 30-second intervals, stirring well, until smooth. Let cool slightly. Transfer the ganache to a small resealable plastic bag and work it toward the corner of the bag. Snip off a tiny bit at the corner of the bag with scissors. Fill each divot with ganache. Let the cookies rest at room temperature until the ganache is firm, about 1 hour, or refrigerate to set in about 30 minutes. Store in an airtight container at room temperature for up to 1 week.

DARK CHOCOLATE-PECAN MANDELBROT

Makes about 2 dozen mandelbrot

TO GET TO THE POINT, *MANDELBROT* IS BASICALLY JEWISH BISCOTTI. ALTHOUGH its origin is fuzzy, Jewish food queen Joan Nathan (bow down) has suggested the large Jewish population in Italy's Piedmont region may have been responsible for adapting biscotti recipes to be dairy-free, and then passing it on to German friends and family. It's possible, then, that mandelbrot first made its appearance in the region in the Upper Midwest between 1850 and 1880 when German Jews began settling in Minnesota and the Dakotas, or a maybe a bit later in the 1880s and '90s, when Russian Jews began arriving in the Midwest. Since this second wave of Jewish immigrants was often poorer than the first, treat-baking was reserved only for religious holidays.

Mandelbrot means "almond bread" and is usually made as a plain cookie with chopped almonds, and sometimes chocolate chips. My recipe here, with pecans and lots of cocoa, is a stretch from the literal interpretation. But I have kept it true to its dairy-free roots, which is one of its best qualities. Made with oil and not butter, mandelbrot's crunch has a tenderness to it, and doesn't require the dunking that a biscotti often does to avoid breaking a tooth. These are sturdy and keep for weeks, making them perfect for holiday cookie tins and gifting.

DOUGH:

1½ teaspoons instant espresso powder

2 teaspoons hot water

¾ teaspoon pure vanilla extract

½ cup/113 g firmly packed dark brown sugar

¼ cup/50 g granulated sugar

¼ cup/57 g vegetable oil

1 large egg

1 large egg yolk

1¼ cups/160 g unbleached all-purpose flour, spooned and leveled, plus more for dusting

⅓ cup/32 g unsweetened cocoa powder

½ teaspoon fine sea salt

½ teaspoon baking powder

¼ teaspoon baking soda

1 cup/120 g raw pecan pieces, roughly chopped, toasted, and cooled

3 ounces/85 g bittersweet chocolate (60% cacao), chopped into ¼-inch/6 mm bits

FINISHING THE COOKIES:

4 ounces/113 g bittersweet chocolate (60% cacao), melted

Prepare the dough: Position an oven rack to the center of the oven and preheat it to 350°F/180°C. Line a 12 x 17-inch/30 x 43 cm baking sheet with parchment paper.

In a small bowl, dissolve the instant espresso powder in the hot water. Stir in the vanilla.

In the bowl of an electric mixer fitted with the whisk attachment, combine the brown sugar, granulated sugar, vegetable oil, egg, egg yolk, and espresso mixture. Beat on high speed until lighter in texture, about 5 minutes.

Switch to the paddle attachment. Add the flour, cocoa powder, salt, baking powder, and baking soda. Stir on low speed until well blended. Stir in the pecans and chocolate bits.

Generously flour a work surface. Shape the dough into a plank,

about 14 inches/35.5 cm long by 2 inches/5 cm wide (the excess flour will be dusted off later). Transfer the log to the prepared baking sheet, placing it diagonally on the sheet.

Bake until firm to the touch, 25 to 30 minutes, rotating the sheet halfway through baking. Place the pan to a wire rack and let cool for about 20 minutes. Lower the oven temperature to 250°F/120°C.

Transfer the plank to a cutting board and use a pastry brush to dust off any excess flour. With a large serrated knife, cut the plank on the diagonal into ½-inch/1.25 cm slices. Arrange the slices flat on the baking sheet and return them to the oven until they are sturdy and dry, about 30 minutes. Let cool completely on the baking sheet.

Drizzle the cooled cookies with the melted chocolate. Allow the chocolate to set before serving. Store in an airtight container for up to 2 weeks.

MARSHMALLOW HAYSTACKS

Makes about 30 haystacks

AS YOU MAY KNOW, I AM A FAN OF MARSHMALLOW. IN FACT, ONCE UPON A TIME, I found a way to write an entire book about them and I loved every fluffy, sticky second of it. You might also notice I've managed to sneak them into several recipes in this book, and for that I offer no apologies. It turns out the marshmallow as we now know it has significant midwestern roots—its inventor was Alex Doumak, a Greek American who created the marshmallow extrusion process in 1954. This development made his family's confectionery business more efficient and profitable. The family moved the company to Bensenville, Illinois, in 1961, and has been a marshmallow-only company ever since, manufacturing several popular brands and exporting mallows across the globe. (If you can think of a more delightful business model, I'd love to hear it.)

This riff on the midwestern favorite, the haystack, celebrates that marshmallow heritage by stuffing as many of them as possible into a kitschy mix of crunchy chow mein noodles and sweet, tan goo. The goo in question here swaps out the typical butterscotch chips for high-quality white chocolate, allowing the peanut butter to really shine.

2 tablespoons/28 g unsalted butter

8 ounces/225 g high-quality white bar chocolate, chopped

¼ cup/65 g creamy peanut butter, such as Skippy brand

⅛ teaspoon fine sea salt

3 cups/170 g crunchy chow mein noodles

½ cup/70 g blanched slivered almonds

3 cups/150 g miniature marshmallows

Sprinkles (optional)

Line 2 baking sheets with parchment paper.

In a 5- to 6-quart/4.7 to 5/7 L, heavy-bottomed pot over low heat, melt the butter. Add the white chocolate and stir constantly until nearly smooth. Turn off the heat. Add the peanut butter and salt and stir until completely smooth. Add the chow mein noodles and almonds and stir to coat. Stir in the marshmallows.

Using 2 spoons, scoop the mixture into portions, 2 heaping tablespoons each, and place on the prepared baking sheets. Decorate with sprinkles, if you wish. Set the baking sheets in the refrigerator to chill until the chocolate is set, about 30 minutes. Transfer to an airtight container and store in a cool place (not the fridge) for up to 1 week.

FORGOTTEN COOKIES

Makes about 3 dozen cookies

THESE SIMPLE, PALE GREEN, COULDN'T-BE-EASIER MERINGUES WERE A STAPLE of our family Christmas cookie menu in my formative sweets-eating years. With my age in the single digits, I recall craving their minty sweetness and crisp, sugary shell that instantly melted on my tongue. At some point, probably due to busyness and discovering new recipes to make and who knows what, everyone just stopped making them. In the early stages of making this book, I found the recipe tucked into Gramma's recipe folder in one of my aunt's junior-high-aged handwriting, recorded in a home ec class from long ago, and I wondered whether they would really be as good as I remembered.

Any hesitation about them was completely dashed when my husband and children sampled one, and then another and another, and then the compliments finally came in the form of shouted interrogations of why it took me so long to make them. Consider these humble gems the dark horse of holiday treats. The ingredient list is short, prep time is laughable, and then you actually *just forget about them* as they dry out in a turned-off oven overnight. What more could you possibly want in this life?

4 large egg whites, at room temperature

1 teaspoon cream of tartar

¼ teaspoon fine sea salt

1½ cups/300 g granulated sugar

1 teaspoon pure vanilla extract

¼ teaspoon pure peppermint extract

Green food coloring

6 ounces/170 g bittersweet chocolate (70% to 72% cacao), finely chopped*

An edgy bittersweet chocolate—with a minimum of 70% and even up to 80% cacao—is the magic here, creating a tweedy network of bitterness within the crisp clouds of sugary meringue.

Position racks to the upper and lower thirds of the oven and preheat it to 350°F/180°C. Line two 12 x 17-inch/30 x 43 cm baking sheets with parchment paper.

In the bowl of an electric mixer fitted with the whisk attachment, combine the egg whites, cream of tartar, and salt. Beat on medium-high speed until the whites reach soft peaks, about 2 minutes. With the mixer running, slowly add the sugar, 1 tablespoon at a time. When all the sugar has been added, beat until the meringue reaches stiff peaks. Beat in the vanilla, peppermint extract, and a few drops of green food coloring to reach a soft, mint green color, like mint chocolate chip ice cream. Remove the bowl from the mixer and fold in the chopped chocolate.

Using 2 spoons, shape the meringue into small mounds, about 1½ tablespoons/22.7 ml each. Space the cookies about 1½ inches/3.8 cm apart on the prepared baking sheets (they won't spread much).

When all the batter has been portioned, turn off the oven. Place the baking sheets in the turned-off oven and close the door. Allow the meringues to dry for at least 4 hours, but overnight is even better. Do not open the oven door at any point during drying. When the meringues are firm to the touch, remove the pans from the oven. Allow the baking sheets to sit at room temperature to let the chocolate bits firm up before storing. The meringues will keep in an airtight container in a cool, dry place for up to 3 weeks.

LEBKUCHEN

Makes about 4 dozen cookies, depending on size

WHEN CHRISTMAS IS ON THE HORIZON, A STROLL THROUGH A LIVELY GERMAN holiday market, like the Christkindlmarket in Chicago or Germania Christkindlmarkt in Cincinnati, is a must-do. It doesn't get much more Christmassy than bundling up with a mug of steaming *Glugwein* and munching on a hot pretzel, sugar-and-spice roasted nuts, or slab of strudel as you peruse the beautiful woodcrafts, sparkling holiday ornaments, and handmade toys, and wonder why you've never had a cuckoo clock in your house.

Iced *lebkuchen* serve as both edibles and decoration at the most authentic Christmas markets, decorated in reds and greens and scrolly German greetings, dangling low from the ceilings of vendors' booths. Lebkuchen is quite possibly the best way to illustrate that Germans seriously know how to Christmas. To do the lebkuchen tradition right, it requires a bit of planning. Mix up a simple, one-bowl dough, and let it ripen for a couple of days. Then, cut, bake, and glaze the cookies. They'll come out awfully similar to a Milk-Bone, and you'll wonder what the heck is going on. But then there's the resting phase, where the cookies are stored with a wedge of apple for moisture, and they transform like the living room on Christmas morning. Soft, but with integrity, and a combination of spices that make it impossible to eat just one.

COOKIES:

¾ cup/252 g clover honey

¾ cup/170 g dark muscovado or organic dark brown sugar*

4 tablespoons/57 g unsalted butter, cut into chunks

1 large egg, beaten

2 teaspoons finely grated lemon zest

1 tablespoon freshly squeezed lemon juice

3 cups/384 g unbleached flour, spooned and leveled, plus more for dusting

¾ teaspoon baking soda

½ teaspoon fine sea salt

2 teaspoons ground cinnamon

½ teaspoon ground allspice

½ teaspoon freshly grated nutmeg

¼ teaspoon ground ginger

¼ teaspoon ground cloves

Oil for bowl

GLAZE:

1 cup/120 g confectioners' sugar, sifted

1 large egg white

1 tablespoon freshly squeezed lemon juice

⅛ teaspoon fine sea salt

If you can find dark muscovado sugar (in natural foods stores or online), it's worth every penny for these special holiday treats. If not, organic dark brown sugar tends to be richer in color and will give you a deeper-hued cookie.

Prepare the cookies: In a 1- to 1½-quart/1 to 1.4 L saucepan, combine the honey and muscovado sugar. Over medium-high heat, stir gently until the sugar begins to dissolve and the mixture just begins to come to a simmer. Remove the pan from the heat and stir in the butter. Let cool until warm to the touch. Whisk in the egg and lemon zest and juice.

In the bowl of an electric mixer fitted with the paddle attachment, stir together the flour, baking soda, salt, and spices.

On low speed, stir in the wet ingredients until a smooth, sticky dough forms. Scrape the dough into a lightly oiled ceramic bowl and cover with a plate—you want the dough to be able to breathe. Allow the dough to "ripen" at cool room temperature for 1 to 2 days—do not refrigerate. (The large amount of honey and sugar will keep bacteria at bay.)

Position racks to the upper and lower thirds of the oven and preheat it to 350°F/180°C. Line 2 baking sheets with parchment paper.

Turn out the dough onto a well-floured work surface. Roll it out to a ¼-inch/6 mm thickness. Use a bench scraper or thin spatula to get under the dough and scoot it around in the flour occasionally to prevent sticking. Cut shapes with 2-inch/5 cm cutters and place 1 inch/2.5 cm apart on the prepared baking sheets. Sweep away any excess flour with a pastry brush. Bake until fragrant and lightly browned, about 12 minutes, rotating the baking sheets from top to bottom and front to back halfway through the baking time. (Watch closely, as the honey in the dough can make the edges catch and burn quickly.)

Prepare the glaze: In a medium bowl, whisk together the confectioners' sugar, egg white, lemon juice, and salt for a smooth, thin, runny glaze. (Add a few drops more of lemon juice, as needed, to achieve this consistency.)

Let the cookies firm up and cool on the baking sheets for 5 minutes. Run an offset spatula under the cookies to gently loosen them from the parchment, leaving them on the sheets.

While still warm, brush the cookies with glaze and transfer to wire racks. Allow the cookies to cool and the glaze to dry completely.

The secret to a perfect lebkuchen texture is in the next resting phase: place the cookies into airtight containers in layers, separated by parchment or waxed paper. Tuck a wedge of apple in the container before sealing. Store in a cool place for at least 3 days, or up to 2 weeks, to allow the cookies to ripen once more before serving.

ITALIAN BAKERY BUTTER COOKIES

Makes 2 to 3 dozen cookies, depending on size and shape

I HAD AN ODD AFFINITY FOR ITALIAN BUTTER COOKIES AS A CHILD, AND HAVE memories of digging through a white waxed cardboard bakery box to find the shell-shaped ones with the most rainbow jimmies on them. It's not that they tasted better than chocolate chip, or were more exciting than an Oreo. Maybe it was the novelty of being able to buy handfuls of cookies by the pound, as so many midwestern bakeries sell them. In fact, I used to think of this type of cookie as being "sprinkle-flavored," probably because most places selling cookies by the pound aren't producing them to be the pinnacle of buttery flavor. And to be honest, with the increase of bakeries using shortening in their cookies, it can be tough to find a good one. As soon as I made my own at home, with really great, rich European-style butter, I think I might have ruined myself for life. My top tip here is to be prepared to pipe the cookies as soon as the dough is finished, so it's easy to pipe and holds a nice shape.

- 8 ounces/225 g unsalted European-style butter, at room temperature

- 1 cup/120 g confectioners' sugar

- 1 large egg, at room temperature

- 1 large egg yolk, at room temperature

- 1 teaspoon pure vanilla extract

- 1/4 teaspoon pure almond, lemon, or anise extract

- 2 cups/256 g unbleached all-purpose flour, spooned and leveled

- 1/2 teaspoon fine sea salt

- 1/4 teaspoon baking powder

- Candied cherries, sprinkles, or sparkling colored sugars (optional)

- Melted dark or white chocolate for drizzling (optional)

Position racks to the upper and lower thirds of the oven and preheat it to 350°F/180°C. Line 2 baking sheets with silicone liners or parchment paper (silicone liners make the piping a little easier, as they don't lift up as the bag pulls away from each cookie). Have ready a heavy-duty piping bag fitted with a large open star tip, such as Ateco #826.

In the bowl of an electric mixer fitted with the paddle attachment, beat the butter on medium-high speed until creamy. Add the confectioners' sugar and continue to beat until very light and fluffy, about 5 minutes. Reduce the mixer speed to medium and beat in the egg, egg yolk, vanilla, and the additional extract of your choice. Blend for 1 minute more. Reduce the mixer speed to low and stir in the flour, salt, and baking powder. Scrape down the bowl well and make sure the dough is well mixed.

Immediately transfer the dough to the prepared piping bag. Pipe the cookies in your desired shapes—aim for cookies about 2 inches/5 cm wide, spaced about 2 inches/5 cm apart (they won't spread much while baking). Decorate with candied cherries, sprinkles, or sparkling colored sugars, if you wish. Refrigerate on the sheets for about 15 minutes, or freeze for 5 minutes.

Bake until lightly golden at the edges, 10 to 12 minutes (cookies on parchment will brown faster; those on silicone mats will need a little more time to color). Allow the cookies to cool on the sheets for 2 or 3 minutes before transferring them to wire racks to cool completely. To finish nonsprinkled cookies, drizzle or sandwich with melted dark or white chocolate.

TIP > *This dough is also suitable for a cookie press.*

SCANDINAVIAN RICE PUDDING

Serves 8 to 10

WHEN IT COMES TO COMFORT FOOD, PUDDING IS RANKED HIGH ON THE LIST. Scandinavian countries love their rice pudding, and making it is truly an art form. To gild the lily, they add a cloud of whipped cream and a pool of ruby red fruit sauce, taking something that can be eaten for breakfast and transforming it into a heavenly dessert. The slight differences in names and serving styles for this creamy, dreamy dish add to its charm. In Denmark, it's known as *risalamande* and topped with cherries, while Norwegian *riskrem* and Swedish *ris à la Malta* can be served with raspberries, lingonberries, or cloudberries, or any combination thereof.

It would stand to reason that the classic midwestern potluck dish called glorified rice was inspired by Scandi rice puddings just like this one. And if you were feeling sprightly, you could take this recipe, up the amount of almonds, add to it canned mandarin oranges, crushed pineapple, and several handfuls of mini marshmallows, and a fine bowl of glorified rice is exactly what you'd have.

4 cups/900 g whole milk

¾ cup/140 g uncooked arborio rice

½ cup/100 g granulated sugar

1 teaspoon finely grated lemon zest

½ teaspoon fine sea salt

½ teaspoon pure almond extract

2 cups/480 g very cold heavy whipping cream

1½ teaspoons pure vanilla bean paste or pure vanilla extract

½ cup/60 g sliced almonds, toasted and finely chopped

In a 3-quart/2.8 L saucepan, combine the milk, rice, sugar, lemon zest, and salt. Bring to simmer over medium heat. Lower the heat to low, cover, and simmer, stirring occasionally and checking to make sure there's always a small bubbling happening inside the pan, for 30 to 35 minutes, or until thickened and rice is tender. Stir in the almond extract. Let cool completely.

In a large bowl and using a handheld mixer, combine the cream with the vanilla bean paste or extract and whip to stiff peaks. Add the pudding to the bowl and fold gently to blend. Fold in the toasted almonds. Spoon into dessert bowls and chill until serving.

SANDBAKKELS

Makes about 3 dozen cookies

AS MUCH AS I WRITE IN PRAISE OF QUICK RECIPES, DURING THE HOLIDAYS I'M A sucker for the kind of baking that requires a bit of shaping and care. Even better if said recipe can be turned into a holiday tradition that calls people to a table and everyone sits around sharing the work, gabbing all the while. These traditions are all too often lost these days, and I'd like to bring them back. I recall a friend from New York who returns home to Ohio every Christmas to her mother's house, and on the second day after she arrives, they have a family baking day, where they churn out dozens upon dozens of cookies together. The stuff of cozy holiday baking dreams.

So if you're thinking this sort of thing might be nice to instill in your own household, might I suggest Norwegian *sandbakkels* as a way to get started? These crisp, buttery sugar cookies (translated as "sand tarts" but also sometimes called "butter tarts") can be eaten straight up, or filled with cream and berries or chocolate or whatever makes your skirt fly up. The dough couldn't be easier, and the fun part comes in the shaping of the shell-like cookies by pressing small hunks of dough into little fluted tins. You can easily find new sets of tins online, often with pretty shapes imprinted in them, and occasionally I'll come across small vintage boxes of round, traditionally shaped ones in thrift stores.

8 ounces/225 g unsalted European-style butter, at room temperature

1/2 cup/60 g confectioners' sugar

1/4 cup/57 g light brown sugar

1/4 cup/50 g granulated sugar

1 large egg, at room temperature

1 teaspoon pure vanilla extract

2 1/4 to 2 1/2 cups/288 to 320 g unbleached all-purpose flour, spooned and leveled

1/2 teaspoon fine sea salt

Nonstick cooking spray for tins

Spoonable Vanilla Custard (page 309), whipped cream, berries for serving (optional)

In the bowl of an electric mixer fitted with the paddle attachment, beat the butter on medium-high speed until creamy, about 30 seconds. Add the confectioners' sugar, brown sugar, and granulated sugar and continue to beat until light and fluffy, about 3 minutes. Reduce the mixer speed to medium and beat in the egg and vanilla. Reduce the mixer speed to low and stir in the flour and salt. Scrape down the bowl well and make sure the dough is well mixed. Cover the bowl tightly and refrigerate the dough until very firm, about 2 hours.

Position racks to the upper and lower thirds of the oven and preheat it to 375°F/190°C. Spritz the interiors of a set of *sandbakkels* tins or other decorative mini (2-inch/5 cm) tart tins with a little nonstick cooking spray. Pinch off walnut-size pieces of the dough and place each in a prepared tin, pressing them evenly across the bottom and up the sides of the tins. (Set aside the remaining dough until after each batch of cookies are baked, as you will be reusing the tins.) Place the filled tins, spaced about 2 inches apart, on baking sheets. Bake until the cookies are golden, 8 to 10 minutes, rotating the sheets from front to back and top to bottom halfway through the baking time.

Line a work surface with newspaper or brown paper grocery bags. When the tins come out of the oven, allow them to cool on the paper for 2 or 3 minutes. Invert the tins onto the paper, and give the bottom of each tin a few taps with your fingertips to encourage the cookies to release from the tins. Let the cookies cool completely on the paper. Allow the tins to cool as well, before shaping the next batch with the remaining dough.

Eat *sandbakkels* straight up, or fill with custard, whipped cream, and/or berries. The baked cookies will keep in an airtight container in layers separated by parchment paper for up to 1 week.

KRANSKAKE

Makes 1 kranskake

THIS TOWERING, FRAGRANT, LIGHTLY SPICED COOKIE-CAKE HYBRID SITS RIGHT IN the center of what I consider to be the ultimate Venn diagram of baking. It's at once wildly impressive, not actually complicated, and can be made well ahead of serving. The bonus point for kranskake is that it's as fun to make as the history surrounding it. Called *kranskake* in Norwegian and *kranskage* in Danish, it's a Scandi stunner that often appears on such special occasions as holidays, baptisms, and weddings. The invention of it is credited to a Danish baker sometime in the 1700s, and it was originally designed to lie on its side, mimicking a cornucopia, filled with candies and chocolates. But one look at an upright, towering version, and the winning posture is clear. One tradition is for the bride and groom to lift the top of the cake together, and the number of rings that pull up indicates the number of children they will have. Position your hands carefully, my friends!

Forming the dough into perfect rings for a kranskake requires a set of special molds obtained easily online or at thrift stores. It's a fun project, especially with multiple ring makers, rolling out the dough into long tubes just the right length to form each circle, part guessing game, part Play-Doh free-for-all. Because the dough is superpliable and gluten-free, it won't toughen up as you squish and reroll dough portions as many times as needed to get each ring just right. The crunchy royal icing drizzled between each layer serves as an edible concrete of sorts, and adds a sweet snap to the chewy almond rings. As precarious as she looks, a good kranskake will not topple for anything, making it an awe-inspiring centerpiece that's a literal taste of history, and magical enough to draw people around the table.

RINGS:

18 ounces/510 g sliced almonds*

4¼ cups/510 g confectioners' sugar, divided

2 teaspoons ground cardamom

1 teaspoon finely grated lemon zest

¼ teaspoon fine sea salt

4 large egg whites

1 teaspoon pure vanilla extract

Nonstick cooking spray for molds

Small sprinkles, edible glitter, or other edible decoration (optional)

ICING:

2 large egg whites

2½ cups/300 g confectioners' sugar

½ teaspoon pure vanilla extract

⅛ teaspoon fine sea salt

1 to 2 teaspoons freshly squeezed lemon juice

I love the nubbly texture, natural look, and flavor of using almonds with the skins. If you can find pre-ground almond meal, you can skip the food processor step.

Prepare the rings: In the bowl of a food processor fitted with the steel S blade, combine the almonds with ½ cup/60 g of the confectioners' sugar. Process continuously until the almonds are very finely ground.

In the bowl of an electric mixer fitted with the paddle attachment, combine the almond mixture, remaining 3¾ cups/450 g of the confectioners' sugar, cardamom, lemon zest, and salt. Mix on low speed to blend. Add the egg whites and vanilla and stir until the dough is evenly mixed. Transfer the dough to a clean bowl, cover tightly, and refrigerate for at least 12 hours, or up to 3 days.

Position racks to the upper and lower thirds of the oven and preheat it to 300°F/150°C. Spray six 3-ring kranskake molds with nonstick cooking spray.

Turn out the dough onto a work surface. Working 1 portion at a time, roll the dough into long ropes, no more than ½ inch/1.25 cm in diameter, just shy of snugly filling each ring—the dough will grow in size during baking and you don't want the rings sticking together. It's a bit of trial and error to guess how much dough you'll need to create a rope that completes each size circle, but it becomes easier to eyeball it as you go. Pinch the ends of each rope together to form a seamless ring.

Set the filled molds directly on the oven racks and bake until the dough rings are somewhat firm to the touch, dry in appearance, and lightly golden, about 20 minutes. Err on the side of giving the rings an extra minute or two of baking if you're not sure—underbaked rings will fall apart upon unmolding. Set the molds on wire racks and allow the rings to cool in the molds before turning them out.

Prepare the icing: In a medium bowl, whisk together the egg whites, confectioners' sugar, vanilla, and salt until smooth and thick. Blend in several drops of lemon juice to adjust the consistency of the icing—you want something fluid but not runny, that can easily be piped but will hold its shape and not drip down the rings as it's applied. Scrape the icing into a piping bag fitted with a small round tip, or use a resealable plastic bag and snip off a tiny corner of the bag with scissors.

Assemble the kranskake: Pipe a few small dabs of icing onto a serving plate, and affix the largest ring to the plate. Pipe thin lines in a zigzag pattern all around the circle. Gently press the next-size ring on top. Continue icing and stacking the rings until the entire kranskake is assembled. If you wish to add small sprinkles or edible glitter to your kranskake, do so layer by layer, after you apply icing and before pressing on the next ring. For slightly larger baubles applied all over the structure, stick them on at the end of construction with small dots of icing. Allow the icing to set completely before displaying and serving.

CHAPTER 11
ELEMENTS

CONSIDER THE FOLLOWING RECIPES TO BE THE KIND
of accoutrements that you can keep in your bakers' toolbox and use
to make any number of recipes extra special.

RHUBARB AND RASPBERRY JAM

Makes about 4 half-pint/500 ml jars

THIS IS A VIBRANT, SWEET-TART JAM CELEBRATING THE AMBROSIAL COMBINATION of rhubarb and raspberries, and is a great way to use up the uncontrollable, fleeting bounty of rhubarb that takes over the Midwest in that hopeful window between April and June. As it's also low-sugar, this jam is best refrigerated or frozen for longer storage, and isn't suitable for canning.

1 pound/453 g rhubarb stalks, cut into ½-inch/1.25 cm pieces (about 4 cups)

6 ounces/170 g fresh raspberries

1¾ cups/350 g granulated sugar

1 tablespoon freshly squeezed lemon juice

¼ teaspoon ground cinnamon

⅛ teaspoon fine sea salt

½ teaspoon pure vanilla extract

Combine all the ingredients except the vanilla in a large, non-reactive bowl. Mix thoroughly and cover. Refrigerate for at least 6 hours, or overnight.

Pour the fruit mixture into a 4- to 5-quart/3.75 to 4.75 L, heavy-bottomed pot. Set the pot over medium heat and bring the mixture to a boil, stirring often. Let boil for 10 to 12 minutes, or until thickened. Remove the pot from the heat and stir in the vanilla. Let cool before ladling into jars or using in recipes. Store in the refrigerator for up to 3 weeks, or freeze for up to 1 year.

HOMEMADE CHERRY PIE FILLING

Makes about 6 cups/1.5 L filling

IN THE EARLY 1900s, FARMERS IN THE MIDWEST GREW DOZENS OF VARIETIES OF sour cherries—the tart, smaller, softer cousin to the sweet cherries we love to eat by the bagful when the season hits. These days, 99 percent of the sour cherries grown in the Midwest are of the Montmorency variety, primarily in Michigan and Door County, Wisconsin. Sour cherry season is fleeting and the harvest quite fragile, so when you are lucky enough to come across some, hoarding them is recommended. For what can't be immediately used, a homemade cherry pie filling is the best way to celebrate your haul.

2¼ pounds/1.2 kg fresh or frozen tart cherries

1 cup/200 g granulated sugar, divided

6 tablespoons/48 g cornstarch

Generous ¼ teaspoon fine sea salt

1 teaspoon freshly squeezed lemon juice (optional)

If using fresh cherries, pit the cherries into a large bowl, discard the pits. Add ½ cup/100 g of the sugar to the bowl and stir to blend. Let sit at room temperature for 1 hour. Drain the cherries, reserving the juice in a small bowl (you should have a little over 1 cup/225 g of juice). Whisk the cornstarch into the juice until dissolved.

If using frozen cherries, thaw them completely, reserving the juice. Drain the cherries, reserving 1 cup plus 2 tablespoons/250 g of the juice in a small bowl (you will have more juice than you need). Lay out the cherries on paper toweling and very gently pat them dry. Whisk the cornstarch into the cherry juice.

In a 3-quart/2.8 L saucepan, combine the cherries, sugar (the remaining ½ cup/100 g if using fresh cherries, 1 cup/200 g if using frozen), cherry juice mixture, and salt. Place the pan over medium-high heat and bring the mixture to a boil. Cook for 2 minutes, stirring gently, until thick and glossy and a clean track remains for 1 to 2 seconds on the bottom of the pot as you stir. Remove the pan from the heat and allow the filling to cool slightly. Taste the filling—if it needs a bit of tartness to really make it sing, add a few drops of lemon juice. Let cool completely before using or ladling into jars. Store in the refrigerator for up to 3 weeks, or in the freezer for up to 1 year.

APRICOT AND ORANGE BLOSSOM LEKVAR

Makes about 2½ cups/800 g lekvar

LEKVAR IS A COARSE, THICK JAM WITH HUNGARIAN ROOTS, AND WORKS BEAUTIFULLY as a filling for kolacky, kolache, cookies, and pastries of just about any origin. This recipe makes a lot, but any leftovers freeze beautifully. This same method can be used for dried cherries, prunes, and figs, adjusting the sugar, acid, and flavorings to taste to suit the sweetness of the fruit.

1 pound/450 g dried apricots

⅔ cup/132 g granulated sugar

1 tablespoon freshly squeezed lemon juice

Pinch of fine sea salt

1 to 1½ teaspoons orange blossom water, to taste

½ teaspoon pure vanilla extract

In a 3-quart/2.8 L lidded saucepan, place the apricots and cover with them water by about 1 inch/2.5 cm. Cover, place over high heat, and bring to a boil. Boil for 5 minutes. Remove the lid, add the sugar, lemon juice, and salt, and stir to combine. Replace the lid. Lower the heat to medium-low and simmer, stirring occasionally, until the fruit is softened, about 20 minutes.

Remove the lid from the pan and continue to simmer, stirring often, until the excess liquid has evaporated and the lekvar becomes thick and jammy and breaks down easily with a fork, about 10 minutes more. Transfer the contents of the pan to a food processor or blender. Blend until nearly smooth. Add 1 teaspoon of the orange blossom water and the vanilla. Blend for 30 seconds more. Taste, adding more orange blossom water, if you like. Pour the lekvar into a heatproof container and let cool. uncovered. at room temperature. Cover tightly and refrigerate for up to 3 weeks, or freeze for up to 1 year.

FIVE-FINGER ICING

Makes about 1/2 cup/120 ml icing

THIS IS A DRIPPY WHITE FINISHING ICING FOR ALL MANNER OF PASTRIES, COFFEE break treats, cookies, and more. Called five-finger icing because so many old-school bakeries use a gloved hand to artfully drizzle it over baked goods, this topping sets up with a firm, matte surface, making anything it touches irresistible.

1 cup/120 g confectioners' sugar

Pinch of fine sea salt

4 teaspoons water

1/2 teaspoon pure vanilla extract, or a squeeze of lemon juice (optional)

Combine the sugar and salt in a small bowl and whisk in just enough water, a little at a time, to form a smooth, opaque glaze—when you lift the whisk, it should easily form a fluid ribbon without breaking, but doesn't drip in little droplets in a runny fashion. (It's often just a matter of a few extra drops of water from your fingertips to get the consistency just right, so don't add too much water in the beginning.) Whisk in the vanilla or lemon juice, if using. Cover with plastic wrap until ready to use.

ITALIAN MERINGUE

Makes about 3 cups/710 ml meringue

PLENTY OF MERINGUE PIE RECIPES HAVE YOU MAKE A FRENCH MERINGUE AS their toppings—the type where egg whites are whipped and granulated sugar gradually added until you get a stiff, glossy meringue. The problem is that this meringue is far from foolproof and all too often ends up grainy, weeping on you, or collapsing. We deserve more certainty from our meringue, I'd say.

My choice for pie topping is Italian meringue. This type of meringue takes a little more doing, but the payoff is its stability—it holds, swoops, and peaks like a dream. Because it's "cooked" by the hot sugar syrup, no further baking is required. For pies, I get a nice controlled toast on it with a kitchen torch, or leave it as is for a silky, fat-free alternative to whipped cream for rich pies that could use a creamy but lighter topping. For the occasional moments that one makes a meringue pie, I say go for the sure thing.

3 large/90 g egg whites, at room temperature

1/4 teaspoon cream of tartar

3/4 cup/150 g granulated sugar

1/3 cup/75 g water

1 tablespoon light corn syrup

1/8 teaspoon fine sea salt

1/2 teaspoon pure vanilla extract

Place the whites in the bowl of an electric mixer fitted with the whisk attachment. Add the cream of tartar. Beat the whites on medium-high speed until soft peaks form, about 3 minutes. Turn off the mixer.

In a small saucepan, combine the sugar, water, corn syrup, and salt. Stirring often, bring the mixture to a full boil. Clip a candy thermometer onto the side of the pot, and cook until the syrup reaches 240°F/115°C.

Turn the mixer back on, on medium speed. In a thin stream, pour just a tablespoon or two of the syrup into the whipping whites. Wait 5 seconds, then pour in 2 more tablespoons. After 5 more seconds, pour in the remaining syrup in a thin, steady stream, aiming for the space between the side of the bowl and the whip. Increase the mixer speed to high and beat until the meringue is thick, glossy, and the bowl is cool to the touch, 7 to 8 minutes. In the last minute of beating, add the vanilla. Store in an airtight container in the refrigerator for up to 2 days.

ERMINE FROSTING

Makes about 3 cups/685 ml frosting

IF YOU'RE ONE OF THOSE PEOPLE WHO CLAIMS TO "HATE FROSTING" BECAUSE it's too sweet, I urge you to give this old-fashioned formula a try. It all starts with a roux of sorts that gives the frosting the kind of body you'd normally get from heaps of confectioners' sugar. With a good whipping, it becomes almost the consistency of whipped cream—remarkably light and so fluffy you'll want to dive right in with a spoon.

This batch is the perfect amount for the Swedish Flop (page 21) and a 9 x 13-inch/23 x 33 cm sheet cake. It will modestly frost a two-layer 8-inch/20 cm cake, so if you like a loftier frosted look for layer cakes, make 1½ batches.

1/4 cup/32 g unbleached all-purpose flour

1 cup/225 g whole milk

1 cup/200 g granulated sugar

1/4 teaspoon fine sea salt

1 cup/225 g unsalted butter, at room temperature

1 teaspoon pure vanilla extract

1/4 teaspoon pure almond extract

In a 2- to 2½-quart/1.9 to 2.4 L saucepan over medium heat, whisk together the flour, milk, sugar, and salt. Continue to whisk until the mixture comes to a full boil. Cook for 1 minute, whisking constantly, until the mixture resembles pudding. Remove the pan from the heat. Let cool completely at room temperature, or to speed up cooling, scrape the mixture into a clean bowl, cover the surface with plastic wrap, and chill in the refrigerator.

In the bowl of an electric mixer fitted with the whisk attachment, whip the butter with the vanilla and almond extract on high speed for 2 minutes. Scrape down the bowl and add the cooled flour mixture. Beat until the frosting becomes very fluffy, almost mousselike in texture, and noticeably lighter in color, about 5 minutes. Use immediately.

SILKY, CREAMY CHOCOLATE FROSTING

Makes about 4 cups/845 ml frosting

WHAT'S MORE CELEBRATORY AND REMINISCENT OF CHILDHOOD THAN MILK chocolate? I know that bittersweet is all the rage, and I love adding edge to baked goods by using it in place of semi-sweet chocolate sometimes. But in the words of the great Nigella Lawson, there are times that only milk chocolate will do. And for me, one of those times is when you're frosting a fluffy yellow birthday cake. This recipe is inspired by one from the brilliant food scientist and author Shirley Corriher. A bit of semisweet chocolate in this silky, flexible, glossy, gloriously swoopable frosting keeps it from being toothachingly sweet, as does the sour cream. It's simply the prettiest frosting you'll ever see.

8 ounces/225 g milk chocolate

6 ounces/170 g semisweet chocolate

2 tablespoons/42 g light or dark corn syrup

1/2 teaspoon pure vanilla extract

1/8 teaspoon fine sea salt

1/2 cup/120 g full-fat sour cream

1/2 cup/120 g heavy whipping cream

In a double boiler, melt together the milk and semisweet chocolate until smooth. Allow the chocolate to cool slightly.

In the bowl of an electric mixer fitted with the paddle attachment, stir together the corn syrup, vanilla, and salt. Add the sour cream and cream. Add the cooled melted chocolate.

Beat on medium speed until the frosting is smooth, glossy, and gorgeous. If it seems a bit sloppy, more like chocolate pudding than frosting, allow it to firm a bit with a 1-hour rest at room temperature. Beat again briefly before using.

THE BEST AMERICAN BUTTERCREAM

Makes about 4 cups/945 ml buttercream

THIS IS MY FAVORITE WAY TO DO A SIMPLE, CONFECTIONERS' SUGAR BUTTER-cream. You'll notice it has a lot more butter than your typical recipe on the back of the sugar box, but because of this, it's creamier, lighter, and much less sweet. It's also really easy to scale it up or down—the formula here is just about equal weights of butter and sugar: one stick of butter, one cup of confectioners' sugar, one tablespoon of milk (or half-and-half or heavy whipping cream, if you're feeling luscious). The key is to whip the heck out of it until it's mousselike in texture—five minutes or more. Slather this on just about any cake. People will ask you for the recipe for this one.

1/4 cup/57 to 60 g whole milk, half-and-half, or heavy whipping cream

Generous 1/4 teaspoon fine sea salt

4 cups/480 g confectioners' sugar

2 cups/450 g unsalted butter, at room temperature, cut into small pieces

2 teaspoons vanilla bean paste or pure vanilla extract

1/4 teaspoon pure almond extract (optional)

In the bowl of an electric mixer fitted with the paddle attachment, combine the milk with the salt. Let it sit for a minute so the salt can dissolve a bit. Dump in the confectioners' sugar. On low speed, mix until the sugar is evenly moistened (it will still look quite dry). Add the butter pieces, vanilla bean paste or extract, and almond extract (if using; I really think you should). Gradually increase the speed from low to high. Beat until the frosting has a light, airy, whipped texture, 5 to 7 minutes depending on your mixer. Adjust the consistency with bit more liquid, if necessary.

Use immediately or store in an airtight container and refrigerate for up to 1 week. Bring the buttercream to room temperature and rewhip before using.

MAKE-AHEAD WHIPPED CREAM

Makes about 4 cups/945 ml whipped cream,
to equal an 8-ounce/225 g container of whipped topping

WHEN I TOLD PEOPLE I WAS WRITING A BOOK ABOUT MIDWESTERN BAKING, I immediately had to follow it up by saying that it wasn't going to be a book full of Cool Whip and Jell-O. Even though those two things make up a fair amount of my own dessert memories, I believe there's a tastier way to get a whipped cream topping that's easily transportable, stable enough to last through a potluck, and made days ahead of when you actually need it, so you're not whipping cream like a crazy person in front of your guests. It's a savior during holidays when you already have one million other things to do.

3 tablespoons/42 g cold water

3/4 teaspoon pure vanilla extract

1 1/2 teaspoons unflavored gelatin

2 cups/480 g heavy whipping cream

6 tablespoons/45 g confectioners' sugar

1/4 teaspoon cream of tartar

In a small, microwave-safe bowl, whisk together the cold water, vanilla, and gelatin until smooth. Let soften for 5 minutes. Microwave on **HIGH** until melted, about 10 seconds.

Pour the cream into a medium bowl or the bowl of an electric mixer. Whisking constantly, add the melted gelatin mixture until blended. Add the confectioners' sugar and cream of tartar and whisk to blend. With handheld beaters or a stand mixer on medium-high speed, whip the cream to smooth, stable peaks, but still soft in appearance (think: shaving cream right out of the can). Do not overwhip—if in doubt, use an electric mixer just until the cream holds its shape, and then finish beating by hand with a whisk. Use immediately, or transfer to an airtight container to refrigerate for up to 3 days. If storing, remove from the refrigerator and whisk energetically to smooth and fluff the cream before using.

TIP › *If you're looking for a substitute for tubs of prepared whipped topping for, say, a dessert salad, I recommend the cream cheese–bolstered whipped cream method in the recipe on page 103.*

SPOONABLE VANILLA CUSTARD

Makes about 3 cups/710 ml custard

ONE OF MY FAVORITE THINGS TO MAKE AND EAT, VANILLA PASTRY CREAM IS definitely a back-pocket recipe. Use this formula as a donut, pie, or cake filling that's sturdy, but luscious. Envelop it with Danish pastry, or dab some on top of individual pastries before baking. Additionally, if you eliminate the whole egg and reduce the cornstarch to 2 tablespoons, you'll have the dreamiest vanilla pudding on the planet, or you can freeze it in ice pop molds to revisit the very best frozen novelty of the 1980s.

2 cups/453 g whole milk*

4 large egg yolks

1 large egg

½ cup/100 g granulated sugar

3 tablespoons/24 g cornstarch

¼ teaspoon fine sea salt

2 tablespoons/28 g unsalted butter, at room temperature

1 teaspoon vanilla bean paste or pure vanilla extract

You can up the richness here by swapping out the whole milk for half-and-half, but whatever you do, don't use low-fat milk. It just comes out tasting . . . beige. Bleh.

In a 3-quart/2.8 L saucepan over medium heat, bring the milk to a bare simmer, but don't let it boil. Meanwhile, in a large bowl, whisk together the egg yolks, egg, sugar, cornstarch, and salt until paler in color, about 1 minute. Slowly whisk in the hot milk until well blended. Pour the mixture back into the saucepan. Set the pan over medium heat and whisk often until the custard is very thick and just beginning to bubble, about 5 minutes. Remove the pan from the heat.

Pour the custard into a blender. Add the butter and vanilla paste or extract and blend on high speed for 1 minute. Pour into a medium bowl. Cover the surface with plastic wrap and refrigerate until cold and firm, at least 3 hours, or up to 2 days ahead. Whisk well before using.

ACKNOWLEDGMENTS

It all began with a big move, a general idea, and the open arms of home. To the countless good folks of the great Midwest, from my closest family members to generous strangers, who inspired and informed this book along the way, thank you for your kindness and never-ending lists of recommendations. I am honored to be one of you.

To my agent, Judy Linden, thank you for always being equal parts advocate, discerning editor, therapist, and cheerleader. Your belief in me is a treasure.

With this book, I am thrilled to join the roster at Running Press. Big thanks to the warm, smart, creative team who brought it to life. My editor, Kristen Green Wiewora, is a gem of a woman and a brilliant culinary editor—thank you for making this book shine. Susan Van Horn lent her mad design skills and I am so grateful to have her artistic touch on these pages. Thank you to Amber Morris for your razor-sharp production management, and Iris Bass for your eagle-eyed copyediting. To the marketing and publicity team of Seta Zink, Cassie Drumm, and Jessica Schmidt, thank you for spreading the Midwest love far and wide.

To my brave brigade of testers, thank you for your time, insight, and making these recipes as good as they can be, especially Megan Swearingen, Kate Leahy, Alana Chernila, Sally Theran, Erin Wilk, and Annelies Zijderveld.

I couldn't be more in love with the photos in this book, and I have a marvelous team of people to thank for them. Paul Strabbing, your talent, humor, and willingness to try just about anything I threw at you—be it a photo concept or a taste of something—is a rare gift. The perfect punctuation on every image came courtesy of Johanna Lowe, who generously provided artistic guidance, excellent libations, and the most beautiful, inspiring shooting locations. To Jane Katte, I would have fallen into a heap without your mad pastry skills, strategic thinking, and enthusiasm—thank you for being a gold-star food styling teammate, and I'm looking forward to seeing your star rise.

Sara Schilling deserves all the cake for her willingness to do whatever it took to keep me sane, including pep talks, testing recipes, style advice, and extra photo shoot help (even lending us your kids!). Everyone should be so lucky to have a friend like you.

I was fortunate enough to encounter some wonderful people who are as passionate about baking and midwestern foodways as I am, and shared their insight without hesitation to help me fine-tune this book and support the journey of making it. Thank you to Ellen F. Steinberg, Gina Guth, Paula Haney, Mindy Segal, James Pelinski, Jessie Sheehan, Jocelyn Delk Adams, Alejandra Ramos, Ann Gray, Brian Hart Hoffman, John Becker, Shauna Niequist and family, Cindy Bendsten, Hannah Agran, Edd Kimber, Amy Thielen, Tracy Weiss, Sara Nelson-Carlson, Luisa Weiss, Trine Hahnemann, Beatrice Ojakangas, Nancy Wall Hopkins, Jan Miller, Irvin Lin, Erin McDowell, Stella Parks, Jennifer Russell, and Zoe Francois.

Huge thanks to Olga Massov for lending your keen editorial eyes to the manuscript right at the finish line—you made this book better, my friend.

To everyone who followed along with #theheartlandbaker and #midwestmadebaking on Instagram for more than three years during the development of this book, I am so grateful for your enthusiasm, good cheer, and patience. I hope this book feels like a triumphant end to all that teasing and waiting.

And lastly and mostly, to Scott, Caroline, and Andrew—thank you for your love, support, understanding, both savage and loving criticism, and endless sweet teeth. I love you so much.

INDEX